ENCYCLICAL LETTER

DILEXIT NOS

OF THE HOLY FATHER
FRANCIS

ON THE HUMAN AND DIVINE LOVE OF
THE HEART OF JESUS CHRIST

*All documents are published
thanks to the generosity of the supporters
of the Catholic Truth Society*

Cover image: Mosaic from the Chapel of St Claude de la Colombiere, Paray-le-Monial, France. Photo by Elena Dijour/Shutterstock.com

This edition first published 2024 by The Incorporated Catholic Truth Society 42-46 Harleyford Road London SE11 5AY.

ISBN 978 1 78469 833 1

CONTENTS

1. "HE LOVED US", St Paul says of Christ (cf. *Rom* 8:37), in order to make us realise that nothing can ever "separate us" from that love (*Rom* 8:39). Paul could say this with certainty because Jesus himself had told his disciples, "I have loved you" (*Jn* 15:9, 12). Even now, thc Lord says to us, "I have called you friends" (*Jn* 15:15). His open heart has gone before us and waits for us, unconditionally, asking only to offer us his love and friendship. For "he loved us first" (cf. *1 Jn* 4:10). Because of Jesus, "we have come to know and believe in the love that God has for us" (*1 Jn* 4:16).

CHAPTER ONE

THE IMPORTANCE OF THE HEART

2. The symbol of the heart has often been used to express the love of Jesus Christ. Some have questioned whether this symbol is still meaningful today. Yet living as we do in an age of superficiality, rushing frenetically from one thing to another without really knowing why, and ending up as insatiable consumers and slaves to the mechanisms of a market unconcerned about the deeper meaning of our lives, all of us need to rediscover the importance of the heart.[1]

WHAT DO WE MEAN BY "THE HEART"?

3. In classical Greek, the word *kardía* denotes the inmost part of human beings, animals and plants. For Homer, it indicates not only the centre of the body, but also the human soul and spirit. In the *Iliad*, thoughts and feelings proceed from the heart and are closely bound one to another.[2] The heart appears as the locus of desire and the place where important decisions take shape.[3] In Plato, the heart serves, as it were, to unite the rational and instinctive aspects of the person, since the impulses of both the higher faculties and the passions were thought to pass through the veins that converge in the heart.[4] From ancient times, then, there has been an appreciation of the fact that human beings are not simply a sum of different skills, but a unity of body and soul with a co-ordinating centre that provides a backdrop of meaning and direction to all that a person experiences.

---

[1] Many of the reflections in this first chapter were inspired by the unpublished writings of the late Fr Diego Fares, S.J. May the Lord grant him eternal rest.

[2] Cf. Homer, *Iliad*, XXI, 441.

[3] Cf. *Iliad*, X, 244.

[4] Cf. Plato, *Timaeus*, 65 c-d; 70.

4. The Bible tells us that, "the Word of God is living and active...
it is able to judge the thoughts and intentions of the heart"
(*Heb* 4:12). In this way, it speaks to us of the heart as a core
that lies hidden beneath all outward appearances, even beneath
the superficial thoughts that can lead us astray. The disciples of
Emmaus, on their mysterious journey in the company of the risen
Christ, experienced a moment of anguish, confusion, despair
and disappointment. Yet, beyond and in spite of this, something
was happening deep within them: "Were not our hearts burning
within us while he was talking to us on the road?" (*Lk* 24:32).

5. The heart is also the locus of sincerity, where deceit and
disguise have no place. It usually indicates our true intentions,
what we really think, believe and desire, the "secrets" that we
tell no one: in a word, the naked truth about ourselves. It is the
part of us that is neither appearance or illusion, but is instead
authentic, real, entirely "who we are". That is why Samson, who
kept from Delilah the secret of his strength, was asked by her,
"How can you say, 'I love you', when your heart is not with me?"
(*Judg* 16:15). Only when Samson opened his heart to her, did she
realise "that he had told her his whole secret" (*Judg* 16:18).

6. This interior reality of each person is frequently concealed
behind a great deal of "foliage", which makes it difficult for us
not only to understand ourselves, but even more to know others:
"The heart is devious above all else; it is perverse, who can
understand it?" (*Jer* 17:9). We can understand, then, the advice
of the Book of Proverbs: "Keep your heart with all vigilance,
for from it flow the springs of life; put away from you crooked
speech" (4:23-24). Mere appearances, dishonesty and deception
harm and pervert the heart. Despite our every attempt to appear
as something we are not, our heart is the ultimate judge, not of
what we show or hide from others, but of who we truly are. It is
the basis for any sound life project; nothing worthwhile can be
undertaken apart from the heart. False appearances and untruths
ultimately leave us empty-handed.

7. As an illustration of this, I would repeat a story I have already told on another occasion. "For the carnival, when we were children, my grandmother would make a pastry using a very thin batter. When she dropped the strips of batter into the oil, they would expand, but then, when we bit into them, they were empty inside. In the dialect we spoke, those cookies were called 'lies'... My grandmother explained why: 'Like lies, they look big, but are empty inside; they are false, unreal'".[5]

8. Instead of running after superficial satisfactions and playing a role for the benefit of others, we would do better to think about the really important questions in life. Who am I, really? What am I looking for? What direction do I want to give to my life, my decisions and my actions? Why and for what purpose am I in this world? How do I want to look back on my life once it ends? What meaning do I want to give to all my experiences? Who do I want to be for others? Who am I for God? All these questions lead us back to the heart.

RETURNING TO THE HEART

9. In this "liquid" world of ours, we need to start speaking once more about the heart and thinking about this place where every person, of every class and condition, creates a synthesis, where they encounter the radical source of their strengths, convictions, passions and decisions. Yet we find ourselves immersed in societies of serial consumers who live from day to day, dominated by the hectic pace and bombarded by technology, lacking in the patience needed to engage in the processes that an interior life by its very nature requires. In contemporary society, people "risk losing their centre, the centre of their very selves".[6] "Indeed, the men and women of our time often find themselves confused and torn apart, almost bereft of an inner principle that

---

[5] *Homily at Morning Mass in Domus Sanctae Marthae*, 14th October 2016: *L'Osservatore Romano*, 15th October 2016, p. 8.

[6] St John Paul II, *Angelus*, 2nd July 2000: *L'Osservatore Romano*, 3rd-4th July 2000, p. 4.

can create unity and harmony in their lives and actions. Models of behaviour that, sadly, are now widespread exaggerate our rational-technological dimension or, on the contrary, that of our instincts".[7] No room is left for the heart.

10. The issues raised by today's liquid society are much discussed, but this depreciation of the deep core of our humanity – the heart – has a much longer history. We find it already present in Hellenic and pre-Christian rationalism, in post-Christian idealism and in materialism in its various guises. The heart has been ignored in anthropology, and the great philosophical tradition finds it a foreign notion, preferring other concepts such as reason, will or freedom. The very meaning of the term is imprecise and hard to situate within our human experience. Perhaps this is due to the difficulty of treating it as a "clear and distinct idea", or because it entails the question of self-understanding, where the deepest part of us is also that which is least known. Even encountering others does not necessarily prove to be a way of encountering ourselves, inasmuch as our thought patterns are dominated by an unhealthy individualism. Many people feel safer constructing their systems of thought in the more readily controllable domain of intelligence and will. The failure to make room for the heart, as distinct from our human powers and passions viewed in isolation from one another, has resulted in a stunting of the idea of a personal centre, in which love, in the end, is the one reality that can unify all the others.

11. If we devalue the heart, we also devalue what it means to speak from the heart, to act with the heart, to cultivate and heal the heart. If we fail to appreciate the specificity of the heart, we miss the messages that the mind alone cannot communicate; we miss out on the richness of our encounters with others; we miss out on poetry. We also lose track of history and our own past, since our real personal history is built with the heart. At the end of our lives, that alone will matter.

---

[7] Id., *Catechesis*, 8th June 1994: *L'Osservatore Romano*, 9th June 1994, p. 5.

12. It must be said, then, that we have a heart, a heart that coexists with other hearts that help to make it a "Thou". Since we cannot develop this theme at length, we will take a character from one of Dostoevsky's novels, Nikolai Stavrogin.[8] Romano Guardini argues that Stavrogin is the very embodiment of evil, because his chief trait is his heartlessness: "Stavrogin has no heart, hence his mind is cold and empty and his body sunken in bestial sloth and sensuality. He has no heart, hence he can draw close to no one and no one can ever truly draw close to him. For only the heart creates intimacy, true closeness between two persons. Only the heart is able to welcome and offer hospitality. Intimacy is the proper activity and the domain of the heart. Stavrogin is always infinitely distant, even from himself, because a man can enter into himself only with the heart, not with the mind. It is not in a man's power to enter into his own interiority with the mind. Hence, if the heart is not alive, man remains a stranger to himself".[9]

13. All our actions need to be put under the "political rule" of the heart. In this way, our aggressiveness and obsessive desires will find rest in the greater good that the heart proposes and in the power of the heart to resist evil. The mind and the will are put at the service of the greater good by sensing and savouring truths, rather than seeking to master them as the sciences tend to do. The will desires the greater good that the heart recognises, while the imagination and emotions are themselves guided by the beating of the heart.

14. It could be said, then, that I am my heart, for my heart is what sets me apart, shapes my spiritual identity and puts me in communion with other people. The algorithms operating in the digital world show that our thoughts and will are much more "uniform" than we had previously thought. They are easily predictable and thus capable of being manipulated. That is not the case with the heart.

---

[8] *The Demons* (1873).

[9] Romano Guardini, *Religiöse Gestalten in Dostojewskijs Werk*, Mainz/Paderborn, 1989, pp. 236ff.

15. The word "heart" proves its value for philosophy and theology in their efforts to reach an integral synthesis. Nor can its meaning be exhausted by biology, psychology, anthropology or any other science. It is one of those primordial words that "describe realities belonging to man precisely in so far as he is one whole (as a corporeo-spiritual person)".[10] It follows that biologists are not being more "realistic" when they discuss the heart, since they see only one aspect of it; the whole is not less real, but even more real. Nor can abstract language ever acquire the same concrete and integrative meaning. The word "heart" evokes the inmost core of our person, and thus it enables us to understand ourselves in our integrity and not merely under one isolated aspect.

16. This unique power of the heart also helps us to understand why, when we grasp a reality with our heart, we know it better and more fully. This inevitably leads us to the love of which the heart is capable, for "the inmost core of reality is love".[11] For Heidegger, as interpreted by one contemporary thinker, philosophy does not begin with a simple concept or certainty, but with a shock: "Thought must be provoked before it begins to work with concepts or while it works with them. Without deep emotion, thought cannot begin. The first mental image would thus be goose bumps. What first stirs one to think and question is deep emotion. Philosophy always takes place in a basic mood (*Stimmung*)".[12] That is where the heart comes in, since it "houses the states of mind and functions as a 'keeper of the state of mind'. The 'heart' listens in a non-metaphoric way to 'the silent voice' of being, allowing itself to be tempered and determined by it".[13]

---

[10] Karl Rahner, *"Some Theses for a Theology of Devotion to the Sacred Heart"*, in *Theological Investigations*, vol. III, Baltimore-London, 1967, p. 332.

[11] Ibid., p. 333.

[12] Byung-Chul Han, *Heideggers Herz. Zum Begriff der Stimmung bei Martin Heidegger*, München, 1996, p. 39.

[13] Ibid., p. 60; cf. p. 176.

THE HEART UNITES THE FRAGMENTS

17. At the same time, the heart makes all authentic bonding possible, since a relationship not shaped by the heart is incapable of overcoming the fragmentation caused by individualism. Two monads may approach one another, but they will never truly connect. A society dominated by narcissism and self-centredness will increasingly become "heartless". This will lead in turn to the "loss of desire", since as other persons disappear from the horizon we find ourselves trapped within walls of our own making, no longer capable of healthy relationships.[14] As a result, we also become incapable of openness to God. As Heidegger puts it, to be open to the divine we need to build a "guest house".[15]

18. We see, then, that in the heart of each person there is a mysterious connection between self-knowledge and openness to others, between the encounter with one's personal uniqueness and the willingness to give oneself to others. We become ourselves only to the extent that we acquire the ability to acknowledge others, while only those who can acknowledge and accept themselves are then able to encounter others.

19. The heart is also capable of unifying and harmonising our personal history, which may seem hopelessly fragmented, yet is the place where everything can make sense. The Gospel tells us this in speaking of Our Lady, who saw things with the heart. She was able to dialogue with the things she experienced by pondering them in her heart, treasuring their memory and viewing them in a greater perspective. The best expression of how the heart thinks is found in the two passages in St Luke's Gospel that speak to us of how Mary "treasured (*synetérei*) all these things and pondered (*symbállousa*) them in her heart" (cf. *Lk* 2:19 and 51). The Greek verb *symbállein*, "ponder", evokes the image of putting two things together ("symbols") in one's

---

[14] Cf. Id., *Agonie des Eros*, Berlin, 2012.

[15] Cf. Martin Heidegger, *Erläuterungen zu Hölderlins Dichtung*, Frankfürt a. M., 1981, p. 120.

mind and reflecting on them, in a dialogue with oneself. In Luke 2:51, the verb used is *dietérei*, which has the sense of "keep". What Mary "kept" was not only her memory of what she had seen and heard, but also those aspects of it that she did not yet understand; these nonetheless remained present and alive in her memory, waiting to be "put together" in her heart.

20. In this age of artificial intelligence, we cannot forget that poetry and love are necessary to save our humanity. No algorithm will ever be able to capture, for example, the nostalgia that all of us feel, whatever our age, and wherever we live, when we recall how we first used a fork to seal the edges of the pies that we helped our mothers or grandmothers to make at home. It was a moment of culinary apprenticeship, somewhere between child-play and adulthood, when we first felt responsible for working and helping one another. Along with the fork, I could also mention thousands of other little things that are a precious part of everyone's life: a smile we elicited by telling a joke, a picture we sketched in the light of a window, the first game of soccer we played with a rag ball, the worms we collected in a shoebox, a flower we pressed in the pages of a book, our concern for a fledgling bird fallen from its nest, a wish we made in plucking a daisy. All these little things, ordinary in themselves yet extraordinary for us, can never be captured by algorithms. The fork, the joke, the window, the ball, the shoebox, the book, the bird, the flower: all of these live on as precious memories "kept" deep in our heart.

21. This profound core, present in every man and woman, is not that of the soul, but of the entire person in his or her unique psychosomatic identity. Everything finds its unity in the heart, which can be the dwelling-place of love in all its spiritual, psychic and even physical dimensions. In a word, if love reigns in our heart, we become, in a complete and luminous way, the persons we are meant to be, for every human being is created above all else for love. In the deepest fibre of our being, we were made to love and to be loved.

22. For this reason, when we witness the outbreak of new wars, with the complicity, tolerance or indifference of other countries, or petty power struggles over partisan interests, we may be tempted to conclude that our world is losing its heart. We need only to see and listen to the elderly women – from both sides – who are at the mercy of these devastating conflicts. It is heartbreaking to see them mourning for their murdered grandchildren, or longing to die themselves after losing the homes where they spent their entire lives. Those women, who were often pillars of strength and resilience amid life's difficulties and hardships, now, at the end of their days, are experiencing, in place of a well-earned rest, only anguish, fear and outrage. Casting the blame on others does not resolve these shameful and tragic situations. To see these elderly women weep, and not feel that this is something intolerable, is a sign of a world that has grown heartless.

23. Whenever a person thinks, questions and reflects on his or her true identity, strives to understand the deeper questions of life and to seek God, or experiences the thrill of catching a glimpse of truth, it leads to the realisation that our fulfilment as human beings is found in love. In loving, we sense that we come to know the purpose and goal of our existence in this world. Everything comes together in a state of coherence and harmony. It follows that, in contemplating the meaning of our lives, perhaps the most decisive question we can ask is, "Do I have a heart?"

FIRE

24. All that we have said has implications for the spiritual life. For example, the theology underlying the *Spiritual Exercises* of St Ignatius Loyola is based on "affection" (*affectus*). The structure of the Exercises assumes a firm and heartfelt desire to "rearrange" one's life, a desire that in turn provides the strength and the wherewithal to achieve that goal. The rules and the compositions of place that Ignatius furnishes are in the service of something much more important, namely, the mystery of the human heart. Michel de Certeau shows how the "movements"

of which Ignatius speaks are the "inbreaking" of God's desire and the desire of our own heart amid the orderly progression of the meditations. Something unexpected and hitherto unknown starts to speak in our heart, breaking through our superficial knowledge and calling it into question. This is the start of a new process of "setting our life in order", beginning with the heart. It is not about intellectual concepts that need to be put into practice in our daily lives, as if affectivity and practice were merely the effects of – and dependent upon – the data of knowledge.[16]

25. Where the thinking of the philosopher halts, there the heart of the believer presses on in love and adoration, in pleading for forgiveness and in willingness to serve in whatever place the Lord allows us to choose, in order to follow in his footsteps. At that point, we realise that in God's eyes we are a "Thou", and for that very reason we can be an "I". Indeed, only the Lord offers to treat each one of us as a "Thou", always and forever. Accepting his friendship is a matter of the heart; it is what constitutes us as persons in the fullest sense of that word.

26. St Bonaventure tells us that in the end we should not pray for light, but for "raging fire".[17] He teaches that, "faith is in the intellect, in such a way as to provoke affection. In this sense, for example, the knowledge that Christ died for us does not remain knowledge, but necessarily becomes affection, love".[18] Along the same lines, St John Henry Newman took as his motto the phrase *cor ad cor loquitur*, since, beyond all our thoughts and ideas, the Lord saves us by speaking to our hearts from his Sacred Heart. This realisation led him, the distinguished intellectual, to recognise that his deepest encounter with himself and with the Lord came not from his reading or reflection, but from his prayerful dialogue, heart to heart, with Christ, alive and

---

[16] Cf. Michel de Certeau, *L'espace du désir ou le «fondement» des Exercises Spirituels: Christus* 77 (1973), pp. 118-128.

[17] *Itinerarium Mentis in Deum*, VII, 6.

[18] Id., *Proemium in I Sent.*, q. 3.

present. It was in the Eucharist that Newman encountered the living heart of Jesus, capable of setting us free, giving meaning to each moment of our lives, and bestowing true peace: "O most Sacred, most loving Heart of Jesus, Thou art concealed in the Holy Eucharist, and Thou beatest for us still... I worship Thee then with all my best love and awe, with my fervent affection, with my most subdued, most resolved will. O my God, when Thou dost condescend to suffer me to receive Thee, to eat and drink Thee, and Thou for a while takest up Thy abode within me, O make my heart beat with Thy Heart. Purify it of all that is earthly, all that is proud and sensual, all that is hard and cruel, of all perversity, of all disorder, of all deadness. So fill it with Thee, that neither the events of the day nor the circumstances of the time may have power to ruffle it, but that in Thy love and Thy fear it may have peace".[19]

27. Before the heart of Jesus, living and present, our mind, enlightened by the Spirit, grows in the understanding of his words and our will is moved to put them into practice. This could easily remain on the level of a kind of self-reliant moralism. Hearing and tasting the Lord, and paying him due honour, however, is a matter of the heart. Only the heart is capable of setting our other powers and passions, and our entire person, in a stance of reverence and loving obedience before the Lord.

THE WORLD CAN CHANGE, BEGINNING WITH THE HEART

28. It is only by starting from the heart that our communities will succeed in uniting and reconciling differing minds and wills, so that the Spirit can guide us in unity as brothers and sisters. Reconciliation and peace are also born of the heart. The heart of Christ is "ecstasy", openness, gift and encounter. In that heart, we learn to relate to one another in wholesome and happy

---

[19] St John Henry Newman, *Meditations and Devotions*, London, 1912, Part III [XVI], par. 3, pp. 573-574.

ways, and to build up in this world God's kingdom of love and justice. Our hearts, united with the heart of Christ, are capable of working this social miracle.

29. Taking the heart seriously, then, has consequences for society as a whole. The Second Vatican Council teaches that, "every one of us needs a change of heart; we must set our gaze on the whole world and look to those tasks we can all perform together in order to bring about the betterment of our race".[20] For "the imbalances affecting the world today are in fact a symptom of a deeper imbalance rooted in the human heart".[21] In pondering the tragedies afflicting our world, the Council urges us to return to the heart. It explains that human beings "by their interior life, transcend the entire material universe; they experience this deep interiority when they enter into their own heart, where God, who probes the heart, awaits them, and where they decide their own destiny in the sight of God".[22]

30. This in no way implies an undue reliance on our own abilities. Let us never forget that our hearts are not self-sufficient, but frail and wounded. They possess an ontological dignity, yet at the same time must seek an ever more dignified life.[23] The Second Vatican Council points out that "the ferment of the Gospel has aroused and continues to arouse in human hearts an unquenchable thirst for human dignity".[24] Yet to live in accordance with this dignity, it is not enough to know the Gospel or to carry out mechanically its demands. We need the help of God's love. Let us turn, then, to the heart of Christ, that core of his being, which is a blazing furnace of divine and human love and the most sublime fulfilment to which humanity can aspire.

---

[20] Pastoral Constitution *Gaudium et Spes*, 82.

[21] Ibid., 10.

[22] Ibid., 14.

[23] Cf. Dicastery for the Doctrine of the Faith, Declaration *Dignitas Infinita* (2nd April 2024), 8. Cf. *L'Osservatore Romano*, 8th April 2024.

[24] Pastoral Constitution *Gaudium et Spes*, 26.

There, in that heart, we truly come at last to know ourselves and we learn how to love.

31. In the end, that Sacred Heart is the unifying principle of all reality, since "Christ is the heart of the world, and the paschal mystery of his death and resurrection is the centre of history, which, because of him, is a history of salvation".[25] All creatures "are moving forward with us and through us towards a common point of arrival, which is God, in that transcendent fullness where the risen Christ embraces and illumines all things".[26] In the presence of the heart of Christ, I once more ask the Lord to have mercy on this suffering world in which he chose to dwell as one of us. May he pour out the treasures of his light and love, so that our world, which presses forward despite wars, socio-economic disparities and uses of technology that threaten our humanity, may regain the most important and necessary thing of all: its heart.

---

[25] St John Paul II, *Angelus*, 28th June 1998: *L'Osservatore Romano*, 30th June-1st July 1998, p. 7.

[26] Encyclical Letter *Laudato Si'* (24th May 2015), 83: AAS 107 (2015), 880.

CHAPTER TWO

ACTIONS AND WORDS OF LOVE

32. The heart of Christ, as the symbol of the deepest and most personal source of his love for us, is the very core of the initial preaching of the Gospel. It stands at the origin of our faith, as the wellspring that refreshes and enlivens our Christian beliefs.

ACTIONS THAT REFLECT THE HEART

33. Christ showed the depth of his love for us not by lengthy explanations but by concrete actions. By examining his interactions with others, we can come to realise how he treats each one of us, even though at times this may be difficult to see. Let us now turn to the place where our faith can encounter this truth: the word of God.

34. The Gospel tells us that Jesus "came to his own" (cf. *Jn* 1:11). Those words refer to us, for the Lord does not treat us as strangers but as a possession that he watches over and cherishes. He treats us truly as "his own". This does not mean that we are his slaves, something that he himself denies: "I do not call you servants" (*Jn* 15:15). Rather, it refers to the sense of mutual belonging typical of friends. Jesus came to meet us, bridging all distances; he became as close to us as the simplest, everyday realities of our lives. Indeed, he has another name, "Emmanuel", which means "God with us", God as part of our lives, God as living in our midst. The Son of God became incarnate and "emptied himself, taking the form of a slave" (*Phil* 2:7).

35. This becomes clear when we see Jesus at work. He seeks people out, approaches them, ever open to an encounter with them. We see it when he stops to converse with the Samaritan woman at the well where she went to draw water (cf. *Jn* 4:5-7).

We see it when, in the darkness of night, he meets Nicodemus, who feared to be seen in his presence (cf. *Jn* 3:1-2). We marvel when he allows his feet to be washed by a prostitute (cf. *Lk* 7:36-50), when he says to the woman caught in adultery, "Neither do I condemn you" (*Jn* 8:11), or again when he chides the disciples for their indifference and quietly asks the blind man on the roadside, "What do you want me to do for you?" (*Mk* 10:51). Christ shows that God is closeness, compassion and tender love.

36. Whenever Jesus healed someone, he preferred to do it, not from a distance but in close proximity: "He stretched out his hand and touched him" (*Mt* 8:3). "He touched her hand" (*Mt* 8:15). "He touched their eyes" (*Mt* 9:29). Once he even stopped to cure a deaf man with his own saliva (cf. *Mk* 7:33), as a mother would do, so that people would not think of him as removed from their lives. "The Lord knows the fine science of the caress. In his compassion, God does not love us with words; he comes forth to meet us and, by his closeness, he shows us the depth of his tender love".[27]

37. If we find it hard to trust others because we have been hurt by lies, injuries and disappointments, the Lord whispers in our ear: "Take heart, son!" (*Mt* 9:2), "Take heart, daughter!" (*Mt* 9:22). He encourages us to overcome our fear and to realise that, with him at our side, we have nothing to lose. To Peter, in his fright, "Jesus immediately reached out his hand and caught him", saying, "You of little faith, why did you doubt?" (*Mt* 14:31). Nor should you be afraid. Let him draw near and sit at your side. There may be many people we distrust, but not him. Do not hesitate because of your sins. Keep in mind that many sinners "came and sat with him" (*Mt* 9:10), yet Jesus was scandalised by none of them. It was the religious élite that complained and treated him as "a glutton and a drunkard, a friend of tax collectors and sinners" (*Mt* 11:19). When the Pharisees criticised him for his closeness

---

[27] *Homily at Morning Mass in Domus Sanctae Marthae*, 7th June 2013: *L'Osservatore Romano*, 8th June 2013, p. 8.

to people deemed base or sinful, Jesus replied, "I desire mercy, not sacrifice" (*Mt* 9:13).

38. That same Jesus is now waiting for you to give him the chance to bring light to your life, to raise you up and to fill you with his strength. Before his death, he assured his disciples, "I will not leave you orphaned; I am coming to you. In a little while the world will no longer see me, but you will see me" (*Jn* 14:18-19). Jesus always finds a way to be present in your life, so that you can encounter him.

JESUS'S GAZE

39. The Gospel tells us that a rich man came up to Jesus, full of idealism yet lacking in the strength needed to change his life. Jesus then "looked at him" (*Mk* 10:21). Can you imagine that moment, that encounter between his eyes and those of Jesus? If Jesus calls you and summons you for a mission, he first looks at you, plumbs the depths of your heart and, knowing everything about you, fixes his gaze upon you. So it was when, "as he walked by the Sea of Galilee, he saw two brothers... and as he went from there, he saw two other brothers" (*Mt* 4:18, 21).

40. Many a page of the Gospel illustrates how attentive Jesus was to individuals and above all to their problems and needs. We are told that, "when he saw the crowds, he had compassion for them, because they were harassed and helpless" (*Mt* 9:36). Whenever we feel that everyone ignores us, that no one cares what becomes of us, that we are of no importance to anyone, he remains concerned for us. To Nathanael, standing apart and busy about his own affairs, he could say, "I saw you under the fig tree before Philip called you" (*Jn* 1:48).

41. Precisely out of concern for us, Jesus knows every one of our good intentions and small acts of charity. The Gospel tells us that once he "saw a poor widow put in two small copper coins" in the Temple treasury (*Lk* 21:2) and immediately brought it to

the attention of his disciples. Jesus thus appreciates the good that he sees in us. When the centurion approached him with complete confidence, "Jesus listened to him and was amazed" (*Mt* 8:10). How reassuring it is to know that, even if others are not aware of our good intentions or actions, Jesus sees them and regards them highly.

42. In his humanity, Jesus learned this from Mary, his mother. Our Lady carefully pondered the things she had experienced; she "treasured them... in her heart" (*Lk* 2:19, 51) and, with St Joseph, she taught Jesus from his earliest years to be attentive in this same way.

JESUS'S WORDS

43. Although the Scriptures preserve Jesus's words, ever alive and timely, there are moments when he speaks to us inwardly, calls us and leads us to a better place. That better place is his heart. There he invites us to find fresh strength and peace: "Come to me, all who are weary and are carrying heavy burdens, and I will give you rest" (*Mt* 11:28). In this sense, he could say to his disciples, "Abide in me" (*Jn* 15:4).

44. Jesus's words show that his holiness did not exclude deep emotions. On various occasions, he demonstrated a love that was both passionate and compassionate. He could be deeply moved and grieved, even to the point of shedding tears. It is clear that Jesus was not indifferent to the daily cares and concerns of people, such as their weariness or hunger: "I have compassion for this crowd...they have nothing to eat...they will faint on the way, and some of them have come from a great distance" (*Mk* 8:2-3).

45. The Gospel makes no secret of Jesus's love for Jerusalem: "As he came near and saw the city, he wept over it" (*Lk* 19:41). He then voiced the deepest desire of his heart: "If you had only recognised on this day the things that make for peace" (*Lk* 19:42).

The evangelists, while at times showing him in his power and glory, also portray his profound emotions in the face of death and the grief felt by his friends. Before recounting how Jesus, standing before the tomb of Lazarus, "began to weep" (*Jn* 11:35), the Gospel observes that, "Jesus loved Martha and her sister and Lazarus" (*Jn* 11:5) and that, seeing Mary and those who were with her weeping, "he was greatly disturbed in spirit and deeply moved" (*Jn* 11:33). The Gospel account leaves no doubt that his tears were genuine, the sign of inner turmoil. Nor do the Gospels attempt to conceal Jesus's anguish over his impending violent death at the hands of those whom he had loved so greatly: he "began to be distressed and agitated" (*Mk* 14:33), even to the point of crying out, "I am deeply grieved, even to death" (*Mk* 14:34). This inner turmoil finds its most powerful expression in his cry from the cross: "My God, my God, why have you forsaken me?" (*Mk* 15:34).

46. At first glance, all this may smack of pious sentimentalism. Yet it is supremely serious and of decisive importance, and finds its most sublime expression in Christ crucified. The cross is Jesus's most eloquent word of love. A word that is not shallow, sentimental or merely edifying. It is love, sheer love. That is why St Paul, struggling to find the right words to describe his relationship with Christ, could speak of "the Son of God, who loved me and gave himself for me" (*Gal* 2:20). This was Paul's deepest conviction: the knowledge that he was loved. Christ's self-offering on the cross became the driving force in Paul's life, yet it only made sense to him because he knew that something even greater lay behind it: the fact that "he loved me". At a time when many were seeking salvation, prosperity or security elsewhere, Paul, moved by the Spirit, was able to see farther and to marvel at the greatest and most essential thing of all: "Christ loved me".

47. Now, after considering Christ and seeing how his actions and words grant us insight into his heart, let us turn to the Church's reflection on the holy mystery of the Lord's Sacred Heart.

CHAPTER THREE

THIS IS THE HEART THAT HAS LOVED SO GREATLY

48. Devotion to the heart of Christ is not the veneration of a single organ apart from the Person of Jesus. What we contemplate and adore is the whole Jesus Christ, the Son of God made man, represented by an image that accentuates his heart. That heart of flesh is seen as the privileged sign of the inmost being of the incarnate Son and his love, both divine and human. More than any other part of his body, the heart of Jesus is "the natural sign and symbol of his boundless love".[28]

WORSHIPPING CHRIST

49. It is essential to realise that our relationship to the Person of Jesus Christ is one of friendship and adoration, drawn by the love represented under the image of his heart. We venerate that image, yet our worship is directed solely to the living Christ, in his divinity and his plenary humanity, so that we may be embraced by his human and divine love.

50. Whatever the image employed, it is clear that the living heart of Christ – not its representation – is the object of our worship, for it is part of his holy risen body, which is inseparable from the Son of God who assumed that body forever. We worship it because it is "the heart of the Person of the Word, to whom it is inseparably united".[29] Nor do we worship it for its own sake, but because with this heart the incarnate Son is alive, loves us and receives our love in return. Any act of love or worship of his

---

[28] Pius XII, Encyclical Letter *Haurietis Aquas* (15th May 1956), I: AAS 48 (1956), 316.

[29] Pius VI, Constitution *Auctorem Fidei* (28th August 1794), 63: DH 2663.

heart is thus "really and truly given to Christ himself",[30] since it spontaneously refers back to him and is "a symbol and a tender image of the infinite love of Jesus Christ".[31]

51. For this reason, it should never be imagined that this devotion may distract or separate us from Jesus and his love. In a natural and direct way, it points us to him and to him alone, who calls us to a precious friendship marked by dialogue, affection, trust and adoration. The Christ we see depicted with a pierced and burning heart is the same Christ who, for love of us, was born in Bethlehem, passed through Galilee healing the sick, embracing sinners and showing mercy. The same Christ who loved us to the very end, opening wide his arms on the cross, who then rose from the dead and now lives among us in glory.

VENERATING HIS IMAGE

52. While the image of Christ and his heart is not in itself an object of worship, neither is it simply one among many other possible images. It was not devised at a desk or designed by an artist; it is "no imaginary symbol, but a real symbol which represents the centre, the source from which salvation flowed for all humanity".[32]

53. Universal human experience has made the image of the heart something unique. Indeed, throughout history and in different parts of the world, it has become a symbol of personal intimacy, affection, emotional attachment and capacity for love. Transcending all scientific explanations, a hand placed on the heart of a friend expresses special affection: when two persons fall in love and draw close to one another, their hearts beat faster; when we are abandoned or deceived by someone we love, our hearts sink. So too, when we want to say something deeply personal, we often say that we are speaking "from the heart".

---

[30] Leo XIII, Encyclical Letter *Annum Sacrum* (25th May 1899): ASS 31 (1898-1899), 649.

[31] Ibid: *"Inest in Sacro Corde symbolum et expressa imago infinitæ Iesu Christi caritatis"*.

[32] *Angelus*, 9th June 2013: *L'Osservatore Romano*, 10th-11th June 2013, p. 8.

The language of poetry reflects the power of these experiences. In the course of history, the heart has taken on unique symbolic value that is more than merely conventional.

54. It is understandable, then, that the Church has chosen the image of the heart to represent the human and divine love of Jesus Christ and the inmost core of his Person. Yet, while the depiction of a heart afire may be an eloquent symbol of the burning love of Jesus Christ, it is important that this heart not be represented apart from him. In this way, his summons to a personal relationship of encounter and dialogue will become all the more meaningful.[33] The venerable image portraying Christ holding out his loving heart also shows him looking directly at us, inviting us to encounter, dialogue and trust; it shows his strong hands capable of supporting us and his lips that speak personally to each of us.

55. The heart, too, has the advantage of being immediately recognisable as the profound unifying centre of the body, an expression of the totality of the person, unlike other individual organs. As a part that stands for the whole, we could easily misinterpret it, were we to contemplate it apart from the Lord himself. The image of the heart should lead us to contemplate Christ in all the beauty and richness of his humanity and divinity.

56. Whatever particular aesthetic qualities we may ascribe to various portrayals of Christ's heart when we pray before them, it is not the case that "something is sought from them or that blind trust is put in images as once was done by the Gentiles". Rather,

---

[33] We can thus understand why the Church has forbidden placing on the altar representations of the heart of Jesus or Mary alone (cf. Response of the Congregation of Sacred Rites to the Reverend Charles Lecoq, P.S.S., 5th April 1879: *Decreta Authentica Congregationis Sacrorum Rituum ex Actis ejusdem Collecta*, vol. III, 107-108, n. 3492). Outside the liturgy, "for private devotion" (ibid.), the symbolism of a heart can be used as a teaching aid, an aesthetic figure or an emblem that invites one to meditate on the love of Christ, but this risks taking the heart as an object of adoration or spiritual dialogue apart from the Person of Christ. On 31st March 1887, the Congregation gave another, similar response (ibid., 187, n. 3673).

"through these images that we kiss, and before which we kneel and uncover our heads, we are adoring Christ".[34]

57. Certain of these representations may indeed strike us as tasteless and not particularly conducive to affection or prayer. Yet this is of little importance, since they are only invitations to prayer, and, to cite an Eastern proverb, we should not limit our gaze to the finger that points us to the moon. Whereas the Eucharist is a real presence to be worshipped, sacred images, albeit blessed, point beyond themselves, inviting us to lift up our hearts and to unite them to the heart of the living Christ. The image we venerate thus serves as a summons to make room for an encounter with Christ, and to worship him in whatever way we wish to picture him. Standing before the image, we stand before Christ, and in his presence, "love pauses, contemplates mystery, and enjoys it in silence".[35]

58. At the same time, we must never forget that the image of the heart speaks to us of the flesh and of earthly realities. In this way, it points us to the God who wished to become one of us, a part of our history, and a companion on our earthly journey. A more abstract or stylised form of devotion would not necessarily be more faithful to the Gospel, for in this eloquent and tangible sign we see how God willed to reveal himself and to draw close to us.

A LOVE THAT IS TANGIBLE

59. On the other hand, love and the human heart do not always go together, since hatred, indifference and selfishness can also reign in our hearts. Yet we cannot attain our fulfilment as human beings unless we open our hearts to others; only through love do we become fully ourselves. The deepest part of us, created for

---

[34] Ecumenical Council of Trent, Session XXV, Decree *Mandat Sancta Synodus* (3rd December 1563): DH 1823.

[35] Fifth General Conference of the Latin American and Caribbean Bishops, *Aparecida Document* (29th June 2007), n. 259.

love, will fulfil God's plan only if we learn to love. And the heart is the symbol of that love.

60. The eternal Son of God, in his utter transcendence, chose to love each of us with a human heart. His human emotions became the sacrament of that infinite and endless love. His heart, then, is not merely a symbol for some disembodied spiritual truth. In gazing upon the Lord's heart, we contemplate a physical reality, his human flesh, which enables him to possess genuine human emotions and feelings, like ourselves, albeit fully transformed by his divine love. Our devotion must ascend to the infinite love of the Person of the Son of God, yet we need to keep in mind that his divine love is inseparable from his human love. The image of his heart of flesh helps us to do precisely this.

61. Since the heart continues to be seen in the popular mind as the affective centre of each human being, it remains the best means of signifying the divine love of Christ, united forever and inseparably to his wholly human love. Pius XII observed that the Gospel, in referring to the love of Christ's heart, speaks "not only of divine charity but also human affection". Indeed, "the heart of Jesus Christ, hypostatically united to the divine Person of the Word, beyond doubt throbbed with love and every other tender affection".[36]

62. The Fathers of the Church, opposing those who denied or downplayed the true humanity of Christ, insisted on the concrete and tangible reality of the Lord's human affections. St Basil emphasised that the Lord's incarnation was not something fanciful, and that "the Lord possessed our natural affections".[37] St John Chrysostom pointed to an example: "Had he not possessed our nature, he would not have experienced sadness from time to time".[38] St Ambrose stated that "in taking a soul,

---

[36] Encyclical Letter *Haurietis Aquas* (15th May 1956), I: AAS 48 (1956), 323-324.

[37] *Ep.* 261, 3: PG 32, 972.

[38] *In Io. homil.* 63, 2: PG 59, 350.

he took on the passions of the soul".[39] For St Augustine, our human affections, which Christ assumed, are now open to the life of grace: "The Lord Jesus assumed these affections of our human weakness, as he did the flesh of our human weakness, not out of necessity, but consciously and freely... lest any who feel grief and sorrow amid the trials of life should think themselves separated from his grace".[40] Finally, St John Damascene viewed the genuine affections shown by Christ in his humanity as proof that he assumed our nature in its entirety in order to redeem and transform it in its entirety: Christ, then, assumed all that is part of human nature, so that all might be sanctified.[41]

63. Here, we can benefit from the thoughts of a theologian who maintains that, "due to the influence of Greek thought, theology long relegated the body and feelings to the world of the pre-human or sub-human or potentially inhuman; yet what theology did not resolve in theory, spirituality resolved in practice. This, together with popular piety, preserved the relationship with the corporal, psychological and historical reality of Jesus. The Stations of the Cross, devotion to Christ's wounds, his Precious Blood and his Sacred Heart, and a variety of Eucharist devotions... all bridged the gaps in theology by nourishing our hearts and imagination, our tender love for Christ, our hope and memory, our desires and feelings. Reason and logic took other directions".[42]

A THREEFOLD LOVE

64. Nor do we remain only on the level of the Lord's human feelings, beautiful and moving as they are. In contemplating Christ's heart we also see how, in his fine and noble sentiments, his kindness and gentleness and his signs of genuine human affection, the deeper truth of his infinite divine love is revealed.

---

[39] *De fide ad Gratianum*, II, 7, 56: PL 16, 594 (ed. 1880).

[40] *Enarr. in Ps.* 87, 3: PL 37, 1111.

[41] Cf. *De fide orth.* 3, 6, 20: PG 94, 1006, 1081.

[42] Olegario González de Cardedal, *La entraña del cristianismo*, Salamanca, 2010, 70-71.

In the words of Benedict XVI, "from the infinite horizon of his love, God wished to enter into the limits of human history and the human condition. He took on a body and a heart. Thus, we can contemplate and encounter the infinite in the finite, the invisible and ineffable mystery in the human heart of Jesus the Nazarene".[43]

65. The image of the Lord's heart speaks to us in fact of a threefold love. First, we contemplate his infinite divine love. Then our thoughts turn to the spiritual dimension of his humanity, in which the heart is "the symbol of that most ardent love which, infused into his soul, enriches his human will". Finally, "it is a symbol also of his sensible love".[44]

66. These three loves are not separate, parallel or disconnected, but together act and find expression in a constant and vital unity. For "by faith, through which we believe that the human and divine nature were united in the Person of Christ, we can see the closest bonds between the tender love of the physical heart of Jesus and the twofold spiritual love, namely human and divine".[45]

67. Entering into the heart of Christ, we feel loved by a human heart filled with affections and emotions like our own. Jesus's human will freely chooses to love us, and that spiritual love is flooded with grace and charity. When we plunge into the depths of his heart, we find ourselves overwhelmed by the immense glory of his infinite love as the eternal Son, which we can no longer separate from his human love. It is precisely in his human love, and not apart from it, that we encounter his divine love: we discover "the infinite in the finite".[46]

---

[43] *Angelus*, 1st June 2008: *L'Osservatore Romano*, 2nd-3rd June 2008, p. 1.

[44] Pius XII, Encyclical Letter *Haurietis Aquas* (15th May 1956), II: AAS 48 (1956), 327-328.

[45] Ibid.: AAS 48 (1956), 343-344.

[46] Benedict XVI, *Angelus*, 1st June 2008: *L'Osservatore Romano*, 2nd-3rd June 2008, p. 1.

68. It is the constant and unequivocal teaching of the Church that our worship of Christ's person is undivided, inseparably embracing both his divine and his human natures. From ancient times, the Church has taught that we are to "adore one and the same Christ, the Son of God and of man, consisting of and in two inseparable and undivided natures".[47] And we do so "with one act of adoration... inasmuch as the Word became flesh".[48] Christ is in no way "worshipped in two natures, whereby two acts of worship are introduced"; instead, we venerate "by one act of worship God the Word made flesh, together with his own flesh".[49]

69. St John of the Cross sought to explain that in mystical experience the infinite love of the risen Christ is not perceived as alien to our lives. The infinite in some way "condescends" to enable us, through the open heart of Christ, to experience an encounter of truly reciprocal love, for "it is indeed credible that a bird of lowly flight can capture the royal eagle of the heights, if this eagle descends with the desire of being captured".[50] He also explains that the Bridegroom, "beholding that the bride is wounded with love for him, because of her moan he too is wounded with love for her. Among lovers, the wound of one is the wound of both".[51] John of the Cross regards the image of Christ's pierced side as an invitation to full union with the Lord. Christ is the wounded stag, wounded when we fail to let ourselves be touched by his love, who descends to the streams of water to quench his thirst and is comforted whenever we turn to him:

---

[47] Vigilius, Constitution *Inter Innumeras Sollicitudines* (14th May 553): DH 420.

[48] Ecumenical Council of Ephesus, *Anathemas of Cyril of Alexandria*, 8: DH 259.

[49] Second Ecumenical Council of Constantinople, Session VIII (2nd June 553), Canon 9: DH 431.

[50] St John of the Cross, *Spiritual Canticle*, red. A, Stanza 22, 4.

[51] Ibid., Stanza 12, 8.

"Return, dove!
The wounded stag
is in sight on the hill,
cooled by the breeze of your flight".[52]

TRINITARIAN PERSPECTIVES

70. Devotion to the heart of Jesus, as a direct contemplation of the Lord that draws us into union with him, is clearly Christological in nature. We see this in the Letter to the Hebrews, which urges us to "run with perseverance the race that is set before us, looking to Jesus" (12:2). At the same time, we need to realise that Jesus speaks of himself as the way to the Father: "I am the way... No one comes to the Father except through me" (*Jn* 14:6). Jesus wants to bring us to the Father. That is why, from the very beginning, the Church's preaching does not end with Jesus, but with the Father. As source and fullness, the Father is ultimately the one to be glorified.[53]

71. If we turn, for example, to the Letter to the Ephesians, we can see clearly how our worship is directed to the Father: "I bow my knees before the Father" (3:14). There is "one God and Father of all, who is above all and through all and in all" (4:6). "Give thanks to God the Father at all times and for everything" (5:20). It is the Father "for whom we exist" (*1 Cor* 8:6). In this sense, St John Paul II could say that, "the whole of the Christian life is like a great pilgrimage to the house of the Father".[54] This too was the experience of St Ignatius of Antioch on his path to martyrdom: "In me there is left no spark of desire for mundane

---

[52] Ibid., Stanza 12, 1.

[53] "There is one God, the Father, from whom are all things and for whom we exist" (*1 Cor* 8:6). "To our God and Father be glory forever and ever. Amen" (*Phil* 4:20). "Blessed be the God and Father of our Lord Jesus Christ, the Father of mercies and the God of all consolation" (*2 Cor* 1:3).

[54] Apostolic Letter *Tertio Millennio Adveniente* (10th November 1994), 49: AAS 87 (1995), 35.

things, but only a murmur of living water that whispers within me, 'Come to the Father'".[55]

72. The Father is, before all else, the Father of Jesus Christ: "Blessed be the God and Father of our Lord Jesus Christ" *(Eph* 1:3). He is "the God of our Lord Jesus Christ, the Father of glory" *(Eph* 1:17). When the Son became man, all the hopes and aspirations of his human heart were directed towards the Father. If we consider the way Christ spoke of the Father, we can grasp the love and affection that his human heart felt for him, this complete and constant orientation towards him.[56] Jesus's life among us was a journey of response to the constant call of his human heart to come to the Father.[57]

73. We know that the Aramaic word Jesus used to address the Father was *"Abba"*, an intimate and familiar term that some found disconcerting (cf. *Jn* 5:18). It is how he addressed the Father in expressing his anguish at his impending death: *"Abba, Father, for you all things are possible; remove this cup from me; yet not what I want, but what you want"* (*Mk* 14:36). Jesus knew well that he had always been loved by the Father: "You loved me before the foundation of the world" (*Jn* 17:24). In his human heart, he had rejoiced at hearing the Father say to him: "You are my Son, the Beloved; with you I am well pleased" (*Mk* 1:11).

74. The Fourth Gospel tells us that the eternal Son was always "close to the Father's heart" (*Jn* 1:18).[58] St Irenaeus thus declares that "the Son of God was with the Father from the beginning".[59] Origen, for his part, maintains that the Son perseveres "in uninterrupted contemplation of the depths of the Father".[60]

---

[55] *Ad Rom.*, 7: PG 5, 694.

[56] "That the world may know that I love the Father" (*Jn* 14:31); "The Father and I are one" (*Jn* 10:30); "I am in the Father and the Father is in me" (*Jn* 14:10).

[57] "I am going to the Father" (*pros ton Patéra*: *Jn* 16:28). "I am coming to you" (*pros se*: *Jn* 17:11).

[58] " *eis ton kolpon tou Patrós*".

[59] *Adv. Haer.*, III, 18, 1: PG 7, 932.

[60] *In Joh*. II, 2: PG 14, 110.

When the Son took flesh, he spent entire nights conversing with his beloved Father on the mountaintop (cf. *Lk* 6:12). He told us, "I must be in my Father's house" (*Lk* 2:49). We see too how he expressed his praise: "Jesus rejoiced in the Holy Spirit and said, 'I thank you, Father, Lord of heaven and earth' (*Lk* 10:21). His last words, full of trust, were, "Father, into your hands I commend my spirit" (*Lk* 23:46).

75. Let us now turn to the Holy Spirit, whose fire fills the heart of Christ. As St John Paul II once said, Christ's heart is "the Holy Spirit's masterpiece".[61] This is more than simply a past event, for even now "the heart of Christ is alive with the action of the Holy Spirit, to whom Jesus attributed the inspiration of his mission (cf. *Lk* 4:18; *Is* 61:1) and whose sending he had promised at the Last Supper. It is the Spirit who enables us to grasp the richness of the sign of Christ's pierced side, from which the Church has sprung (cf. *Sacrosanctum Concilium*, 5)".[62] In a word, "only the Holy Spirit can open up before us the fullness of the 'inner man', which is found in the heart of Christ. He alone can cause our human hearts to draw strength from that fullness, step by step".[63]

76. If we seek to delve more deeply into the mysterious working of the Spirit, we learn that he groans within us, saying "Abba!" Indeed, "the proof that you are children is that God has sent the Spirit of his Son into our hearts, crying, 'Abba! Father!'" (*Gal* 4:6). For "the Spirit bears witness with our spirit that we are children of God" (*Rom* 8:16). The Holy Spirit at work in Christ's human heart draws him unceasingly to the Father. When the Spirit unites us to the sentiments of Christ through grace, he makes us sharers in the Son's relationship to the Father, whereby we receive "a spirit of adoption through which we cry out, 'Abba! Father!'" (*Rom* 8:15).

---

[61] *Angelus*, 23rd June 2002: *L'Osservatore Romano*, 24th-25th June 2002, p. 1.

[62] St John Paul II, *Message on the Hundredth Anniversary of the Consecration of the Human Race to the Divine Heart of Jesus*, Warsaw, 11th June 1999, Solemnity of the Sacred Heart of Jesus, 3: *L'Osservatore Romano*, 12th June 1999, p. 5.

[63] Id., *Angelus*, 8th June 1986: *L'Osservatore Romano*, 9th-10th June 1986, p. 5

77. Our relationship with the heart of Christ is thus changed, thanks to the prompting of the Spirit who guides us to the Father, the source of life and the ultimate wellspring of grace. Christ does not expect us simply to remain in him. His love is "the revelation of the Father's mercy",[64] and his desire is that, impelled by the Spirit welling up from his heart, we should ascend to the Father "with him and in him". We give glory to the Father "through" Christ,[65] "with" Christ,[66] and "in" Christ.[67] St John Paul II taught that, "the Saviour's heart invites us to return to the Father's love, which is the source of every authentic love".[68] This is precisely what the Holy Spirit, who comes to us through the heart of Christ, seeks to nurture in our hearts. For this reason, the liturgy, through the enlivening work of the Spirit, always addresses the Father from the risen heart of Christ.

RECENT TEACHINGS OF THE MAGISTERIUM

78. In numerous ways, Christ's heart has always been present in the history of Christian spirituality. In the Scriptures and in the early centuries of the Church's life, it appeared under the image of the Lord's wounded side, as a fountain of grace and a summons to a deep and loving encounter. In this same guise, it has reappeared in the writings of numerous saints, past and present. In recent centuries, this spirituality has gradually taken on the specific form of devotion to the Sacred Heart of Jesus.

79. A number of my Predecessors have spoken in various ways about the heart of Christ and exhorted us to unite ourselves to it.

---

[64] *Homily*, Visit to the Gemelli Hospital and to the Faculty of Medicine of the Catholic University of the Sacred Heart, 27th June 2014: *L'Osservatore Romano*, 29th June 2014, p. 7.

[65] *Eph* 1:5, 7; 2:18; 3:12.

[66] *Eph* 2:5, 6; 4:15.

[67] *Eph* 1:3, 4, 6, 7, 11, 13, 15; 2:10, 13, 21, 22; 3:6, 11, 21.

[68] *Message on the Hundredth Anniversary of the Consecration of the Human Race to the Divine Heart of Jesus, Warsaw,* 11th June 1999, Solemnity of the Sacred Heart of Jesus, 2: *L'Osservatore Romano*, 12th June 1999, p. 5.

At the end of the nineteenth century, Leo XIII encouraged us to consecrate ourselves to the Sacred Heart, thus uniting our call to union with Christ and our wonder before the magnificence of his infinite love.[69] Some thirty years later, Pius XI presented this devotion as a "summa" of the experience of Christian faith.[70] Pius XII went on to declare that adoration of the Sacred Heart expresses in an outstanding way, as a sublime synthesis, the worship we owe to Jesus Christ.[71]

80. More recently, St John Paul II presented the growth of this devotion in recent centuries as a response to the rise of rigorist and disembodied forms of spirituality that neglected the richness of the Lord's mercy. At the same time, he saw it as a timely summons to resist attempts to create a world that leaves no room for God. "Devotion to the Sacred Heart, as it developed in Europe two centuries ago, under the impulse of the mystical experiences of St Margaret Mary Alacoque, was a response to

[69] "Since there is in the Sacred Heart a symbol and the express image of the infinite love of Jesus Christ that moves us to love one another, it is fit and proper that we should consecrate ourselves to his most Sacred Heart – an act that is nothing else than an offering and a binding of oneself to Jesus Christ, for whatever honour, veneration and love is given to this divine Heart is really and truly given to Christ himself...And now, today, behold another blessed and heavenly token is offered to our sight – the most Sacred Heart of Jesus, with a cross rising from it and shining forth with dazzling splendour amidst flames of love. In that Sacred Heart all our hopes should be placed, and from it the salvation of men is to be confidently besought" (Encyclical Letter *Annum Sacrum* [25th May 1899]: ASS 31 [1898-1899], 649, 651).

[70] "For is not the sum of all religion and therefore the pattern of more perfect life, contained in that most auspicious sign and in the form of piety that follows from it inasmuch as it more readily leads the minds of men to an intimate knowledge of Christ our Lord, and more efficaciously moves their hearts to love him more vehemently and to imitate him more closely?" (Encyclical Letter *Miserentissimus Redemptor* [8th May 1928]: AAS 20 [1928], 167).

[71] "For it is perfectly clear that this devotion, if we examine its proper nature, is a most excellent act of religion, inasmuch as it demands the full and absolute determination of surrendering and consecrating oneself to the love of the divine Redeemer whose wounded heart is the living sign and symbol of that love... In it, we can contemplate not only the symbol, but also, as it were, the synthesis of the whole mystery of our redemption... Christ expressly and repeatedly pointed to his heart as the symbol by which men are drawn to recognise and acknowledge his love, and at the same time constituted it as the sign and pledge of his mercy and his grace for the needs of the Church in our time" (Encyclical Letter *Haurietis Aquas* [15th May 1956], Proemium, III, IV: AAS 48 [1956], 311, 336, 340).

Jansenist rigour, which ended up disregarding God's infinite mercy... The men and women of the third millennium need the heart of Christ in order to know God and to know themselves; they need it to build the civilisation of love".[72]

81. Benedict XVI asked us to recognise in the heart of Christ an intimate and daily presence in our lives: "Every person needs a 'centre' for his or her own life, a source of truth and goodness to draw upon in the events, situations and struggles of daily existence. All of us, when we pause in silence, need to feel not only the beating of our own heart, but deeper still, the beating of a trustworthy presence, perceptible with faith's senses and yet much more real: the presence of Christ, the heart of the world".[73]

FURTHER REFLECTIONS AND RELEVANCE FOR OUR TIMES

82. The expressive and symbolic image of Christ's heart is not the only means granted us by the Holy Spirit for encountering the love of Christ, yet it is, as we have seen, an especially privileged one. Even so, it constantly needs to be enriched, deepened and renewed through meditation, the reading of the Gospel and growth in spiritual maturity. Pius XII made it clear that the Church does not claim that "we must contemplate and adore in the heart of Jesus a 'formal' image, that is, a perfect and absolute sign of his divine love, for the essence of this love can in no way be adequately expressed by any created image whatsoever".[74]

83. Devotion to Christ's heart is essential for our Christian life to the extent that it expresses our openness in faith and adoration to the mystery of the Lord's divine and human love. In this sense, we can once more affirm that the Sacred Heart is a synthesis of

---

[72] *Catechesis*, 8th June 1994, 2: *L'Osservatore Romano*, 9th June 1994, p. 5.

[73] *Angelus*, 1st June 2008: *L'Osservatore Romano*, 2nd-3rd June 2008, p. 1.

[74] Encyclical Letter *Haurietis Aquas* (15th May 1956), IV: AAS 48 (1956), 344.

the Gospel.[75] We need to remember that the visions or mystical showings related by certain saints who passionately encouraged devotion to Christ's heart are not something that the faithful are obliged to believe as if they were the word of God.[76] Nonetheless, they are rich sources of encouragement and can prove greatly beneficial, even if no one need feel forced to follow them should they not prove helpful on his or her own spiritual journey. At the same time, however, we should be mindful that, as Pius XII pointed out, this devotion cannot be said "to owe its origin to private revelations".[77]

84. The promotion of Eucharistic communion on the first Friday of each month, for example, sent a powerful message at a time when many people had stopped receiving communion because they were no longer confident of God's mercy and forgiveness and regarded communion as a kind of reward for the perfect. In the context of Jansenism, the spread of this practice proved immensely beneficial, since it led to a clearer realisation that in the Eucharist the merciful and ever-present love of the heart of Christ invites us to union with him. It can also be said that this practice can prove similarly beneficial in our own time, for a different reason. Amid the frenetic pace of today's world and our obsession with free time, consumption and diversion, smart phones and social media, we forget to nourish our lives with the strength of the Eucharist.

85. While no one should feel obliged to spend an hour in adoration each Thursday, the practice ought surely to be recommended. When we carry it out with devotion, in union with many of our brothers and sisters and discover in the Eucharist the immense love of the heart of Christ, we "adore, together with the Church,

---

[75] Cf. ibid.: AAS 48 (1956), 336.

[76] "The value of private revelations is essentially different from that of the one public revelation: the latter demands faith... A private revelation... is a help which is proffered, but its use is not obligatory" (Benedict XVI, Apostolic Exhortation *Verbum Domini* [30th September 2010], 14: AAS 102 [2010]), 696).

[77] Encyclical Letter *Haurietis Aquas* (15th May 1956), IV: AAS 48 (1956), 340.

the sign and manifestation of the divine love that went so far as to love, through the heart of the incarnate Word, the human race".[78]

86. Many Jansenists found this difficult to comprehend, for they looked askance on all that was human, affective and corporeal, and so viewed this devotion as distancing us from pure worship of the Most High God. Pius XII described as "false mysticism"[79] the elitist attitude of those groups that saw God as so sublime, separate and distant that they regarded affective expressions of popular piety as dangerous and in need of ecclesiastical oversight.

87. It could be argued that today, in place of Jansenism, we find ourselves before a powerful wave of secularisation that seeks to build a world free of God. In our societies, we are also seeing a proliferation of varied forms of religiosity that have nothing to do with a personal relationship with the God of love, but are new manifestations of a disembodied spirituality. I must warn that within the Church too, a baneful Jansenist dualism has re-emerged in new forms. This has gained renewed strength in recent decades, but it is a recrudescence of that Gnosticism which proved so great a spiritual threat in the early centuries of Christianity because it refused to acknowledge the reality of "the salvation of the flesh". For this reason, I turn my gaze to the heart of Christ and I invite all of us to renew our devotion to it. I hope this will also appeal to today's sensitivities and thus help us to confront the dualisms, old and new, to which this devotion offers an effective response.

88. I would add that the heart of Christ also frees us from another kind of dualism found in communities and pastors excessively caught up in external activities, structural reforms that have little to do with the Gospel, obsessive reorganisation plans, worldly projects, secular ways of thinking and mandatory

---

[78] Ibid.: AAS 48 (1956), 344.
[79] Ibid.

programmes. The result is often a Christianity stripped of the tender consolations of faith, the joy of serving others, the fervour of personal commitment to mission, the beauty of knowing Christ and the profound gratitude born of the friendship he offers and the ultimate meaning he gives to our lives. This too is the expression of an illusory and disembodied otherworldliness.

89. Once we succumb to these attitudes, so widespread in our day, we tend to lose all desire to be cured of them. This leads me to propose to the whole Church renewed reflection on the love of Christ represented in his Sacred Heart. For there we find the whole Gospel, a synthesis of the truths of our faith, all that we adore and seek in faith, all that responds to our deepest needs.

90. As we contemplate the heart of Christ, the incarnate synthesis of the Gospel, we can, following the example of St Thérèse of the Child Jesus, "place heartfelt trust not in ourselves but in the infinite mercy of a God who loves us unconditionally and has already given us everything in the cross of Jesus Christ".[80] Thérèse was able to do this because she had discovered in the heart of Christ that God is love: "To me he has granted his infinite mercy, and through it I contemplate and adore the other divine perfections".[81] That is why a popular prayer, directed like an arrow towards the heart of Christ, says simply: "Jesus, I trust in you".[82] No other words are needed.

91. In the following chapters, we will emphasise two essential aspects that contemporary devotion to the Sacred Heart needs to combine, so that it can continue to nourish us and bring us closer to the Gospel: personal spiritual experience and communal missionary commitment.

---

[80] Apostolic Exhortation *C'est la Confiance* (15th October 2023), 20: *L'Osservatore Romano*, 16th October 2023.

[81] St Thérèse of the Child Jesus, *Autobiography*, Ms A, 83v°.

[82] St Maria Faustina Kowalska, *Diary*, 47 (22nd February 1931) , Marian Press, Stockbridge, 2011, p. 46.

CHAPTER FOUR

A LOVE THAT GIVES ITSELF AS DRINK

92. Let us now return to the Scriptures, the inspired texts where, above all, we encounter God's revelation. There, and in the Church's living Tradition, we hear what the Lord has wished to tell us in the course of history. By reading several texts from the Old and the New Testaments, we will gain insight into the word of God that has guided the great spiritual pilgrimage of his people down the ages.

A GOD WHO THIRSTS FOR LOVE

93. The Bible shows that the people that journeyed through the desert and yearned for freedom received the promise of an abundance of life-giving water: "With joy you will draw water from the wells of salvation" (*Is* 12:3). The messianic prophecies gradually coalesced around the imagery of purifying water: "I will sprinkle clean water upon you, and you shall be clean... a new spirit I will put within you" (*Ezek* 36:25-26). This water would bestow on God's people the fullness of life, like a fountain flowing from the Temple and bringing a wealth of life and salvation in its wake. "I saw on the bank of the river a great many trees on the one side and on the other... and wherever that river goes, every living creature will live... and when that river enters the sea, its waters will become fresh; everything will live where the river goes" (*Ezek* 47:7-9).

94. The Jewish festival of Booths (*Sukkot*), which recalls the forty-year sojourn of Israel in the desert, gradually adopted the symbolism of water as a central element. It included a rite of offering water each morning, which became most solemn on the final day of the festival, when a great procession took place

towards the Temple, the altar was circled seven times and the water was offered to God amid loud cries of joy.[83]

95. The dawn of the messianic era was described as a fountain springing up for the people: "I will pour out a spirit of compassion and supplication on the house of David and the inhabitants of Jerusalem, and they shall look on him whom they have pierced... On that day, a fountain shall be opened for the house of David and the inhabitants of Jerusalem, to cleanse them from sin and impurity" (*Zech* 12:10; 13:1).

96. One who is pierced, a flowing fountain, the outpouring of a spirit of compassion and supplication: the first Christians inevitably considered these promises fulfilled in the pierced side of Christ, the wellspring of new life. In the Gospel of John, we contemplate that fulfilment. From Jesus's wounded side, the water of the Spirit poured forth: "One of the soldiers pierced his side with a spear, and at once blood and water flowed out" (*Jn* 19:34). The evangelist then recalls the prophecy that had spoken of a fountain opened in Jerusalem and the pierced one (*Jn* 19:37; cf. *Zech* 12:10). The open fountain is the wounded side of Christ.

97. Earlier, John's Gospel had spoken of this event, when on "the last day of the festival" (*Jn* 7:37), Jesus cried out to the people celebrating the great procession: "Let anyone who is thirsty come to me and drink... out of his heart shall flow rivers of living water" (*Jn* 7:37-38). For this to be accomplished, however, it was necessary for Jesus's "hour" to come, for he "was not yet glorified" (*Jn* 7:39). That fulfilment was to come on the cross, in the blood and water that flowed from the Lord's side.

98. The Book of Revelation takes up the prophecies of the pierced one and the fountain: "every eye will see him, even those who pierced him" (*Rev* 1:7); "Let everyone who is thirsty come; let anyone who wishes take the water of life as a gift" (*Rev* 22:17).

---

[83] Mishnah Sukkah, IV, 5, 9.

99. The pierced side of Jesus is the source of the love that God had shown for his people in countless ways. Let us now recall some of his words:

"Because you are precious in my sight and honoured, I love you" (*Is* 43:4).

"Can a woman forget her nursing child, or show no compassion for the child of her womb? Even if these may forget, yet I will not forget you. See, I have inscribed you on the palms of my hands" (*Is* 49:15-16).

"For the mountains may depart, and the hills be removed, but my steadfast love shall not depart from you, and my covenant of peace shall not be removed" (*Is* 54:10).

"I have loved you with an everlasting love; therefore I have continued my faithfulness to you" (*Jer* 31:3).

"The Lord, your God, is in your midst, a warrior who gives you victory; he will rejoice over you with gladness, he will renew you in his love; he will exult over you with loud singing" (*Zeph* 3:17).

100. The prophet Hosea goes so far as to speak of the heart of God, who "led them with cords of human kindness, with bands of love" (*Hos* 11:4). When that love was spurned, the Lord could say, "My heart is stirred within me; my compassion grows warm and tender" (*Hos* 11:8). God's merciful love always triumphs (cf. *Hos* 11:9), and it was to find its most sublime expression in Christ, his definitive Word of love.

101. The pierced heart of Christ embodies all God's declarations of love present in the Scriptures. That love is no mere matter of words; rather, the open side of his Son is a source of life for those whom he loves, the fount that quenches the thirst of his people. As St John Paul II pointed out, "the essential elements of devotion [to the Sacred Heart] belong in a permanent fashion to the spirituality of the Church throughout her history; for since

the beginning, the Church has looked to the heart of Christ pierced on the Cross".[84]

ECHOES OF THE WORD IN HISTORY

102. Let us consider some of the ways that, in the history of the Christian faith, these prophecies were understood to have been fulfilled. Various Fathers of the Church, especially those in Asia Minor, spoke of the wounded side of Jesus as the source of the water of the Holy Spirit: the word, its grace and the sacraments that communicate it. The courage of the martyrs is born of "the heavenly fount of living waters flowing from the side of Christ"[85] or, in the version of Rufinus, "the heavenly and eternal streams that flow from the heart of Christ".[86] We believers, reborn in the Spirit, emerge from the cleft in the rock; "we have come forth from the heart of Christ".[87] His wounded side, understood as his heart, filled with the Holy Spirit, comes to us as a flood of living water. "The fount of the Spirit is entirely in Christ".[88] Yet the Spirit whom we have received does not distance us from the risen Lord, but fills us with his presence, for by drinking of the Spirit we drink of the same Christ. In the words of St Ambrose: "Drink of Christ, for he is the rock that pours forth a flood of water. Drink of Christ, for he is the source of life. Drink of Christ, for he is the river whose streams gladden the city of God. Drink of Christ, for he is our peace. Drink of Christ, for from his side flows living water".[89]

103. St Augustine opened the way to devotion to the Sacred Heart as the locus of our personal encounter with the Lord. For

---

[84] *Letter to the Superior General of the Society of Jesus*, Paray-le-Monial (France), 5th October 1986: *L'Osservatore Romano*, 7th October 1986, p. IX.

[85] *Acta Martyrum Lugdunensium*, in Eusebius OF Caesarea, *Historia Ecclesiastica*, V, 1: PG 20, 418.

[86] Rufinus, V, 1, 22, in GCS, *Eusebius* II, 1, p. 411, 13ff.

[87] St Justin, *Dial.* 135, 3: PG 6, 787

[88] Novatian, *De Trinitate*, 29: PL 3, 994; cf. St Gregory of Elvira, *Tractatus Origenis de libris Sanctarum Scripturarum*, XX, 12: CSSL 69, 144.

[89] *Expl. Ps.* 1:33: PL 14, 983-984.

Augustine, Christ's wounded side is not only the source of grace and the sacraments, but also the symbol of our intimate union with Christ, the setting of an encounter of love. There we find the source of the most precious wisdom of all, which is knowledge of him. In effect, Augustine writes that John, the beloved disciple, reclining on Jesus's bosom at the Last Supper, drew near to the secret place of wisdom.[90] Here we have no merely intellectual contemplation of an abstract theological truth. As St Jerome explains, a person capable of contemplation "does not delight in the beauty of that stream of water, but drinks of the living water flowing from the side of the Lord".[91]

104. St Bernard takes up the symbolism of the pierced side of the Lord and understands it explicitly as a revelation and outpouring of all of the love of his heart. Through that wound, Christ opens his heart to us and enables us to appropriate the boundless mystery of his love and mercy: "I take from the bowels of the Lord what is lacking to me, for his bowels overflow with mercy through the holes through which they stream. Those who crucified him pierced his hands and feet, they pierced his side with a lance. And through those holes I can taste wild honey and oil from the rocks of flint, that is, I can taste and see that the Lord is good… A lance passed through his soul even to the region of his heart. No longer is he unable to take pity on my weakness. The wounds inflicted on his body have disclosed to us the secrets of his heart; they enable us to contemplate the great mystery of his compassion".[92]

105. This theme reappears especially in William of St-Thierry, who invites us to enter into the heart of Jesus, who feeds us from his own breast.[93] This is not surprising if we recall that for William, "the art of arts is the art of love… Love is awakened by the Creator of nature, and is a power of the soul that leads it, as if

---

[90] Cf. *Tract. in Ioannem* 61, 6: PL 35, 1801.

[91] *Ep. ad Rufinum*, 3, 4.3: PL 22, 334.

[92] *Sermones in Cant.* 61, 4: PL 183, 1072.

[93] *Expositio altera super Cantica Canticorum*, c. 1: PL 180, 487.

by its natural gravity, to its proper place and end".[94] That proper place, where love reigns in fullness, is the heart of Christ: "Lord, where do you lead those whom you embrace and clasp to your heart? Your heart, Jesus, is the sweet manna of your divinity that you hold within the golden jar of your soul (cf. *Heb* 9:4), and that surpasses all knowledge. Happy those who, having plunged into those depths, have been hidden by you in the recess of your heart".[95]

106. St Bonaventure unites these two spiritual currents. He presents the heart of Christ as the source of the sacraments and of grace, and urges that our contemplation of that heart become a relationship between friends, a personal encounter of love.

107. Bonaventure makes us appreciate first the beauty of the grace and the sacraments flowing from the fountain of life that is the wounded side of the Lord. "In order that from the side of Christ sleeping on the cross, the Church might be formed and the Scripture fulfilled that says: 'They shall look upon him whom they pierced', one of the soldiers struck him with a lance and opened his side. This was permitted by divine Providence so that, in the blood and water flowing from that wound, the price of our salvation might flow from the hidden wellspring of his heart, enabling the Church's sacraments to confer the life of grace and thus to be, for those who live in Christ, like a cup filled from the living fount springing up to life eternal".[96]

108. Bonaventure then asks us to take another step, in order that our access to grace not be seen as a kind of magic or neo-platonic emanation, but rather as a direct relationship with Christ, a dwelling in his heart, so that whoever drinks from that source becomes a friend of Christ, a loving heart. "Rise up, then, O soul who are a friend of Christ, and be the dove that nests in the cleft in

---

[94] William of St-Thierry, *De natura et dignitate amoris*, 1: PL 184, 379.

[95] Id., *Meditivae Orationes*, 8, 6: PL 180, 230.

[96] St Bonaventure, *Lignum Vitae. De mysterio passionis*, 30.

the rock; be the sparrow that finds a home and constantly watches over it; be the turtledove that hides the offspring of its chaste love in that most holy cleft".[97]

THE SPREAD OF DEVOTION TO
THE HEART OF CHRIST

109. Gradually, the wounded side of Christ, as the abode of his love and the wellspring of the life of grace, began to be associated with his heart, especially in monastic life. We know that in the course of history, devotion to the heart of Christ was not always expressed in the same way, and that its modern developments, related to a variety of spiritual experiences, cannot be directly derived from the mediæval forms, much less the biblical forms in which we glimpse the seeds of that devotion. This notwithstanding, the Church today rejects nothing of the good that the Holy Spirit has bestowed on us down the centuries, for she knows that it will always be possible to discern a clearer and deeper meaning in certain aspects of that devotion, and to gain new insights over the course of time.

110. A number of holy women, in recounting their experiences of encounter with Christ, have spoken of resting in the heart of the Lord as the source of life and interior peace. This was the case with Saints Lutgarde and Mechtilde of Hackeborn, St Angela of Foligno and Dame Julian of Norwich, to mention only a few. St Gertrude of Helfta, a Cistercian nun, tells of a time in prayer when she reclined her head on the heart of Christ and heard its beating. In a dialogue with St John the Evangelist, she asked him why he had not described in his Gospel what he experienced when he did the same. Gertrude concludes that "the sweet sound of those heartbeats has been reserved for modern times, so that, hearing them, our ageing and lukewarm world may be renewed in the love of God".[98] Might we think that this

---

[97] Ibid., 47.

[98] *Legatus divinae pietatis*, IV, 4, 4: SCh 255, 66.

is indeed a message for our own times, a summons to realise how our world has indeed "grown old", and needs to perceive anew the message of Christ's love? St Gertrude and St Mechtilde have been considered among "the most intimate confidants of the Sacred Heart".[99]

111. The Carthusians, encouraged above all by Ludolph of Saxony, found in devotion to the Sacred Heart a means of growth in affection and closeness to Christ. All who enter through the wound of his heart are inflamed with love. St Catherine of Siena wrote that the Lord's sufferings are impossible for us to comprehend, but the open heart of Christ enables us to have a lively personal encounter with his boundless love. "I wished to reveal to you the secret of my heart, allowing you to see it open, so that you can understand that I have loved you so much more than I could have proved to you by the suffering that I once endured".[100]

112. Devotion to the heart of Christ slowly passed beyond the walls of the monasteries to enrich the spirituality of saintly teachers, preachers and founders of religious congregations, who then spread it to the farthest reaches of the earth.[101]

113. Particularly significant was the initiative taken by St John Eudes, who, "after preaching with his confrères a fervent mission in Rennes, convinced the bishop of that diocese to approve the celebration of the feast of the Adorable Heart of our Lord Jesus Christ. This was the first time that such a feast was officially authorised in the Church. Following this, between the years 1670 and 1671, the bishops of Coutances, Evreux, Bayeux, Lisieux and Rouen authorised the celebration of the feast for their respective dioceses".[102]

---

[99] Léon Dehon, *Directoire spirituel des prêtres su Sacré Cœur de Jésus*, Turnhout, 1936, II, ch. VII, n. 141.

[100] *Dialogue on Divine Providence*, LXXV: Fiorilli M.-Caramella S., eds., Bari, 1928, 144.

[101] Cf., for example, Angelus Walz, *De veneratione divini cordis Iesu in Ordine Prædicatorum*, Pontificium Institutum Angelicum, Rome, 1937.

[102] Rafael García Herreros , *Vida de San Juan Eudes*, Bogotá, 1943, 42.

ST FRANCIS DE SALES

114. In modern times, mention should be made of the important contribution of St Francis de Sales. Francis frequently contemplated Christ's open heart, which invites us to dwell therein, in a personal relationship of love that sheds light on the mysteries of his life. In his writings, the saintly Doctor of the Church opposes a rigorous morality and a legalistic piety by presenting the heart of Jesus as a summons to complete trust in the mysterious working of his grace. We see this expressed in his letter to St Jane Frances de Chantal: "I am certain that we will remain no longer in ourselves...but dwell forever in the Lord's wounded side, for apart from him not only can we do nothing, but even if we were able, we would lack the desire to do anything".[103]

115. For Francis de Sales, true devotion had nothing to do with superstition or perfunctory piety, since it entails a personal relationship in which each of us feels uniquely and individually known and loved by Christ. "This most adorable and lovable heart of our Master, burning with the love which he professes to us, [is] a heart on which all our names are written... Surely it is a source of profound consolation to know that we are loved so deeply by our Lord, who constantly carries us in his heart".[104] With the image of our names written on the heart of Christ, St Francis sought to express the extent to which Christ's love for each of us is not something abstract and generic, but utterly personal, enabling each believer to feel known and respected for who he or she is. "How lovely is this heaven, in which the Lord is its sun and his breast a fountain of love from which the blessed drink to their heart's content! Each of us can look therein and see our name carved in letters of love, which true love alone can read and true love has written. Dear God! And what too, beloved

---

[103] St Francis de Sales, *Letter to Jane Frances de Chantal*, 24th April 1610.
[104] *Sermon for the Second Sunday of Lent*, 20th February 1622.

daughter, of our loved ones? Surely they will be there too; for even if our hearts have no love, they nonetheless possess a desire for love and the beginnings of love".[105]

116. Francis saw this experience of Christ's love as essential to the spiritual life, indeed one of the great truths of faith: "Yes, my beloved daughter, he thinks of you and not only, but even the smallest hair of your head: this is an article of faith and in no way must it be doubted".[106] It follows that the believer becomes capable of complete abandonment in the heart of Christ, in which he or she finds repose, comfort and strength: "Oh God! What happiness to be thus embraced and to recline in the bosom of the Saviour. Remain thus, beloved daughter, and like another little one, St John, while others are tasting different kinds of food at the table of the Lord, lay your head, your soul and your spirit, in a gesture of utter trust, on the loving bosom of this dear Lord".[107] "I hope that you are resting in the cleft of the turtledove and in the pierced side of our beloved Saviour... How good is this Lord, my beloved daughter! How loving is his Heart! Let us remain here, in this holy abode".[108]

117. At the same time, faithful to his teaching on the sanctification of ordinary life, Francis proposes that this experience take place in the midst of the activities, tasks and obligations of our daily existence. "You asked me how souls that are attracted in prayer to this holy simplicity, to this perfect abandonment in God, should conduct themselves in all their actions? I would reply that, not only in prayer, but also in the conduct of everyday life they should advance always in the spirit of simplicity, abandoning and completely surrendering their soul, their actions and their accomplishments to God's will. And to do so with a love marked by perfect and absolute trust, abandoning themselves to grace

---

[105] *Letter to Jane Frances de Chantal*, Solemnity of the Ascension, 1612.

[106] *Letter to Marie Aimée de Blonay*, 18th February 1618.

[107] *Letter to Jane Frances de Chantal*, late November 1609.

[108] *Letter to Jane Frances de Chantal*, ca. 25th February 1610.

and to the care of the eternal love that divine Providence feels for them".[109]

118. For this reason, when looking for a symbol to convey his vision of spiritual life, Francis de Sales concluded: "I have thought, dear Mother, if you agree, that we should take as our emblem a single heart pierced by two arrows, the whole enclosed in a crown of thorns".[110]

A NEW DECLARATION OF LOVE

119. Under the salutary influence of this Salesian spirituality, the events of Paray-le-Monial took place at the end of the seventeenth century. St Margaret Mary Alacoque reported a remarkable series of apparitions of Christ between the end of December 1673 and June of 1675. Fundamental to these was a declaration of love that stood out in the first apparition. Jesus said: "My divine Heart is so inflamed with love for men, and for you in particular, that, no longer able to contain in itself the flames of its ardent charity, it must pour them out through you and be manifested to them, in order to enrich them with its precious treasures which I now reveal to you".[111]

120. St Margaret Mary's account is powerful and deeply moving: "He revealed to me the wonders of his love and the inexplicable secrets of his Sacred Heart which he had hitherto kept hidden from me, until he opened it to me for the first time, in such a striking and sensible manner that he left me no room for doubt".[112] In subsequent appearances, that consoling message was reiterated: "He revealed to me the ineffable wonders of his pure love and to what extremes it had led him to love mankind".[113]

---

[109] *Entretien XIV*, on religious simplicity and prudence.

[110] *Letter to Jane Frances de Chantal,* 10th June 1611.

[111] St Margaret Mary Alacoque, *Autobiography*, n. 53.

[112] Ibid.

[113] Ibid., n. 55.

121. This powerful realisation of the love of Jesus Christ bequeathed to us by St Margaret Mary can spur us to greater union with him. We need not feel obliged to accept or appropriate every detail of her spiritual experience, in which, as often happens, God's intervention combines with human elements related to the individual's own desires, concerns and interior images.[114] Such experiences must always be interpreted in the light of the Gospel and the rich spiritual tradition of the Church, even as we acknowledge the good they accomplish in many of our brothers and sisters. In this way, we can recognise the gifts of the Holy Spirit present in those experiences of faith and love. More important than any individual detail is the core of the message handed on to us, which can be summed up in the words heard by St Margaret Mary: "This is the heart that so loved human beings that it has spared nothing, even to emptying and consuming itself in order to show them its love".[115]

122. This apparition, then, invites us to grow in our encounter with Christ, putting our trust completely in his love, until we attain full and definitive union with him. "It is necessary that the divine heart of Jesus in some way replace our own; that he alone live and work in us and for us; that his will... work absolutely and without any resistance on our part; and finally that its affections, thoughts and desires take the place of our own, especially his love, so that he is loved in himself and for our sakes. And so, this lovable heart being our all in all, we can say with St Paul that we no longer live our own lives, but it is he who lives within us".[116]

123. In the first message that St Margaret Mary received, this invitation was expressed in vivid, fervent and loving terms. "He asked for my heart, which I asked him to take, which he did and then placed myself in his own adorable heart, from which

---

[114] Cf. Dicastery for the Doctrine of the Faith, *Norms for Proceeding in the Discernment of Alleged Supernatural Phenomena*, 17th May 2024, I, A, 12.

[115] St Margaret Mary Alacoque, *Autobiography*, n. 92.

[116] *Letter to Sœur de la Barge*, 22nd October 1689.

he made me see mine like a little atom consumed in the fiery furnace of his own".[117]

124. At another point, we see that the one who gives himself to us is the risen and glorified Christ, full of life and light. If indeed, at different times, he spoke of the suffering that he endured for our sake and of the ingratitude with which it is met, what we see here are not so much his blood and painful wounds, but rather the light and fire of the Lord of life. The wounds of the passion have not disappeared, but are now transfigured. Here we see the paschal mystery in all its splendour: "Once, when the Blessed Sacrament was exposed, Jesus appeared, resplendent in glory, with his five wounds that appeared as so many suns blazing forth from his sacred humanity, but above all from his adorable breast, which seemed a fiery furnace. Opening his robe, he revealed his most loving and lovable heart, which was the living source of those flames. Then it was that I discovered the ineffable wonders of his pure love, with which he loves men to the utmost, yet receives from them only ingratitude and indifference".[118]

ST CLAUDE DE LA COLOMBIÈRE

125. When St Claude de La Colombière learned of the experiences of St Margaret Mary, he immediately undertook her defence and began to spread word of the apparitions. St Claude played a special role in developing the understanding of devotion to the Sacred Heart and its meaning in the light of the Gospel.

126. Some of the language of St Margaret Mary, if poorly understood, might suggest undue trust in our personal sacrifices and offerings. St Claude insists that contemplation of the heart of Jesus, when authentic, does not provoke self-complacency or a vain confidence in our own experiences or human efforts, but rather an ineffable abandonment in Christ that fills our life

---

[117] *Autobiography*, n. 53.

[118] Ibid., n. 55.

with peace, security and decision. He expressed this absolute confidence most eloquently in a celebrated prayer:

"My God, I am so convinced that you keep watch over those who hope in you, and that we can want for nothing when we look for all in you, that I am resolved in the future to live free from every care and to turn all my anxieties over to you... I shall never lose my hope. I shall keep it to the last moment of my life; and at that moment all the demons in hell will strive to tear it from me... Others may look for happiness from their wealth or their talents; others may rest on the innocence of their life, or the severity of their penance, or the amount of their alms, or the fervour of their prayers. As for me, Lord, all my confidence is confidence itself. This confidence has never deceived anyone... I am sure, therefore, that I shall be eternally happy, since I firmly hope to be, and because it is from you, O God, that I hope for it".[119]

127. In a note of January 1677, after mentioning the assurance he felt regarding his mission, Claude continued: "I have come to know that God wanted me to serve him by obtaining the fulfilment of his desires regarding the devotion that he suggested to a person to whom he communicates in confidence, and for whose sake he has desired to make use of my weakness. I have already used it to help several persons".[120]

128. It should be recognised that the spirituality of St Claude de La Colombière resulted in a fine synthesis of the profound and moving spiritual experience of St Margaret Mary and the vivid and concrete form of contemplation found in the *Spiritual Exercises* of St Ignatius Loyola. At the beginning of the third week of the Exercises, Claude reflected: "Two things have moved me in a striking way. First, the attitude of Christ towards those who sought to arrest him. His heart is full of bitter sorrow;

---

[119] *Sermon on Trust in God*, in *Œuvres du R.P de La Colombière*, t. 5, Perisse, Lyon, 1854, p. 100.

[120] *Spiritual Exercises in London*, 1st-8th February 1677, in *Œuvres du R.P de La Colombière*, t. 7, Seguin, Avignon, 1832, p. 93.

every violent passion is unleashed against him and all nature is in turmoil, yet amid all this confusion, all these temptations, his heart remains firmly directed to God. He does not hesitate to take the part that virtue and the highest virtue suggested to him. Second, the attitude of that same heart towards Judas who betrayed him, the apostles who cravenly abandoned him, the priests and the others responsible for the persecution he suffered; none of these things was able to arouse in him the slightest sentiment of hatred or indignation. I present myself anew to this heart free of anger, free of bitterness, filled instead with genuine compassion towards its enemies".[121]

ST CHARLES DE FOUCAULD AND ST THÉRÈSE OF THE CHILD JESUS

129. St Charles de Foucauld and St Thérèse of the Child Jesus, without intending to, reshaped certain aspects of devotion to the heart of Christ and thus helped us understand it in an even more evangelical spirit. Let us now examine how this devotion found expression in their lives. In the following chapter, we will return to them, in order to illustrate the distinctively missionary dimension that each of them brought to the devotion.

Iesus Caritas

130. In Louye, Charles de Foucauld was accustomed to visit the Blessed Sacrament with his cousin, Marie de Bondy. One day she showed him an image of the Sacred Heart.[122] His cousin played a fundamental role in Charles's conversion, as he himself acknowledged: "Since God has made you the first instrument of his mercies towards me, from you everything else began. Had you not converted me, brought me to Jesus and taught me little by little, letter by letter, all that is holy and good, where would

---

[121] *Spiritual Exercises in Lyon*, October-November 1674, ibid., p. 45.

[122] St Charles de Foucauld, *Letter to Madame de Bondy*, 27th April 1897.

I be today?"[123] What Marie awakened in him was an intense awareness of the love of Jesus. That was the essential thing, and centred on devotion to the heart of Jesus, in which he encountered unbounded mercy: "Let us trust in the infinite mercy of the one whose heart you led me to know".[124]

131. Later, his spiritual director, Fr Henri Huvelin, helped Charles to deepen his understanding of the inestimable mystery of "this blessed heart of which you spoke to me so often".[125] On 6th June 1889, Charles consecrated himself to the Sacred Heart, in which he found a love without limits. He told Christ, "You have bestowed on me so many benefits, that it would appear ingratitude towards your heart not to believe that it is disposed to bestow on me every good, however great, and that your love and your generosity are boundless".[126] He was to become a hermit "under the name of the heart of Jesus".[127]

132. On 17th May 1906, the same day in which Brother Charles, alone, could no longer celebrate Mass, he wrote of his promise "to let the heart of Jesus live in me, so that it is no longer I who live, but the heart of Jesus that lives in me, as he lived in Nazareth".[128] His friendship with Jesus, heart to heart, was anything but a privatised piety. It inspired the austere life he led in Nazareth, born of a desire to imitate Christ and to be conformed to him. His loving devotion to the heart of Jesus had a concrete effect on his style of life, and his Nazareth was nourished by his personal relationship with the heart of Christ.

---

[123] *Letter to Madame de Bondy*, 28th April 1901. Cf. *Letter to Madame de Bondy*, 5th April 1909: "Through you I came to know the adoration of the Blessed Sacrament, the benedictions and the Sacred Heart".

[124] *Letter to Madame de Bondy*, 7th April 1890.

[125] *Letter to l'Abbé Huvelin*, 27th June 1892.

[126] St Charles de Foucauld, *Méditations sur l'Ancien Testament (1896-1897)*, XXX, 1-21.

[127] Id., *Letter to l'Abbé Huvelin*, 16th May 1900.

[128] Id., *Diary*, 17th May 1906.

St Thérèse of the Child Jesus

133. Like St Charles de Foucauld, St Thérèse of the Child Jesus was influenced by the great renewal of devotion that swept nineteenth-century France. Fr Almire Pichon, the spiritual director of her family, was seen as a devoted apostle of the Sacred Heart. One of her sisters took as her name in religion "Sr Marie of the Sacred Heart", and the monastery that Thérèse entered was dedicated to the Sacred Heart. Her devotion nonetheless took on certain distinctive traits with regard to the customary piety of that age.

134. When Thérèse was fifteen, she could speak of Jesus as the one "whose heart beats in unison with my own".[129] Two years later, speaking of the image of Christ's heart crowned with thorns, she wrote in a letter: "You know that I myself do not see the Sacred Heart as everyone else. I think that the Heart of my Spouse is mine alone, just as mine is his alone, and I speak to him then in the solitude of this delightful heart to heart, while waiting to contemplate him one day face to face".[130]

135. In one of her poems, Thérèse voiced the meaning of her devotion, which had to do more with friendship and assurance than with trust in her sacrifices:

"I need a heart burning with tenderness,
Who will be my support forever,
Who loves everything in me, even my weakness…
And who never leaves me day or night…
I must have a God who takes on my nature,
And becomes my brother and is able to suffer!…
Ah! I know well, all our righteousness
Is worthless in your sight…
So I, for my purgatory,
Choose your burning love, O heart of my God!"[131]

---

[129] *Letter 67 to Mme. Guérin*, 18th November 1888.

[130] *Letter 122 to Céline, 14th October 1890.*

[131] *Poem 23, "To the Sacred Heart of Jesus"*, June or October 1895.

136. Perhaps the most important text for understanding the devotion of Thérèse to the heart of Christ is a letter that she wrote three months before her death to her friend Maurice Bellière. "When I see Mary Magdalene walking up before the many guests, washing with her tears the feet of her adored Master, whom she is touching for the first time, I feel that her heart has understood the abysses of love and mercy of the heart of Jesus, and, sinner though she is, this heart of love was disposed not only to pardon her but to lavish on her the blessings of his divine intimacy, to lift her to the highest summits of contemplation. Ah! dear little Brother, ever since I have been given the grace to understand also the love of the heart of Jesus, I admit that it has expelled all fear from my heart. The remembrance of my faults humbles me, draws me never to depend on my strength which is only weakness, but this remembrance speaks to me of mercy and love even more".[132]

137. Those moralisers who want to keep a tight rein on God's mercy and grace might claim that Thérèse could say this because she was a saint, but a simple person could not say the same. In that way, they excise from the spirituality of St Thérèse its wonderful originality, which reflects the heart of the Gospel. Sadly, in certain Christian circles we often encounter this attempt to fit the Holy Spirit into a certain preconceived pattern in a way that enables them to keep everything under their supervision. Yet this astute Doctor of the Church reduces them to silence and directly contradicts their reductive view in these clear words: "If I had committed all possible crimes, I would always have the same confidence; I feel that this whole multitude of offences would be like a drop of water thrown into a fiery furnace".[133]

138. To Sr Marie, who praised her generous love of God, prepared even to embrace martyrdom, Thérèse responded at length in a letter that is one of the great milestones in the history

---

[132] *Letter 247 to l'Abbé Maurice Bellière*, 21st June 1897.
[133] *Last Conversations. Yellow Notebook*, 11th July 1897, 6.

of spirituality. This page ought to be read a thousand times over for its depth, clarity and beauty. There, Thérèse helps her sister, "Marie of the Sacred Heart", to avoid focusing this devotion on suffering, since some had presented reparation primarily in terms of accumulating sacrifices and good works. Thérèse, for her part, presents confidence as the greatest and best offering, pleasing to the heart of Christ: "My desires of martyrdom are nothing; they are not what give me the unlimited confidence that I feel in my heart. They are, to tell the truth, the spiritual riches that render one unjust, when one rests in them with complacence and one believes that they are something great…what pleases [Jesus] is that he sees me loving my littleness and my poverty, the blind hope that I have in his mercy… That is my only treasure… If you want to feel joy, to have an attraction for suffering, it is your consolation that you are seeking… Understand that to be his victim of love, the weaker one is, without desires or virtues, the more suited one is for the workings of this consuming and transforming Love… Oh! How I would like to be able to make you understand what I feel!… It is confidence and nothing but confidence that must lead us to Love".[134]

139. In many of her writings, Thérèse speaks of her struggle with forms of spirituality overly focused on human effort, on individual merit, on offering sacrifices and carrying out certain acts in order to "win heaven". For her, "merit does not consist in doing or in giving much, but rather in receiving".[135] Let us read once again some of these deeply meaningful texts where she emphasises this and presents it as a simple and rapid means of taking hold of the Lord "by his heart".

140. To her sister Léonie she writes, "I assure you that God is much better than you believe. He is content with a glance, a

---

[134] *Letter 197 to Sister Marie of the Sacred Heart*, 17th September 1896. This does not mean that Thérèse did not offer sacrifices, sorrows and troubles as a way of associating herself with the suffering of Christ, but that, in the end, she was concerned not to give these offerings an importance they did not have.

[135] *Letter 142 to Céline*, 6th July 1893.

sigh of love... As for me, I find perfection very easy to practise because I have understood it is a matter of taking hold of Jesus by his heart... Look at a little child who has just annoyed his mother... If he comes to her, holding out his little arms, smiling and saying: 'Kiss me, I will not do it again', will his mother be able not to press him to her heart tenderly and forget his childish mischief? However, she knows her dear little one will do it again on the next occasion, but this does not matter; if he takes her again by her heart, he will not be punished".[136]

141. So too, in a letter to Fr Adolphe Roulland she writes, "[M]y way is all confidence and love. I do not understand souls who fear a friend so tender. At times, when I am reading certain spiritual treatises in which perfection is shown through a thousand obstacles, surrounded by a crowd of illusions, my poor little mind quickly tires; I close the learned book that is breaking my head and drying up my heart, and I take up Holy Scripture. Then all seems luminous to me; a single word uncovers for my soul infinite horizons, perfection seems simple to me. I see that it is sufficient to recognise one's nothingness and to abandon oneself like a child into God's arms".[137]

142. In yet another letter, she relates this to the love shown by a parent: "I do not believe that the heart of [a] father could resist the filial confidence of his child, whose sincerity and love he knows. He realises, however, that more than once his son will fall into the same faults, but he is prepared to pardon him always, if his son always takes him by his heart".[138]

RESONANCES WITHIN THE SOCIETY OF JESUS

143. We have seen how St Claude de La Colombière combined the spiritual experience of St Margaret Mary with the aim of the

---

[136] *Letter 191 to Léonie*, 12th July 1896.

[137] *Letter 226 to Father Roulland*, 9th May 1897.

[138] *Letter 258 to l'Abbé Maurice Bellière*, 18th July 1897.

Spiritual Exercises. I believe that the place of the Sacred Heart in the history of the Society of Jesus merits a few brief words.

144. The spirituality of the Society of Jesus has always proposed an "interior knowledge of the Lord in order to love and follow him more fully".[139] St Ignatius invites us in his *Spiritual Exercises* to place ourselves before the Gospel that tells us that, "[Christ's] side was pierced by the lance and blood and water flowed forth".[140] When retreatants contemplate the wounded side of the crucified Lord, Ignatius suggests that they enter into the heart of Christ. Thus we have a way to enlarge our own hearts, recommended by one who was a "master of affections", to use the words of St Peter Faber in one of his letters to St Ignatius.[141] Fr Juan Alfonso de Polanco echoed that same expression in his biography of St Ignatius: "He [Cardinal Gasparo Contarini] realised that in Fr Ignatius he had encountered a master of affections".[142] The colloquies that St Ignatius proposed are an essential part of this training of the heart, for in them we sense and savour with the heart a Gospel message and converse about it with the Lord. St Ignatius tells us that we can share our concerns with the Lord and seek his counsel. Anyone who follows the Exercises can readily see that they involve a dialogue, heart to heart.

145. St Ignatius brings his contemplations to a crescendo at the foot of the cross and invites the retreatant to ask the crucified Lord with great affection, "as one friend to another, as a servant to his master", what he or she must do for him.[143] The progression of the Exercises culminates in the "Contemplation to Attain Love", which gives rise to thanksgiving and the offering of one's "memory, understanding and will" to the heart which is the fount

---

[139] Cf. St Ignatius Loyola, *Spiritual Exercises*, 104.

[140] Ibid., 297.

[141] Cf. *Letter to Ignatius Loyola*, 23rd January 1541.

[142] *De Vita P. Ignatii et Societatis Iesu initiis*, ch. 8. 96.

[143] *Spiritual Exercises*, 54.

and origin of every good thing.[144] This interior contemplation is not the fruit of our understanding and effort, but is to be implored as a gift.

146. This same experience inspired the great succession of Jesuit priests who spoke explicitly of the heart of Jesus: St Francis Borgia, St Peter Faber, St Alphonsus Rodriguez, Fr Álvarez de Paz, Fr Vincent Carafa, Fr Kasper Drużbicki and countless others. In 1883, the Jesuits declared that, "the Society of Jesus accepts and receives with an overflowing spirit of joy and gratitude the most agreeable duty entrusted to it by our Lord Jesus Christ to practise, promote and propagate devotion to his divine heart".[145] In September 1871, Fr Pieter Jan Beckx consecrated the Society to the Sacred Heart of Jesus and, as a sign that it remains an outstanding element in the life of the Society, Fr Pedro Arrupe renewed that consecration in 1972, with a conviction that he explained in these words: "I therefore wish to say to the Society something about which I feel I cannot remain silent. From my novitiate on, I have always been convinced that what we call devotion to the Sacred Heart contains a symbolic expression of what is most profound in Ignatian spirituality, and of an extraordinary efficacy – *ultra quam speraverint* – both for its own perfection and for its apostolic fruitfulness. I continue to have this same conviction... In this devotion I encounter one of the deepest sources of my interior life".[146]

147. When St John Paul II urged "all the members of the Society to be even more zealous in promoting this devotion, which corresponds more than ever to the expectations of our time", he did so because he recognised the profound connection between devotion to the heart of Christ and Ignatian spirituality. For "the desire to 'know the Lord intimately' and to 'have a conversation'

---

[144] Ibid., 230ff.

[145] Thirty-Third General Congregation of the Society of Jesus, Decree 46, 1: *Institutum Societatis Iesu*, 2, Florence, 1893, 511.

[146] *In Him Alone is Our Hope. Texts on the Heart of Christ*, St. Louis, 1984.

with him, heart to heart, is characteristic of the Ignatian spiritual and apostolic dynamism, thanks to the *Spiritual Exercises*, and this dynamism is wholly at the service of the love of the heart of God".[147]

A BROAD CURRENT OF THE INTERIOR LIFE

148. Devotion to the heart of Christ reappears in the spiritual journey of many saints, all quite different from each other; in every one of them, the devotion takes on new hues. St Vincent de Paul, for example, used to say that what God desires is the heart: "God asks primarily for our heart – our heart – and that is what counts. How is it that a man who has no wealth will have greater merit than someone who has great possessions that he gives up? Because the one who has nothing does it with greater love; and that is what God especially wants..."[148] This means allowing one's heart to be united to that of Christ. "What blessing should a Sister not hope for from God if she does her utmost to put her heart in the state of being united with the heart of our Lord!"[149]

149. At times, we may be tempted to consider this mystery of love as an admirable relic from the past, a fine spirituality suited to other times. Yet we need to remind ourselves constantly that, as a saintly missionary once said, "this divine heart, which let itself be pierced by an enemy's lance in order to pour forth through that sacred wound the sacraments by which the Church was formed, has never ceased to love".[150] More recent saints, like St Pius of Pietrelcina, St Teresa of Calcutta and many others, have spoken with deep devotion of the heart of Christ. Here I would also mention the experiences of St Faustina Kowalska, which re-propose devotion to the heart of Christ by greatly emphasising

---

[147] *Letter to the Superior General of the Society of Jesus*, Paray-le-Monial, 5th October 1986: *L'Osservatore Romano*, 6th October 1986, p. 7.

[148] *Conference to Priests, "Poverty"*, 13th August 1655.

[149] *Conference to the Daughters of Charity, "Mortification, Correspondence, Meals and Journeys"0* (*Common Rules*, art. 24-27), 9th December 1657.

[150] St Daniele Comboni, *Gli scritti*, Bologna, 1991, 998 (n. 3324).

the glorious life of the risen Lord and his divine mercy. Inspired by her experiences and the spiritual legacy of St Józef Sebastian Pelczar (1842-1924),[151] St John Paul II intimately linked his reflections on divine mercy with devotion to the heart of Christ: "The Church seems in a singular way to profess the mercy of God and to venerate it when she directs herself to the heart of Christ. In fact, it is precisely this drawing close to Christ in the mystery of his heart which enables us to dwell on this point of the revelation of the merciful love of the Father, a revelation that constituted the central content of the messianic mission of the Son of Man".[152] St John Paul also spoke of the Sacred Heart in very personal terms, acknowledging that, "it has spoken to me ever since my youth".[153]

150. The enduring relevance of devotion to the heart of Christ is especially evident in the work of evangelisation and education carried out by the numerous male and female religious congregations whose origins were marked by this profoundly Christological devotion. Mentioning all of them by name would be an endless undertaking. Let us simply consider two examples taken at random: "The Founder [St Daniele Comboni] discovered in the mystery of the heart of Jesus the source of strength for his missionary commitment".[154] "Caught up as we are in the desires of the heart of Jesus, we want people to grow in dignity, as human beings and as children of God. Our starting point is the Gospel, with all that it demands from us of love, forgiveness and justice, and of solidarity with those who are poor and rejected by the world".[155] So too, the many shrines worldwide that are consecrated to the heart of Christ continue to be an impressive

---

[151] *Homily at the Mass of Canonization*, 18th May 2003: *L'Osservatore Romano*, 19th-20th May 2003, p. 6.

[152] St John Paul II, Encyclical Letter *Dives in Misericordia* (30th November 1980), 1: AAS 72 (1980), 1219.

[153] Id., *Catechesis*, 20th June 1979: *L'Osservatore Romano*, 22nd June 1979, 1.

[154] Combonian Missionaries of the Heart of Jesus, *Rule of Life*, 3.

[155] Society of the Sacred Heart, *Constitutions of 1982*, 7.

source of renewal in prayer and spiritual fervour. To all those who in any way are associated with these spaces of faith and charity I send my paternal blessing.

THE DEVOTION OF CONSOLATION

151. The wound in Christ's side, the wellspring of living water, remains open in the risen body of the Saviour. The deep wound inflicted by the lance and the wounds of the crown of thorns that customarily appear in representations of the Sacred Heart are an inseparable part of this devotion, in which we contemplate the love of Christ who offered himself in sacrifice to the very end. The heart of the risen Lord preserves the signs of that complete self-surrender, which entailed intense sufferings for our sake. It is natural, then, that the faithful should wish to respond not only to this immense outpouring of love, but also to the suffering that the Lord chose to endure for the sake of that love.

With Jesus on the cross

152. It is fitting to recover one particular aspect of the spirituality that has accompanied devotion to the heart of Christ, namely, the interior desire to offer consolation to that heart. Here I will not discuss the practice of "reparation", which I deem better suited to the social dimension of this devotion to be discussed in the next chapter. I would like instead to concentrate on the desire often felt in the hearts of the faithful who lovingly contemplate the mystery of Christ's passion and experience it as a mystery which is not only recollected but becomes present to us by grace, or better, allows us to be mystically present at the moment of our redemption. If we truly love the Lord, how could we not desire to console him?

153. Pope Pius XI wished to ground this particular devotion in the realisation that the mystery of our redemption by Christ's passion transcends, by God's grace, all boundaries of time and space. On the cross, Jesus offered himself for all sins, including

those yet to be committed, including our own sins. In the same way, the acts we now offer for his consolation, also transcending time, touch his wounded heart. "If, because of our sins too, as yet in the future but already foreseen, the soul of Jesus became sorrowful unto death, it cannot be doubted that at the same time he derived some solace from our reparation, likewise foreseen, at the moment when 'there appeared to him an angel from heaven' (*Lk* 22:43), in order that his heart, oppressed with weariness and anguish, might find consolation. And so even now, in a wondrous yet true manner, we can and ought to console that Most Sacred Heart, which is continually wounded by the sins of thankless men".[156]

Reasons of the heart

154. It might appear to some that this aspect of devotion to the Sacred Heart lacks a firm theological basis, yet the heart has its reasons. Here the *sensus fidelium* perceives something mysterious, beyond our human logic, and realises that the passion of Christ is not merely an event of the past, but one in which we can share through faith. Meditation on Christ's self-offering on the cross involves, for Christian piety, something much more than mere remembrance. This conviction has a solid theological grounding.[157] We can also add the recognition of our own sins, which Jesus took upon his bruised shoulders, and our inadequacy in the face of that timeless love, which is always infinitely greater.

155. We may also question how we can pray to the Lord of life, risen from the dead and reigning in glory, while at the same time comforting him in the midst of his sufferings. Here we need to realise that his risen heart preserves its wound as a constant memory, and that the working of grace makes possible

---

[156] Encyclical Letter *Miserentissimus Redemptor* (8th May 1928): AAS 20 (1928), 174.

[157] The believer's act of faith has as its object not simply the doctrine proposed, but also union with Christ himself in the reality of his divine life (cf. St Thomas Aquinas, *Summa Theologiae*, II-II, q. 1, a. 2, ad 2; q. 4, a. 1).

an experience that is not restricted to a single moment of the past. In pondering this, we find ourselves invited to take a mystical path that transcends our mental limitations yet remains firmly grounded in the word of God. Pope Pius XI makes this clear: "How can these acts of reparation offer solace now, when Christ is already reigning in the beatitude of heaven? To this question, we may answer in the words of St Augustine, which are very apposite here – 'Give me the one who loves, and he will understand what I say'. Anyone possessed of great love for God, and who looks back to the past, can dwell in meditation on Christ, and see him labouring for man, sorrowing, suffering the greatest hardships, 'for us men and for our salvation', well-nigh worn out with sadness, with anguish, nay 'bruised for our sins' (*Is* 53:5), and bringing us healing by those very bruises. The more the faithful ponder all these things, the more clearly they see that the sins of mankind, whenever they were committed, were the reason why Christ was delivered up to death".[158]

156. Those words of Pius XI merit serious consideration. When Scripture states that believers who fail to live in accordance with their faith "are crucifying again the Son of God" (*Heb* 6:6), or when Paul, offering his sufferings for the sake of others, says that, "in my flesh I am completing what is lacking in Christ's afflictions" (*Col* 1:24), or again, when Christ in his passion prays not only for his disciples at that time, but also for "those who will believe in me through their word" (*Jn* 17:20), all these statements challenge our usual way of thinking. They show us that it is not possible to sever the past completely from the present, however difficult our minds find this to grasp. The Gospel, in all its richness, was written not only for our prayerful meditation, but also to enable us to experience its reality in our works of love and in our interior life. This is certainly the case with regard to the mystery of Christ's death and resurrection. The temporal distinctions that our minds employ appear incapable of

---

[158] Pius XI, Encyclical Letter *Miserentissimus Redemptor* (8th May 1928): AAS 20 (1928), 174.

embracing the fullness of this experience of faith, which is the basis both of our union with Christ in his suffering and of the strength, consolation and friendship that we enjoy with him in his risen life.

157. We see, then, the unity of the paschal mystery in these two inseparable and mutually enriching aspects. The one mystery, present by grace in both these dimensions, ensures that whenever we offer some suffering of our own to Christ for his consolation, that suffering is illuminated and transfigured in the paschal light of his love. We share in this mystery in our own life because Christ himself first chose to share in that life. He wished to experience first, as Head, what he would then experience in his Body, the Church: both our wounds and our consolations. When we live in God's grace, this mutual sharing becomes for us a spiritual experience. In a word, the risen Lord, by the working of his grace, mysteriously unites us to his passion. The hearts of the faithful, who experience the joy of the resurrection, yet at the same time desire to share in the Lord's passion, understand this. They desire to share in his sufferings by offering him the sufferings, the struggles, the disappointments and the fears that are part of their own lives. Nor do they experience this as isolated individuals, since their sufferings are also a participation in the suffering of the mystical Body of Christ, the holy pilgrim People of God, which shares in the passion of Christ in every time and place. The devotion of consolation, then, is in no way ahistorical or abstract; it becomes flesh and blood in the Church's pilgrimage through history.

Compunction

158. The natural desire to console Christ, which begins with our sorrow in contemplating what he endured for us, grows with the honest acknowledgement of our bad habits, compulsions, attachments, weak faith, vain goals and, together with our actual sins, the failure of our hearts to respond to the Lord's love and

his plan for our lives. This experience proves purifying, for love needs the purification of tears that, in the end, leave us more desirous of God and less obsessed with ourselves.

159. In this way, we see that the deeper our desire to console the Lord, the deeper will be our sincere sense of "compunction". Compunction is "not a feeling of guilt that makes us discouraged or obsessed with our unworthiness, but a beneficial 'piercing' that purifies and heals the heart. Once we acknowledge our sin, our hearts can be opened to the working of the Holy Spirit, the source of living water that wells up within us and brings tears to our eyes... This does not mean weeping in self-pity, as we are so often tempted to do... To shed tears of compunction means seriously to repent of grieving God by our sins; recognising that we always remain in God's debt... Just as drops of water can wear down a stone, so tears can slowly soften hardened hearts. Here we see the miracle of sorrow, that 'salutary sorrow' which brings great peace... Compunction, then, is not our work but a grace and, as such, it must be sought in prayer."[159] It means, "asking for sorrow in company with Christ in his sorrow, for anguish with Christ in his anguish, for tears and a deep sense of pain at the great pains that Christ endured for my sake".[160]

160. I ask, then, that no one make light of the fervent devotion of the holy faithful people of God, which in its popular piety seeks to console Christ. I also encourage everyone to consider whether there might be greater reasonableness, truth and wisdom in certain demonstrations of love that seek to console the Lord than in the cold, distant, calculated and nominal acts of love that are at times practised by those who claim to possess a more reflective, sophisticated and mature faith.

---

[159] *Homily at the Chrism Mass*, 28th March 2024: *L'Osservatore Romano*, 28th March 2024, p. 2.

[160] St Ignatius Loyola, *Spiritual Exercises*, 203.

Consoled ourselves in order to console others

161. In contemplating the heart of Christ and his self-surrender even to death, we ourselves find great consolation. The grief that we feel in our hearts gives way to complete trust and, in the end, what endures is gratitude, tenderness, peace; what endures is Christ's love reigning in our lives. Compunction, then, "is not a source of anxiety but of healing for the soul, since it acts as a balm on the wounds of sin, preparing us to receive the caress of the Lord".[161] Our sufferings are joined to the suffering of Christ on the cross. If we believe that grace can bridge every distance, this means that Christ by his sufferings united himself to the sufferings of his disciples in every time and place. In this way, whenever we endure suffering, we can also experience the interior consolation of knowing that Christ suffers with us. In seeking to console him, we will find ourselves consoled.

162. At some point, however, in our contemplation, we should likewise hear the urgent plea of the Lord: "Comfort, comfort my people!" (*Is* 40:1). As St Paul tells us, God offers us consolation "so that we may be able to console those who are in any affliction, with the consolation by which we ourselves are consoled by God" (*2 Cor* 1:4).

163. This then challenges us to seek a deeper understanding of the communitarian, social and missionary dimension of all authentic devotion to the heart of Christ. For even as Christ's heart leads us to the Father, it sends us forth to our brothers and sisters. In the fruits of service, fraternity and mission that the heart of Christ inspires in our lives, the will of the Father is fulfilled. In this way, we come full circle: "My Father is glorified by this, that you bear much fruit" (*Jn* 15:8).

---

[161] *Homily at the Chrism Mass*, 28th March 2024: *L'Osservatore Romano*, 28th March 2024, p. 2.

CHAPTER FIVE

LOVE FOR LOVE

164. In the spiritual experiences of St Margaret Mary Alacoque, we encounter, along with an ardent declaration of love for Jesus Christ, a profoundly personal and challenging invitation to entrust our lives to the Lord. The knowledge that we are loved, and our complete confidence in that love, in no way lessens our desire to respond generously, despite our frailty and our many shortcomings.

A LAMENT AND A REQUEST

165. Beginning with his second great apparition to St Margaret Mary, Jesus spoke of the sadness he feels because his great love for humanity receives in exchange "nothing but ingratitude and indifference", "coldness and contempt". And this, he added, "is more grievous to me than all that I endured in my Passion".[162]

166. Jesus spoke of his thirst for love and revealed that his heart is not indifferent to the way we respond to that thirst. In his words, "I thirst, but with a thirst so ardent to be loved by men in the Most Blessed Sacrament, that this thirst consumes me; and I have not encountered anyone who makes an effort, according to my desire, to quench my thirst, giving back a return for my love".[163] Jesus asks for love. Once the faithful heart realises this, its spontaneous response is one of love, not a desire to multiply sacrifices or simply discharge a burdensome duty: "I received from my God excessive graces of his love, and I felt moved by the desire to respond to some of them and to respond with love

---

[162] St Margaret Mary Alacoque, *Autobiography*, n. 55.
[163] *Letter 133 to Father Croiset.*

72

for love".[164] As my Predecessor Leo XIII pointed out, through the image of his Sacred Heart, the love of Christ "moves us to return love for love".[165]

EXTENDING CHRIST'S LOVE TO OUR BROTHERS AND SISTERS

167. We need once more to take up the word of God and to realise, in doing so, that our best response to the love of Christ's heart is to love our brothers and sisters. There is no greater way for us to return love for love. The Scriptures make this patently clear:

"Just as you did it to one of the least of these my brethren, you did it to me" (*Mt* 25:40).

"For the whole law is summed up in a single commandment: 'You shall love your neighbour as yourself'" (*Gal* 5:14).

"We know that we have passed from death to life because we love one another. Whoever does not love abides in death" (*1 Jn* 3:14).

"Those who do not love a brother or sister whom they have seen, cannot love God whom they have not seen" (*1 Jn* 4:20).

168. Love for our brothers and sisters is not simply the fruit of our own efforts; it demands the transformation of our selfish hearts. This realisation gave rise to the oft-repeated prayer: "Jesus, make our hearts more like your own". St Paul, for his part, urged his hearers to pray not for the strength to do good works, but "to have the same mind among you that was in Christ Jesus" (*Phil* 2:5).

169. We need to remember that in the Roman Empire many of the poor, foreigners and others who lived on the fringes of society met with respect, affection and care from Christians.

---

[164] *Autobiography*, n. 92.

[165] Encyclical Letter *Annum Sacrum* (25th May 1899): ASS 31 (1898-1899), 649.

This explains why the apostate emperor Julian, in one of his letters, acknowledged that one reason why Christians were respected and imitated was the assistance they gave the poor and strangers, who were ordinarily ignored and treated with contempt. For Julian, it was intolerable that the Christians whom he despised, "in addition to feeding their own, also feed our poor and needy, who receive no help from us".[166] The emperor thus insisted on the need to create charitable institutions to compete with those of the Christians and thus gain the respect of society: "There should be instituted in each city many accommodations so that the immigrants may enjoy our philanthropy… and make the Greeks accustomed to such works of generosity".[167] Julian did not achieve his objective, no doubt because underlying those works there was nothing comparable to the Christian charity that respected the unique dignity of each person.

170. By associating with the lowest ranks of society (cf. *Mt* 25:31-46), "Jesus brought the great novelty of recognising the dignity of every person, especially those who were considered 'unworthy'. This new principle in human history – which emphasises that individuals are even more 'worthy' of our respect and love when they are weak, scorned, or suffering, even to the point of losing the human 'figure' – has changed the face of the world. It has given life to institutions that take care of those who find themselves in disadvantaged conditions, such as abandoned infants, orphans, the elderly who are left without assistance, the mentally ill, people with incurable diseases or severe deformities, and those living on the streets".[168]

171. In contemplating the pierced heart of the Lord, who "took our infirmities and bore our diseases" (*Mt* 8:17), we too are inspired to be more attentive to the sufferings and needs of others,

[166] Iulianus IMP., *Ep. XLIX ad Arsacium Pontificem Galatiae*, Mainz, 1828, 90-91.

[167] Ibid.

[168] Dicastery for the Doctrine of the Faith, Declaration *Dignitas Infinita* (2nd April 2024), 19: *L'Osservatore Romano*, 8th April 2024.

and confirmed in our efforts to share in his work of liberation as instruments for the spread of his love.[169] As we meditate on Christ's self-offering for the sake of all, we are naturally led to ask why we too should not be ready to give our lives for others: "We know love by this, that he laid down his life for us – and that we ought to lay down our lives for one another" (*1 Jn* 3:16).

ECHOES IN THE HISTORY OF SPIRITUALITY

172. This bond between devotion to the heart of Jesus and commitment to our brothers and sisters has been a constant in the history of Christian spirituality. Let us consider a few examples.

Being a fountain from which others can drink

173. Starting with Origen, various Fathers of the Church reflected on the words of John 7:38 – "out of his heart shall flow rivers of living water" – which refer to those who, having drunk of Christ, put their faith in him. Our union with Christ is meant not only to satisfy our own thirst, but also to make us springs of living water for others. Origen wrote that Christ fulfils his promise by making fountains of fresh water well up within us: "The human soul, made in the image of God, can itself contain and pour forth wells, fountains and rivers".[170]

174. St Ambrose recommended drinking deeply of Christ, "in order that the spring of water welling up to eternal life may overflow in you".[171] Marius Victorinus was convinced that the Holy Spirit has given of himself in such abundance that, "whoever receives him becomes a heart that pours forth rivers of living water".[172] St Augustine saw this stream flowing from the

---

[169] Cf. Benedict XVI, *Letter to the Superior General of the Society of Jesus on the Fiftieth Anniversary of the Encyclical "Haurietis Aquas"* (15th May 2006): AAS 98 (2006), 461.

[170] *In Num. homil.* 12, 1: PG 12, 657.

[171] *Epist.* 29, 24: PL 16, 1060.

[172] *Adv. Arium* 1, 8: PL 8, 1044.

believer as benevolence.[173] St Thomas Aquinas thus maintained that whenever someone "hastens to share various gifts of grace received from God, living water flows from his heart".[174]

175. Although "the sacrifice offered on the cross in loving obedience renders most abundant and infinite satisfaction for the sins of mankind",[175] the Church, born of the heart of Christ, prolongs and bestows, in every time and place, the fruits of that one redemptive passion, which lead men and women to direct union with the Lord.

176. In the heart of the Church, the mediation of Mary, as our intercessor and mother, can only be understood as "a sharing in the one source, which is the mediation of Christ himself",[176] the sole Redeemer. For this reason, "the Church does not hesitate to profess the subordinate role of Mary".[177] Devotion to the heart of Mary in no way detracts from the sole worship due the heart of Christ, but rather increases it: "Mary's function as mother of humanity in no way obscures or diminishes this unique mediation of Christ, but rather shows its power".[178] Thanks to the abundant graces streaming from the open side of Christ, in different ways the Church, the Virgin Mary and all believers become themselves streams of living water. In this way, Christ displays his glory in and through our littleness.

Fraternity and mysticism

177. St Bernard, in exhorting us to union with the heart of Christ, draws upon the richness of this devotion to call for a conversion grounded in love. Bernard believed that our affections, enslaved

---

[173] *Tract. in Joannem* 32, 4: PL 35, 1643.

[174] *Expos. in Ev. S. Joannis*, cap. VII, lectio 5.

[175] Pius XII, Encyclical Letter *Haurietis Aquas*, 15th May 1956: AAS 48 (1956), 321.

[176] St John Paul II, Encyclical Letter *Redemptoris Mater* (25th March 1987), 38: AAS 79 (1987), 411.

[177] Second Vatican Ecumenical Council, Dogmatic Constitution *Lumen Gentium*, 62.

[178] Ibid., 60.

by pleasures, may nonetheless be transformed and set free, not by blind obedience to a commandment but rather in response to the delectable love of Christ. Evil is overcome by good, conquered by the flowering of love: "Love the Lord your God with the full and deep affection of all your heart; love him with your mind wholly alert and intent; love him with all your strength, so much so that you would not even fear to die for love of him... Your affection for the Lord Jesus should be both sweet and intimate, to oppose the sweet enticements of the sensual life. Sweetness conquers sweetness, as one nail drives out another".[179]

178. St Francis de Sales was particularly taken by Jesus's words, "Learn from me; for I am gentle and humble in heart" (*Mt* 11:29). Even in the most simple and ordinary things, he said, we can "steal" the Lord's heart. "Those who would serve him acceptably must give heed not only to lofty and important matters, but to things mean and little, since by both alike we may win his heart and love... I mean the acts of daily forbearance, the headache, the toothache, the heavy cold; the tiresome peculiarities of a husband or wife, the broken glass, the loss of a ring, a handkerchief, a glove; the sneer of a neighbour; the effort of going to bed early in order to rise early for prayer or communion, the little shyness some people feel in openly performing religious duties... Be sure that all these sufferings, small as they are, if accepted lovingly, are most pleasing to God's goodness".[180] Ultimately, however, our response to the love of the heart of Christ is manifested in love of our neighbour: "a love that is firm, constant, steady, unconcerned with trivial matters or people's station in life, not subject to changes or animosity... Our Lord loves us unceasingly, puts up with so many of our defects and our flaws. Precisely because of this, we must do the same with our brothers and sisters, never tiring of putting up with them".[181]

---

[179] *Sermones super Cant.*, XX, 4: PL 183, 869.

[180] *Introduction to the Devout Life*, Part III, xxxv.

[181] *Sermon for the XVII Sunday after Pentecost.*

179. St Charles de Foucauld sought to imitate Jesus by living and acting as he did, in a constant effort to do what Jesus would have done in his place. Only by being conformed to the sentiments of the heart of Christ could he fully achieve this goal. Here too we find the idea of "love for love". In his words, "I desire sufferings in order to return love for love, to imitate him... to enter into his work, to offer myself with him, the nothingness that I am, as a sacrifice, as a victim, for the sanctification of men".[182] The desire to bring the love of Jesus to others, his missionary outreach to the poorest and most forgotten of our world, led him to take as his emblem the words, "Iesus-Caritas", with the symbol of the heart of Christ surmounted by a cross.[183] Nor was this a light decision: "With all my strength I try to show and prove to these poor lost brethren that our religion is all charity, all fraternity, and that its emblem is a heart".[184] He wanted to settle with other brothers "in Morocco, in the name of the heart of Jesus".[185] In this way, their evangelising work could radiate outwards: "Charity has to radiate from our fraternities, as it radiates from the heart of Jesus".[186] This desire gradually made him a "universal brother". Allowing himself to be shaped by the heart of Christ, he sought to shelter the whole of suffering humanity in his fraternal heart: "Our heart, like that of Jesus, must embrace all men and women".[187] "The love of the heart of Jesus for men and women, the love that he demonstrated in his passion, this is what we need to have for all human beings".[188]

---

[182] *Écrits spirituels*, Paris 1947, 67.

[183] After 19th March 1902, all his letters begin with the words *Jesus Caritas* separated by a heart surmounted by the cross.

[184] *Letter to l'Abbé Huvelin*, 15th July 1904.

[185] *Letter to Dom Martin*, 25th January 1903.

[186] Cited in René Voillaume , *Les fraternités du Père de Foucauld*, Paris, 1946, 173.

[187] *Méditations des saints Évangiles sur les passages relatifs à quinze vertus*, Nazareth, 1897-1898, *Charité* (*Mt* 13:3), 60.

[188] Ibid., *Charité* (*Mt* 22:1), 90.

180. Fr Henri Huvelin, the spiritual director of St Charles de Foucauld, observed that, "when our Lord dwells in a heart, he gives it such sentiments, and this heart reaches out to the least of our brothers and sisters. Such was the heart of St Vincent de Paul... When our Lord lives in the soul of a priest, he makes him reach out to the poor".[189] It is important to realise that the apostolic zeal of St Vincent, as Fr Huvelin describes it, was also nurtured by devotion to the heart of Christ. St Vincent urged his confrères to "find in the heart of our Lord a word of consolation for the poor sick person".[190] If that word is to be convincing, our own heart must first have been changed by the love and tenderness of the heart of Christ. St Vincent often reiterated this conviction in his homilies and counsels, and it became a notable feature of the Constitutions of his Congregation: "We should make a great effort to learn the following lesson, also taught by Christ: 'Learn from me, for I am gentle and humble of heart'. We should remember that he himself said that by gentleness we inherit the earth. If we act on this, we will win people over so that they will turn to the Lord. That will not happen if we treat people harshly or sharply".[191]

REPARATION: BUILDING ON THE RUINS

181. All that has been said thus far enables us to understand in the light of God's word the proper meaning of the "reparation" to the heart of Christ that the Lord expects us, with the help of his grace, to "offer". The question has been much discussed, but St John Paul II has given us a clear response that can guide Christians today towards a spirit of reparation more closely attuned to the Gospels.

---

[189] H. Huvelin, *Quelques directeurs d'âmes au XVII siècle*, Paris, 1911, 97.

[190] *Conference, "Service of the Sick and Care of One's own Health"*, 11th November 1657.

[191] *Common Rules of the Congregation of the Mission*, 17th May 1658, c. 2, 6.

The social significance of reparation to the heart of Christ

182. St John Paul explained that by entrusting ourselves together to the heart of Christ, "over the ruins accumulated by hatred and violence, the greatly desired civilisation of love, the Kingdom of the heart of Christ, can be built". This clearly requires that we "unite filial love for God and love of neighbour", and indeed this is "the true reparation asked by the heart of the Saviour".[192] In union with Christ, amid the ruins we have left in this world by our sins, we are called to build a new civilisation of love. That is what it means to make reparation as the heart of Christ would have us do. Amid the devastation wrought by evil, the heart of Christ desires that we co-operate with him in restoring goodness and beauty to our world.

183. All sin harms the Church and society; as a result, "every sin can undoubtedly be considered as a social sin" and this is especially true for those sins that "by their very matter constitute a direct attack on one's neighbour".[193] St John Paul II explained that the repetition of these sins against others often consolidates a "structure of sin" that has an effect on the development of peoples.[194] Frequently, this is part of a dominant mind-set that considers normal or reasonable what is merely selfishness and indifference. This then gives rise to social alienation: "A society is alienated if its forms of social organisation, production and consumption make it more difficult to offer the gift of self and to establish solidarity between people".[195] It is not only a moral norm that leads us to expose and resist these alienated social structures and to support efforts within society to restore and consolidate the common good. Rather, it is our "conversion of

---

[192] *Letter to the Superior General of the Society of Jesus*, Paray-le-Monial, 5th October 1986: *L'Osservatore Romano*, 6th October 1986, p. 7.

[193] St John Paul II, Post-Synodal Apostolic Exhortation *Reconciliatio et Pœnitentia* (2nd December 1984), 16: AAS 77 (1985), 215.

[194] Cf. Encyclical Letter *Sollicitudo Rei Socialis* (30th December 1987), 36: AAS 80 (1988), 561-562.

[195] Encyclical Letter *Centesimus Annus* (1st May 1991), 41: AAS 83 (1991), 844-845.

heart" that "imposes the obligation"[196] to repair these structures. It is our response to the love of the heart of Jesus, which teaches us to love in turn.

184. Precisely because evangelical reparation possesses this vital social dimension, our acts of love, service and reconciliation, in order to be truly reparative, need to be inspired, motivated and empowered by Christ. St John Paul II also observed that "to build the civilisation of love",[197] our world today needs the heart of Christ. Christian reparation cannot be understood simply as a congeries of external works, however indispensable and at times admirable they may be. These need a "mystique", a soul, a meaning that grants them strength, drive and tireless creativity. They need the life, the fire and the light that radiate from the heart of Christ.

Mending wounded hearts

185. Nor is a merely outward reparation sufficient, either for our world or for the heart of Christ. If each of us considers his or her own sins and their effect on others, we will realise that repairing the harm done to this world also calls for a desire to mend wounded hearts where the deepest harm was done, and the hurt is most painful.

186. A spirit of reparation thus "leads us to hope that every wound can be healed, however deep it may be. Complete reparation may at times seem impossible, such as when goods or loved ones are definitively lost, or when certain situations have become irremediable. Yet the intention to make amends, and to do so in a concrete way, is essential for the process of reconciliation and a return to peace of heart".[198]

---

[196] *Catechism of the Catholic Church*, 1888.

[197] *Catechesis*, 8th June 1994, 2: *L'Osservatore Romano*, 4th May 1994, p. 5.

[198] *Address to the Participants in the International Colloquium "Réparer L'Irréparable"*, on the 350th Anniversary of the Apparitions of Jesus in Paray-le-Monial, 4th May 2024: *L'Osservatore Romano*, 4th May 2024, p. 12.

The beauty of asking forgiveness

187. Good intentions are not enough. There has to be an inward desire that finds expression in our outward actions. "Reparation, if it is to be Christian, to touch the offended person's heart and not be a simple act of commutative justice, presupposes two demanding things: acknowledging our guilt and asking forgiveness... It is from the honest acknowledgement of the wrong done to our brother or sister, and from the profound and sincere realisation that love has been compromised, that the desire to make amends arises".[199]

188. We should never think that acknowledging our sins before others is somehow demeaning or offensive to our human dignity. On the contrary, it demands that we stop deceiving ourselves and acknowledge our past for what it is, marred by sin, especially in those cases when we caused hurt to our brothers and sisters. "Self-accusation is part of Christian wisdom... It is pleasing to the Lord, because the Lord accepts a contrite heart".[200]

189. Part of this spirit of reparation is the custom of asking forgiveness from our brothers and sisters, which demonstrates great nobility amid our human weakness. Asking forgiveness is a means of healing relationships, for it "re-opens dialogue and manifests the will to re-establish the bond of fraternal charity... It touches the heart of our brother or sister, brings consolation and inspires acceptance of the forgiveness requested. Even if the irreparable cannot be completely repaired, love can always be reborn, making the hurt bearable".[201]

---

[199] Ibid.

[200] *Homily at Morning Mass in Domus Sanctae Marthae*, 6th March 2018: *L'Osservatore Romano*, 5th-6th March 2018, p. 8.

[201] *Address to the Participants in the International Colloquium "Réparer L'Irréparable"*, on the 350th Anniversary of the Apparitions of Jesus in Paray-le-Monial, 4th May 2024: *L'Osservatore Romano*, 4th May 2024, p. 12.

190. A heart capable of compunction will grow in fraternity and solidarity. Otherwise, "we regress and grow old within", whereas when "our prayer becomes simpler and deeper, grounded in adoration and wonder in the presence of God, we grow and mature. We become less attached to ourselves and more attached to Christ. Made poor in spirit, we draw closer to the poor, those who are dearest to God".[202] This leads to a true spirit of reparation, for "those who feel compunction of heart increasingly feel themselves brothers and sisters to all the sinners of the world; renouncing their airs of superiority and harsh judgements, they are filled with a burning desire to show love and make reparation".[203] The sense of solidarity born of compunction also enables reconciliation to take place. The person who is capable of compunction, "rather than feeling anger and scandal at the failings of our brothers and sisters, weeps for their sins. There occurs a sort of reversal, where the natural tendency to be indulgent with ourselves and inflexible with others is overturned and, by God's grace, we become strict with ourselves and merciful towards others".[204]

REPARATION: AN EXTENSION OF
THE HEART OF CHRIST

191. There is another, complementary, approach to reparation, which allows us to set it in an even more direct relationship with the heart of Christ, without excluding the aspect of concrete commitment to our brothers and sisters.

192. Elsewhere I have suggested that, "God has in some way sought to limit himself in such a way that many of the things we think of as evils, dangers or sources of suffering, are in reality part of the pains of childbirth which he uses to draw us into the act of

---

[202] *Homily at the Chrism Mass*, 28th March 2024: *L'Osservatore Romano*, 28th March 2024, p. 2.

[203] Ibid.

[204] Ibid

co-operation with the Creator".[205] This co-operation on our part can allow the power and the love of God to expand in our lives and in the world, whereas our refusal or indifference can prevent it. Several passages of the Bible express this metaphorically, as when the Lord cries out, "If only you would return to me, O Israel!" (cf. *Jer* 4:1). Or when, confronted with rejection by his people, he says, "My heart recoils within me; my compassion grows warm and tender" (*Hos* 11:8).

193. Even though it is not possible to speak of new suffering on the part of the glorified Lord, "the paschal mystery of Christ... and all that Christ is – all that he did and suffered for all men – participates in the divine eternity, and so transcends all times while being made present in them all".[206] We can say that he has allowed the expansive glory of his resurrection to be limited and the diffusion of his immense and burning love to be contained, in order to leave room for our free co-operation with his heart. Our rejection of his love erects a barrier to that gracious gift, whereas our trusting acceptance of it opens a space, a channel enabling it to pour into our hearts. Our rejection or indifference limits the effects of his power and the fruitfulness of his love in us. If he does not encounter openness and confidence in me, his love is deprived – because he himself has willed it – of its extension, unique and unrepeatable, in my life and in this world, where he calls me to make him present. Again, this does not stem from any weakness on his part but rather from his infinite freedom, his mysterious power and his perfect love for each of us. When God's power is revealed in the weakness of our human freedom, "only faith can discern it". [207]

194. St Margaret Mary recounted that, in one of Christ's appearances, he spoke of his heart's passionate love for us, telling her that, "unable to contain the flames of his burning

---

[205] Encyclical Letter *Laudato Si'* (24th May 2015), 80: AAS 107 (2015), 879.

[206] *Catechism of the Catholic Church*, 1085.

[207] Ibid., No. 268.

charity, he must spread them abroad".[208] Since the Lord, who can do all things, desired in his divine freedom to require our co-operation, reparation can be understood as our removal of the obstacles we place before the expansion of Christ's love in the world by our lack of trust, gratitude and self-sacrifice.

An Oblation to Love

195. To help us reflect more deeply on this mystery, we can turn once more to the luminous spirituality of St Thérèse of the Child Jesus. Thérèse was aware that in certain quarters an extreme form of reparation had developed, based on a willingness to offer oneself in sacrifice for others, and to become in some sense a "lightning rod" for the chastisements of divine justice. In her words, "I thought about the souls who offer themselves as victims of God's justice in order to turn away the punishments reserved to sinners, drawing them upon themselves".[209] However, as great and generous as such an offering might appear, she did not find it overly appealing: "I was far from feeling attracted to making it".[210] So great an emphasis on God's justice might eventually lead to the notion that Christ's sacrifice was somehow incomplete or only partly efficacious, or that his mercy was not sufficiently powerful.

196. With her great spiritual insight, St Thérèse discovered that we can offer ourselves in another way, without the need to satisfy divine justice but by allowing the Lord's infinite love to spread freely: "O my God! Is your disdained love going to remain closed up within your heart? It seems to me that if you were to find souls offering themselves as victims of holocaust to your love, you would consume them rapidly; it seems to me, too, that you would be happy not to hold back the waves of infinite tenderness within you".[211]

---

[208] *Autobiography*, n. 53.

[209] Ms A, 84r.

[210] Ibid.

[211] Ibid.

197. While nothing need be added to the one redemptive sacrifice of Christ, it remains true that our free refusal can prevent the heart of Christ from spreading the "waves of his infinite tenderness" in this world. Again, this is because the Lord wishes to respect our freedom. More than divine justice, it was the fact that Christ's love might be refused that troubled the heart of St Thérèse, because for her, God's justice is understood only in the light of his love. As we have seen, she contemplated all God's perfections through his mercy, and thus saw them transfigured and resplendent with love. In her words, "even his justice (and perhaps this even more so than the others) seems to me clothed in love".[212]

198. This was the origin of her Act of Oblation, not to God's justice but to his merciful love. "I offer myself as a victim of holocaust to your merciful love, asking you to consume me incessantly, allowing the waves of infinite tenderness shut up within you to overflow into my soul, and that thus I may become a martyr of your love".[213] It is important to realise that, for Thérèse, this was not only about allowing the heart of Christ to fill her heart, through her complete trust, with the beauty of his love, but also about letting that love, through her life, spread to others and thus transform the world. Again, in her words, "In the heart of the Church, my Mother, I shall be love… and thus my dream will be realised".[214] The two aspects were inseparably united.

199. The Lord accepted her oblation. We see that shortly thereafter she stated that she felt an intense love for others and maintained that it came from the heart of Christ, prolonged through her. So she told her sister Léonie: "I love you a thousand times more tenderly than ordinary sisters love each other, for I can love you with the heart of our celestial spouse".[215] Later, to Maurice Bellière she wrote, "How I would like to make you

[212] Ms A, 83v.; cf. *Letter 226 to Father Roulland*, 9th May 1897.

[213] *Act of Oblation to Merciful Love*, 9th June 1895, 2r-2v.

[214] Ms B, 3v.

[215] *Letter 186 to Léonie*, 11th April 1896.

understand the tenderness of the heart of Jesus, what he expects from you!"[216]

Integrity and Harmony

200. Sisters and brothers, I propose that we develop this means of reparation, which is, in a word, to offer the heart of Christ a new possibility of spreading in this world the flames of his ardent and gracious love. While it remains true that reparation entails the desire to "render compensation for the injuries inflicted on uncreated Love, whether by negligence or grave offence",[217] the most fitting way to do this is for our love to offer the Lord a possibility of spreading, in amends for all those occasions when his love has been rejected or refused. This involves more than simply the "consolation" of Christ of which we spoke in the previous chapter; it finds expression in acts of fraternal love by which we heal the wounds of the Church and of the world. In this way, we offer the healing power of the heart of Christ new ways of expressing itself.

201. The sacrifices and sufferings required by these acts of love of neighbour unite us to the passion of Christ. In this way, "by that mystic crucifixion of which the Apostle speaks, we shall receive the abundant fruits of its propitiation and expiation, for ourselves and for others".[218] Christ alone saves us by his offering on the cross; he alone redeems us, for "there is one God; there is also one mediator between God and men, the man Christ Jesus, who gave himself as a ransom for all" (1 *Tim* 2:5-6). The reparation that we offer is a freely accepted participation in his redeeming love and his one sacrifice. We thus complete in our flesh "what is lacking in Christ's afflictions for the sake of his body, that is, the Church" (*Col* 1:24); and Christ himself prolongs through us the effects of his complete and loving self-oblation.

---

[216] *Letter 258 to l'Abbé Bellière*, 18th July 1897.

[217] Cf. PIUS XI, Encyclical Letter *Miserentissimus Redemptor*, 8th May 1928: AAS 20 (1928), 169.

[218] Ibid.: AAS 20 (1928), 172.

202. Often, our sufferings have to do with our own wounded ego. The humility of the heart of Christ points us towards the path of abasement. God chose to come to us in condescension and littleness. The Old Testament had already shown us, with a variety of metaphors, a God who enters into the heart of history and allows himself to be rejected by his people. Christ's love was shown amid the daily life of his people, begging, as it were, for a response, as if asking permission to manifest his glory. Yet "perhaps only once did the Lord Jesus refer to his own heart, in his own words. And he stresses this sole feature: 'gentleness and lowliness', as if to say that only in this way does he wish to win us to himself".[219] When he said, "Learn from me, for I am gentle and humble in heart" (*Mt* 11:29), he showed us that "to make himself known, he needs our littleness, our self-abasement".[220]

203. In what we have said, it is important to note several inseparable aspects. Acts of love of neighbour, with the renunciation, self-denial, suffering and effort that they entail, can only be such when they are nourished by Christ's own love. He enables us to love as he loved, and in this way he loves and serves others through us. He humbles himself to show his love through our actions, yet even in our slightest works of mercy, his heart is glorified and displays all its grandeur. Once our hearts welcome the love of Christ in complete trust, and enable its fire to spread in our lives, we become capable of loving others as Christ did, in humility and closeness to all. In this way, Christ satisfies his thirst and gloriously spreads the flames of his ardent and gracious love in us and through us. How can we fail to see the magnificent harmony present in all this?

204. Finally, in order to appreciate this devotion in all of its richness, it is necessary to add, in the light of what we have

---

[219] St John Paul II , *Catechesis, 20th June 1979*: *L'Osservatore Romano*, 22nd June 1979, p. 1.

[220] *Homily at Mass in Domus Sanctae Marthae*, 27th June 2014: *L'Osservatore Romano*, 28th June 2014, p. 8.

said about its Trinitarian dimension, that the reparation made by Christ in his humanity is offered to the Father through the working of the Holy Spirit in each of us. Consequently, the reparation we offer to the heart of Christ is directed ultimately to the Father, who is pleased to see us united to Christ whenever we offer ourselves through him, with him and in him.

BRINGING LOVE TO THE WORLD

205. The Christian message is attractive when experienced and expressed in its totality: not simply as a refuge for pious thoughts or an occasion for impressive ceremonies. What kind of worship would we give to Christ if we were to rest content with an individual relationship with him and show no interest in relieving the sufferings of others or helping them to live a better life? Would it please the heart that so loved us, if we were to bask in a private religious experience while ignoring its implications for the society in which we live? Let us be honest and accept the word of God in its fullness. On the other hand, our work as Christians for the betterment of society should not obscure its religious inspiration, for that, in the end, would be to seek less for our brothers and sisters than what God desires to give them. For this reason, we should conclude this chapter by recalling the missionary dimension of our love for the heart of Christ.

206. St John Paul II spoke of the social dimension of devotion to the heart of Christ, but also about "reparation, which is apostolic co-operation in the salvation of the world".[221] Consecration to the heart of Christ is thus "to be seen in relation to the Church's missionary activity, since it responds to the desire of Jesus's heart to spread throughout the world, through the members of his Body, his complete commitment to the Kingdom".[222] As a result, "through the witness of Christians, love will be poured

---

[221] *Message for the Centenary of the Consecration of the Human Race to the Divine Heart of Jesus, Warsaw,* 11th June 1999, Solemnity of the Sacred Heart of Jesus. *L'Osservatore Romano,* 12th June 1999, p. 5.

[222] Ibid.

into human hearts, to build up the body of Christ which is the Church, and to build a society of justice, peace and fraternity".[223]

207. The flames of love of the Sacred Heart of Jesus also expand through the Church's missionary outreach, which proclaims the message of God's love revealed in Christ. St Vincent de Paul put this nicely when he invited his disciples to pray to the Lord for "this spirit, this heart that causes us to go everywhere, this heart of the Son of God, the heart of our Lord, that disposes us to go as he went...he sends us, like [the apostles], to bring fire everywhere".[224]

208. St Paul VI, addressing religious Congregations dedicated to the spread of devotion to the Sacred Heart, made the following observation. "There can be no doubt that pastoral commitment and missionary zeal will fan into flame, if priests and laity alike, in their desire to spread the glory of God, contemplate the example of eternal love that Christ has shown us, and direct their efforts to make all men and women sharers in the unfathomable riches of Christ".[225] As we contemplate the Sacred Heart, mission becomes a matter of love. For the greatest danger in mission is that, amid all the things we say and do, we fail to bring about a joyful encounter with the love of Christ who embraces us and saves us.

209. Mission, as a radiation of the love of the heart of Christ, requires missionaries who are themselves in love and who, enthralled by Christ, feel bound to share this love that has changed their lives. They are impatient when time is wasted discussing secondary questions or concentrating on truths and rules, because their greatest concern is to share what they have

---

[223] *Letter to the Archbishop of Lyon on the occasion of the Pilgrimage of Paray-le-Monial for the Centenary of the Consecration of the Human Race to the Divine Heart of Jesus*, 4th June 1999: *L'Osservatore Romano*, 12th June 1999, p. 4.

[224] *Conference, "Repetition of Prayer"*, 22nd August 1655.

[225] Letter *Diserti interpretes* (25th May 1965), 4: *Enchiridion della Vita Consacrata*, Bologna-Milano, 2001, n. 3809.

experienced. They want others to perceive the goodness and beauty of the Beloved through their efforts, however inadequate they may be. Is that not the case with any lover? We can take as an example the words with which Dante Alighieri sought to express this logic of love:

"Io dico che, pensando al suo valore
amor si dolce si mi si fa sentire,
che s'io allora non perdessi ardire
farei parlando innamorar la gente". [226]

210. To be able to speak of Christ, by witness or by word, in such a way that others seek to love him, is the greatest desire of every missionary of souls. This dynamism of love has nothing to do with proselytism; the words of a lover do not disturb others, they do not make demands or oblige, they only lead others to marvel at such love. With immense respect for their freedom and dignity, the lover simply waits for them to inquire about the love that has filled his or her life with such great joy.

211. Christ asks you never to be ashamed to tell others, with all due discretion and respect, about your friendship with him. He asks that you dare to tell others how good and beautiful it is that you found him. "Everyone who acknowledges me before others, I also will acknowledge before my Father in heaven" (*Mt* 10:32). For a heart that loves, this is not a duty but an irrepressible need: "Woe to me if I do not proclaim the Gospel!" (*1 Cor* 9:16). "Within me there is something like a burning fire shut up in my bones; I am weary with holding it in, and I cannot" (*Jer* 20:9).

In communion of service

212. We should not think of this mission of sharing Christ as something only between Jesus and me. Mission is experienced

---

[226] *Vita Nuova* XIX, 5-6: "I declare that, in thinking of its worth, love so sweet makes me feel that, if my courage did not fail me, I would speak out and make everyone else fall in love".

in fellowship with our communities and with the whole Church. If we turn aside from the community, we will be turning aside from Jesus. If we turn our back on the community, our friendship with Jesus will grow cold. This is a fact, and we must never forget it. Love for the brothers and sisters of our communities – religious, parochial, diocesan and others – is a kind of fuel that feeds our friendship with Jesus. Our acts of love for our brothers and sisters in community may well be the best and, at times, the only way that we can witness to others our love for Jesus Christ. He himself said, "By this everyone will know that you are my disciples, if you have love for one another" (*Jn* 13:35).

213. This love then becomes service within the community. I never tire of repeating that Jesus told us this in the clearest terms possible: "Just as you did it to one of the least of these my brethren, you did it to me" (*Mt* 25:40). He now asks you to meet him there, in every one of our brothers and sisters, and especially in the poor, the despised and the abandoned members of society. What a beautiful encounter that can be!

214. If we are concerned with helping others, this in no way means that we are turning away from Jesus. Rather, we are encountering him in another way. Whenever we try to help and care for another person, Jesus is at our side. We should never forget that, when he sent his disciples on mission, "the Lord worked with them" (*Mk* 16:20). He is always there, always at work, sharing our efforts to do good. In a mysterious way, his love becomes present through our service. He speaks to the world in a language that at times has no need of words.

215. Jesus is calling you and sending you forth to spread goodness in our world. His call is one of service, a summons to do good, perhaps as a physician, a mother, a teacher or a priest. Wherever you may be, you can hear his call and realise that he is sending you forth to carry out that mission. He himself told us, "I am sending you out" (*Lk* 10:3). It is part of our being friends with him. For this friendship to mature, however, it is up to you

to let him send you forth on a mission in this world, and to carry it out confidently, generously, freely and fearlessly. If you stay trapped in your own comfort zone, you will never really find security; doubts and fears, sorrow and anxiety will always loom on the horizon. Those who do not carry out their mission on this earth will find not happiness, but disappointment. Never forget that Jesus is at your side at every step of the way. He will not cast you into the abyss, or leave you to your own devices. He will always be there to encourage and accompany you. He has promised, and he will do it: "For I am with you always, to the end of the age" (*Mt* 28:20).

216. In your own way, you too must be a missionary, like the apostles and the first disciples of Jesus, who went forth to proclaim the love of God, to tell others that Christ is alive and worth knowing. St Thérèse experienced this as an essential part of her oblation to merciful Love: "I wanted to give my Beloved to drink and I felt myself consumed with a thirst for souls".[227] That is your mission as well. Each of us must carry it out in his or her own way; you will come to see how you can be a missionary. Jesus deserves no less. If you accept the challenge, he will enlighten you, accompany you and strengthen you, and you will have an enriching experience that will bring you much happiness. It is not important whether you see immediate results; leave that to the Lord who works in the secret of our hearts. Keep experiencing the joy born of our efforts to share the love of Christ with others.

---

[227] Ms A, 45v.

CONCLUSION

217. The present document can help us see that the teaching of the social Encyclicals *Laudato Si'* and *Fratelli Tutti* is not unrelated to our encounter with the love of Jesus Christ. For it is by drinking of that same love that we become capable of forging bonds of fraternity, of recognising the dignity of each human being, and of working together to care for our common home.

218. In a world where everything is bought and sold, people's sense of their worth appears increasingly to depend on what they can accumulate with the power of money. We are constantly being pushed to keep buying, consuming and distracting ourselves, held captive to a demeaning system that prevents us from looking beyond our immediate and petty needs. The love of Christ has no place in this perverse mechanism, yet only that love can set us free from a mad pursuit that no longer has room for a gratuitous love. Christ's love can give a heart to our world and revive love wherever we think that the ability to love has been definitively lost.

219. The Church also needs that love, lest the love of Christ be replaced with outdated structures and concerns, excessive attachment to our own ideas and opinions, and fanaticism in any number of forms, which end up taking the place of the gratuitous love of God that liberates, enlivens, brings joy to the heart and builds communities. The wounded side of Christ continues to pour forth that stream which is never exhausted, never passes away, but offers itself time and time again to all those who wish to love as he did. For his love alone can bring about a new humanity.

220. I ask our Lord Jesus Christ to grant that his Sacred Heart may continue to pour forth the streams of living water that can heal the hurt we have caused, strengthen our ability to love and serve others, and inspire us to journey together towards a just, solidary and fraternal world. Until that day when we will rejoice

in celebrating together the banquet of the heavenly kingdom in the presence of the risen Lord, who harmonises all our differences in the light that radiates perpetually from his open heart. May he be blessed forever.

Franciscus

Given in Rome, at St Peter's, on 24th October of the year 2024, the twelfth of my Pontificate.

IR

Goetz von Berli
play, written wh
hero, 'Goetz of t
knight of the late middle ages – a choice
which reflects the revolt of Goethe's generation against the staleness and corruption of
polite society in pre-revolutionary Europe.
John Arden's free adaptation of this fast-
moving prose play preserves the vigour and
broad scope of the original: he has, however, balanced the somewhat one-sided,
romantic presentation of Goetz by strength-
ening the character of Weislingen, the free
knight turned statesman. *Ironhand* is a rich,
vivid and ironic drama of early sixteenth-
century Germany, when the old way of life
was challenged as much by the revolt of the
peasants – who sought to make Goetz their
champion – as by the new order of the
princes and the new middle class.

The photograph on the front cover shows
Christopher Benjamin in a scene from the
Bristol production. Photo: David Sim, repro-
duced by courtesy of The Observer

IRONHAND

adapted by John Arden
from Goethe's
GOETZ VON BERLICHINGEN

EYRE METHUEN LTD
11 NEW FETTER LANE, LONDON, EC4

First published 1965 *by Methuen & Co. Ltd.*
Reprinted 1973
This translation © 1965 *by John Arden*
All rights reserved
Printed in Great Britain by
Whitstable Litho, Straker Brothers Ltd.
SBN 413 31050 7

Introductory Note

This is not an accurate translation of *Goetz von Berlichingen* – it is more in the nature of a free paraphrase, for which I make no apologies. *Goetz* was Goethe's first play. He wrote it in 1773, when he was twenty-four, and it is not surprising to find it full of all the technical faults that are normally and greedily looked for in young and revolutionary work. As a result, its reputation has suffered in comparison with that of his later and more mature writings. As far as I can discover, there is not one stageworthy English version – I have used as a crib Sir Walter Scott's translation of 1799, which has the merit of being reasonably close in date to the original, but the demerit of being literary and unsuited to theatrical performance. The blame for this lies perhaps less with Scott than with the state of the British theatre in his time. It was apparently impossible for a dramatist writing in English at the end of the eighteenth century to understand the appeal of a play that treated of historical personages in vernacular prose, that varied that prose from the stately conversation of princes and emperors to the slang of soldiers and the regional dialect of peasants, and that included in its scope not only battles, chivalry, and romantic love, but also such wide-ranging historical questions as the dispute between the partisans of the Roman and Common Laws, the Peasants' Revolt of 1525, and the ideas of the young Luther.

Goethe was writing in excited reaction from the dried-up classical theatre, hung over one hundred years from Racine and Corneille, and his natural inspiration was, of course, Shakespeare. It is therefore scarcely to be wondered at that *Goetz* is even more episodic in structure than *Antony and Cleopatra*. But the vernacular vigour of the language is, I believe, both new and truly wonderful – the usual result of Shakespearian influence being a fanatical devotion to the iambic pentameter and the verbiage of Wardour Street, used extremely well by

Schiller and considerably less well by such English poets as Keats, Wordsworth, and Byron. *Goetz* in many ways fore-shadows Scott's handling of Scottish history in the better of the Waverley Novels. Had he made his translation at the end instead of the beginning of his literary life, it is possible that he might have found his way through to the strength and spirit of the original.

In preparing a version of *Goetz* for the modern English theatre a number of problems automatically present themselves. Its hero is seen almost entirely from his own point of view. As Goethe was working from Goetz's own apologetic auto-biography, this is perhaps only to be expected: but today it is impossible to look upon the bloody exploits of a late-medieval robber-knight with the tolerance and enthusiasm of the eighteenth century. To a poet bored to death with the polite decorum of pre-revolutionary European society, the life led by such men as Goetz, with their Gothic castles, their armour, their bands of hard-riding, hard-drinking horse-troopers etcetera, must have seemed one of unalloyed excitement. But the very intelligence and imagination with which Goethe captures the personalities and events of his story makes us refuse to accept his romantic view of them. Goetz in particular lives so strongly as a man that in justice to him and to his creator some sort of judgement must be made upon his actions. The natural way of doing this is to strengthen the role of his opponent Weislingen. Weislingen is an unsatisfactory character in the original. His part in the story is very important, and he is seen to rise from a subordinate position in a local Episcopal Court to a place of high responsibility in the Imperial adminis-tration – but unfortunately, the personality given to him by Goethe is frankly so wet and his vacillations so miserable as to leave a modern audience both incredulous and bored. The commentators suggest that Goethe was to a large degree pre-senting his own weaknesses through this character. This seems to me highly likely – we often find that when a dramatist deliberately puts himself into one of his plays he cannot avoid a certain sentimental Narcissism.

I have accordingly taken the liberty of 'reconstructing' Weislingen to fit his part in the plot, which, I hope, has the effect of improving the argument against Goetz and at the same time making more plausible the latter's final misfortunes. Another character with whom I have tinkered is the mysterious Brother Martin of Act One. An English audience has, I think, the right to know if it is supposed to be listening to Luther or not – Goethe purposely leaves the identification open – in the same way as a German audience would expect to be told whether a man called only 'Oliver', in some hypothetical English play set in the seventeenth century, was in fact Cromwell. In committing myself to a definite Luther, I have found it necessary to work towards a more clearly historical portrait than Goethe was concerned with, and it is possible that I have thereby slightly distorted the meaning of the episode.

The loose structure of the whole play appeals to me, but I did in many places find it altogether *too* loose – particularly in the second half. I have tried to retain all the turns of the plot, but by amalgamating several very short scenes I have somewhat simplified its expression. At the same time I have found it necessary to provide logical links between various apparently unrelated episodes. For instance, the melodramatic 'Secret Tribunal' of the last act is entirely unprepared for – but the play is so filled with references to the appalling state of German justice that Goethe seems to have intuitively placed the scene in exactly the right spot. I have inserted an early reference into the legal conversation at the Bishop's dinner-party to make it comprehensible to an audience unacquainted with the details of German history. I have found this sort of thing time after time while working on the play. Continually one *knows* that such and such an episode is entirely right, but one remains exasperated by the author's failure to explain, connect, or comment. I hope I have not overdone the explanations, but it does seem to me that *Goetz* is written in a highly articulate style that demands an equally articulate treatment of the plotting.

I am only too well aware of the difficulties this play presents to a producer. I have decided not to allow these to exert too great an influence on my version, because to attempt to bring the work within the compass of normal English theatrical practice would be to destroy its essential quality. The cast is simply enormous (though there are many parts that can be doubled or trebled without difficulty). The original text specifies definite localities for even the shortest scenes – sometimes with suggestions of quite elaborate stage pictures. These I have retained, because I think that Goethe regarded them as important. He was imitating Shakespeare in the number and brevity of his scenes, but being unaware of Elizabethan theatrical convention, he conceived them as taking place upon a proscenium-arch stage with elaborate décor. This is something of a bastard style: but I see no reason why a contemporary producer should not find an acceptable compromise – by means, say, of a wide bare stage with certain permanent features, and either back-projection or motifs flown-in to provide the locations required by the author. It is conceivable that these might counterpoint rather than illustrate – for instance, the use of reasonably relevant pictures by Dürer, Cranach, or Urs Graf could suggest both the historical period and the emotional climate of many scenes with economy and aptness.

By the same token, I have employed Goethe's fairly circumstantial stage directions, which imply naturalistic settings: but obviously these could be modified in production. The only feature of his dramatic method I have cut out almost completely is his use of the soliloquy, which I find tiresome and unnecessary, being in most cases only a misunderstood survival of the direct-address technique of Shakespeare, and out of place in this sort of play.

I owe a great deal to George Brandt of Bristol University, who has given me much assistance and encouragement in preparing this version, and also to Mr A. E. Hammer, of Sedbergh School, under whose supervision I first read the original some years ago, and who managed to preserve interest and enthusiasm for it throughout the protracted routine of studying it as an examination 'set-book'.

JOHN ARDEN, 1961

Dramatis Personae

THE EMPEROR MAXIMILIAN I
GOETZ VON BERLICHINGEN, a free knight of the Empire
ELISABETH, his wife
MARIA, his sister
KARL, his son
GEORG, his page
LERSE, a mercenary soldier
HANS VON SELBITZ
FRANZ VON SICKINGEN } free knights of the Empire
THE BISHOP OF BAMBERG
ADELBERT VON WEISLINGEN, a knight in his service
FRANZ, Weislingen's squire
LIEBETRAUT, a courtier in the Bishop's service
ADELHEID VON WALLDORF, a lady at the Episcopal Court
MARGARET, her lady-in-waiting
THE ABBOT OF FULDA
OLEARIUS, a Doctor of Law
METZLER
SIEVERS
KOHL } peasant leaders
WILD

Other Peasants including:

    A BRIDEGROOM
    A BRIDE
    HER FATHER
    BOY

Civilian Refugees including:

    AN OLD MAN
    A MOTHER
    A WOMAN

Gipsies including:

CAPTAIN
OLD WOMAN
YOUNG WOMAN
BOY

BROTHER MARTIN, a monk
THE LANDLORD of an Inn
THE GAOLER of Heilbronn
COURTIERS and SERVANTS in the service of the Bishop
BURGOMASTER and CITIZENS of Heilbronn
OFFICERS of the City of Heilbronn
CAPTAIN and OFFICERS of the Imperial Army
HORSE-TROOPERS in the service of The Emperor
                                    The Bishop
                                    Berlichingen
                                    Selbitz
PIKEMEN in the service of Sickingen
The Members of the TRIBUNAL OF SECRET JUSTICE
IMPERIAL COMMISSIONERS OF JUSTICE
SERJEANT-AT-ARMS

The action of the play takes place in various parts of Germany.
The period is the early years of the sixteenth century.

Act One

SCENE ONE

Schwarzenberg in Franconia.
An Inn.

METZLER *and* SIEVERS (*peasants*) *are sitting drinking at a table. Two* TROOPERS *wearing the* BISHOP OF BAMBERG'S *badge are at the other side of the room, eating by the fire.*

SIEVERS. Hey, Hansel: more brandy!

The LANDLORD *comes at his call to refill his glass.* SIEVERS *looks crossly at the amount poured out.*

D'you call that Christianity ? Fill it up.

LANDLORD (*pouring out some more*). Day *you* find yourself filled up, we'll give a cheer. . . . Do you ?

SIEVERS. It'll do.

The LANDLORD *fills* METZLER'S *glass and retires.*

METZLER (*in a low tone*). What you wor telling me just now about Goetz Ironhand – those two Bamberg men heard it; they didn't like it, so tell it again.

SIEVERS (*in the same tone*). What are they doing here, any road ?

METZLER. Weislingen's up at the castle having a word wi' your Count. He's off back to Bamberg tonight. They're part of his escort.

SIEVERS. Them ? I thought they wor the Bishop's men.

METZLER. They are. So's Weislingen. His right-hand man, they *call* him. *I'd* call him his running dog: but he knows where he's running. He's running after Goetz. He's got troops o' men from the Bishop and they're out to lay an ambush. I heard that in Bamberg: it's true.

SIEVERS. An ambush for Goetz? He'll have to be fair crafty if he wants to do that!

METZLER. That's right: he had. So tell it again.

He raises his voice for the TROOPERS *to hear.*

First *I* knew o' Goetz having more quarrels wi' the Bishop.

SIEVERS. The Bishop of Bamberg.

METZLER. The Bishop of Bamberg. I thought that wor all passed up and smoothed over.

SIEVERS. Passed up in a parson's gut! Look, the Bishop turns rough, so Goetz turns dirty. Swords out and highway fighting: he can't take that, the Bishop, so he runs to the Princes and hollers for an Arbitration. What d'you think? Judgement against Goetz.

METZLER. O' *course*. It always is. Nobility and Justice.

SIEVERS. Goetz von Berlichingen I call a good man.

METZLER. He's a nobleman.

SIEVERS. But a good man.

METZLER. He is.

SIEVERS. But listen at this: *after* your Arbitration, *after*, your bloody great Bishop catches one of Ironhand's lads and claps him into Bamberg. No crime and no charge: but your bloody great Bishop –

FIRST BAMBERG TROOPER (*standing up*). Hey. You. You're talking about our Bishop.

SIEVERS. *We're* set at *this* table.

SECOND BAMBERG TROOPER. Who put you up to talk about our Bishop?

SIEVERS. We don't have to answer none o' your questions. . . . Look at 'em there, guzzling their fat goose in front of our fire –

FIRST TROOPER *hits him.*

METZLER. Do him, Sievers, do him!

SECOND BAMBERG TROOPER (*running at him*). Come on then: *I'm* ready!

All four fight. The LANDLORD *rushes in between them.*

LANDLORD. Keep it quiet, you bloody wolves, or take it out-side. *My* house, this: and it's a quiet house. Go on, get out.

He pushes the TROOPERS *towards the door. They glance at each other and go.*

You, you stupid donkeys, what are you playing at?

METZLER. Now then, Hansel – is that what you call him? – Hansel: you wouldn't want all them glittering glasses broke, would you, Hansel? No. All right, we're off.

As they approach the door they meet two more TROOPERS (GOETZ'S *men, but without badges) on their way in.*

FIRST GOETZ TROOPER. Hey up. What's the matter?

SIEVERS. Aye, Peter! How are you, man? How's Goetz –

SECOND GOETZ TROOPER (*cuts him short*). Ss-sh: no names.

FIRST GOETZ TROOPER. I said, what's going on?

SIEVERS. Bamberg men. Did you see 'em?

FIRST GOETZ TROOPER. What are they doing here?

METZLER. They came to the castle wi' Weislingen. Who are you?

FIRST GOETZ TROOPER (*to his companion*). Weislingen!

SECOND GOETZ TROOPER. We've found him!

FIRST GOETZ TROOPER. Ss-sh.

SECOND GOETZ TROOPER (*to* METZLER). How long's he been here?

METZLER. Two days: but he's off. Lend us a fist, friend. They're waiting outside.

FIRST GOETZ TROOPER (*to his companion*). We'd better look sharp. We might lose him yet. Come on.

SIEVERS. Hey, boy, the Bamberg men: they're waiting. Aren't you going to help us?

SECOND GOETZ TROOPER. We've no time. There's two on you, ent there? Go on, kill 'em: you can do it.

The TROOPERS *go.*

SIEVERS. Horse-troopers for ever! You want one o' *them* in a fight, you've got to *pay* him first.

METZLER. Whose are they?

SIEVERS. Eh? Oh, I'm not supposed to tell. . . . Don't say no names, but his hand's made of iron.

METZLER. Ah, Goetz? That accounts then. . . . Right, have you got your stick? We're going to knock those devils down, swords or no swords.

SIEVERS. I'd sooner knock their masters. Princes and the Bishops, why, they drag our poor mucky skins off over our ears like shirts – I can tell you, I—

METZLER. *We'll* knock 'em, boy, one day. I've not been travelling this country for nowt, you know. You just wait, you'll see. Come on.

They go.

SCENE TWO

Outside a hovel in the forest. Dusk.

GOETZ *is walking up and down. He has a leather bottle from which he drinks at intervals. He is in armour, and on his left hand wears a gauntlet. His right hand is made of iron, but is designed in such a way that at first glance it, too, appears to be gauntleted.*

GOETZ. What the devil's keeping them? They ought to have found him by now, they ought to be here! Five days and nights of it. Lurking about in hovels. No sleep. Oatmeal rations. Riding in the rain. . . . Where *are* those incompetent scouts! I said I must have news by sunset. If they leave it any later, all they'll come to tell me is that Weis-

lingen's back in Bamberg and we've lost him yet again. . . .
No sleep. No. Walk up, and down: and so, we keep
awake. . . .

He discovers he has finished all his wine.

Empty. Georg! Keep this full and keep awake: not a prince
in Germany can drive my helmet down. I stand up awake and
stand by right of knighthood – Georg! . . . Nor no bishops
neither! I know, Bamberg, I know what you're after: you
spoon out your pious injustices from your high cathedral
stool while Weislingen your viper slanders my good name in
every kinsman's hall and houseplace! We'll see how much
longer he can carry on at *that*! Bishop, I'm awake: Ironhand
walks and wakes! . . . Georg! Georg, boy, here!

GEORG, *his page, runs out of the cottage. He is struggling to
unfasten a grown man's breastplate from his body.*

GEORG. Yes, sir, ready . . .

GOETZ. Where have you been, boy? Sleeping?

He sees the breastplate.

What have you got there? Look, if you want to act in the
Christmas play, go back to my castle and tell the minstrel to
give you some ribbons and bells. We've not come here for
foolery! . . . Oh, never mind, never mind. I daresay it'll fit
you in a couple of years. Whose is it, Johann's?

GEORG. He wanted to sleep, you see, so he told me to unbuckle
it, and I thought, like, I could—

GOETZ. Wanted to sleep, did he? That's what you'd call the
world turned upside-down – the squire reclines and snorts,
while the knight walks out on sentry. I'll live to survive it.
Take him back his breastplate, tell him to wake up, and give
him a drink of wine to make sure that he does! And before
you give *him* one, you can fill this up for *me*!

GEORG. It was just I wanted to practise swinging a sword in the
full gear, and—

GOETZ. Wait a minute – d'you hear horses?

GEORG (*listens a moment*). No.

GOETZ. Jesus, Mary and Joseph, why aren't they here! Tell Johann he can start getting our own horses ready. When these lads do come, we shan't have any time to lose.

GEORG. The horses *are* ready.

GOETZ. Are they, by God's feet? Is that you?

GEORG. Yes, sir, I've just looked after it.

GOETZ. Not so bad, boy: you're improving.

GEORG. Then when can I ride?

GOETZ. What?

GEORG. I'm old enough to ride. If I do a squire's work, I can fight a squire's battle. Let me ride tonight.

GOETZ. Eh? What? No, of course you can't: no. Far too tricky tonight. D'you not understand, boy, I'm out to catch *Weislingen*? To have you without experience in an ambush like that – you might as well wear Bamberg's badge and that's all about it. . . . If you really think you're old enough to ride, wait while there's something easy before you begin. Like, an undefended wagon-train on the road to Frankfurt Fair – now you come to me *then*, boy: I'll give you a proper horse, I'll give you your gear, and I'll be only too pleased for you to show me what you can do! But for just now, fill my wine up, and don't be a nuisance. . . .

He sees GEORG *is staring into the distance.*

What is it? Someone coming?

GEORG. It's only a man walking. Looks like a monk.

GOETZ. A monk? In the middle of the forest at this time of night? . . . All right, in.

GEORG *goes in with the bottle as a young* MONK *enters, with a traveller's pack and staff.*

Good evening. For a man of religion, you are keeping late hours, are you not? Have you come far?

MONK. I am on my way home from pilgrimage. I have been to the Holy City.

GOETZ. Jerusalem?

MONK. No, sir: Rome. But a hard enough distance for one man's feet to travel.

GOETZ. So I should imagine.

GEORG re-enters with the full bottle.

Wine. You will join me?

The MONK *shakes his head.*

Not? It replenishes the diminished humours, particularly the sanguine. I need not remind *you* of St Paul's very sensible words on the subject. Georg, bring him a cup.

MONK. Only water, if you please, boy. St Paul was a hardy man, sir, and I revere his memory: but he did not have to live by the Rule of Augustine. When I take a vow, I keep it. Chastity is absolute. Therefore, though it is not specifically in my vow: for me, no wine.

GOETZ (*to* GEORG). Water.

GEORG goes inside again.

MONK. And furthermore, not only danger of lasciviousness: but also sloth. I dare not, for my soul, fall into sloth!

GOETZ. Since I was *that* high, sir, I've drunk *this* much wine a day. You look at *me*: lazy?

MONK. Ah no indeed, not you, no, no, indeed not! You ride and fight and eat and drink, I look and I can see it: there is a man! And his life is the golden wine and the wine can re-create that life and every day his deeds tower up in strength!

GEORG returns with a cup and a jug of water. He pours some out for the MONK.

I thank you. Your good health, sir.

He drinks it off thirstily, and holds out for more. GOETZ *proffers the wine.*

GOETZ. Come on, one cup of this. It won't destroy you. If you're drinking to me, you should drink it my way. There you are.

MONK (*accepting with a smile*). Ah well, a little. . . .

GOETZ. There you are, sir. You're a sanguine man! Excuse me –

He suddenly takes GEORG *aside.*

Any sound of their horses yet?

GEORG. Not yet.

GOETZ. Then go down the Dachsbach road and put your ear to the ground. They must be coming soon!

Exit GEORG.

MONK. I spent last night at the Priory of St Veit. The Prior was most courteous: he showed me into his garden, and do you know – for two hours I was able to *think*. I walked among the beanstalks, saw the salad greens, the cabbages – oh, sir, the cabbages! . . . And cauliflowers and artichokes like between the four rivers of Eden!

GOETZ. I should hardly have thought you were a gardener.

MONK. No, that is true. I often wish I were. You may not believe this, as your life has little to do with it, but *my* life as a cloisterer, shutting out the world, is manacled and banded to the edge of despair by the very world it shuts out! Business, politics, ecclesiastical administration: I might as well be living in the town hall of Wittenberg – why, I even had to fight to be permitted this pilgrimage.

GOETZ. I am not over-surprised – I have had *some* knowledge of ecclesiastical affairs. . . . What did you think of Rome?

MONK. An extraordinary city. I am still astonished by it. In that city I was able to pursue such spiritual exercises that I was nearly a dead man before I had finished.

GOETZ. What about the wine?

MONK. Oh yes, they drink their wine there, oh yes, they drink it. . . . Rome is a deadly city, sir. I do not altogether know

what I should think of it. It is, I suppose, the centre of the
world. . . .

GOETZ. Have another drink – what are you looking at ?

MONK. Your armour, your gear – the working gear of a soldier.
It fascinates me.

GOETZ. It would fascinate me more if it weighed a little less.
Do you fancy yourself wearing it ?

MONK. Poverty, chastity, and obedience are just as heavy and
just as inconvenient – and sometimes I wonder if they are not
just as unnatural. I have carried them a long way: and I
know. Do you have a wife ?

GOETZ. I do indeed. A very fine one.

MONK. I drink to her health.

GOETZ. Thank you.

MONK. She must be the crown of your life. The crown of
creation!

GOETZ. Oh, come, sir, come. . . .

MONK. When I say how terrible it is for me to be denied such a
blessing, you must not imagine that I am just one of your
concupiscent clerics with a bramble bush beneath their
girdles and courage of the will neither to root it out nor let it
flower! The vows I take, I keep. But I know what I am doing!

GEORG *runs in.*

GEORG. Sir, sir, I can hear them – two horses at the gallop!

GOETZ. God's feet, at last! Call Johann, tell him to mount. My
own horse, bring it out – hurry, boy, hurry!

GEORG *hastens into the cottage.*

Sir, I must leave you! This gear of mine has found its work!

MONK. Tell me your name.

GOETZ. I had rather not, if you don't mind. But here is my
hand.

He offers him his left hand.

MONK. Your left hand? I suppose a virgin monk is not regarded as worthy of your knightly sword-arm. I am sorry.

GOETZ. If you were the Emperor himself you would have to put up with this. I have only been wearing one gauntlet – do you see?

MONK. Goetz of the Iron Hand.

GOETZ. That's right. You have heard of me.

MONK. I once met a monk who served in the hospital where your hand was amputated after the Battle of Landshut. He said you turned your face to the wall and would speak to nobody until one day a knight came in who had lost his hand also and yet fought with a sword for a generation afterwards. So you seized hold of your courage and your courage brought back liberty and God could take twelve hands from you and still you would fight! Sir, that is strength. That is pride and knighthood. Brother Martin, Doctor of Theology, sometime known as Martin Luther the law-student, sir, here I do this!

> *He kisses the iron hand.*
> GOETZ'S *two* TROOPERS (*from Scene One*) *hurry in.*

FIRST TROOPER. Berlichingen, we've found him!

GOETZ. Can we catch him?

SECOND TROOPER. We can.

FIRST TROOPER. Five miles out of Schwarzenberg with only four riders!

GOETZ. Johann, are you ready! Brother Martin, good night: I hope you sleep well! Johann—

> GOETZ *runs out with the* TROOPERS.

MONK (*calls after him*). God go with you, sir. I shall not forget this meeting!

> GEORG *reappears from the cottage.*

GEORG. Were you wanting to sleep here?

MONK. Is there a bed?

GEORG. No. There's some straw.

MONK. Very well, boy: straw. They leave you behind, I see, when they ride. You would prefer to be with them?

GEORG. One of these days I'm going to kill as many men as my master. They'll know it, when I do.

MONK. What do they call you?

GEORG. Georg.

MONK. Then your patron saint is St George.

He takes his breviary out of his wallet and turns to a picture, which he tears out and gives to GEORG.

Look, here he is, and there is his dragon. Follow his example. Be brave, ride down the devil, look neither to the right nor the left as you travel the forest of this world. God cannot abide complexity. Show me where I may sleep.

Monk stays with them

GEORG *takes him into the building.*

SCENE THREE

Bamberg.
A hall in the Bishop's Palace.

The BISHOP *at dinner with the* ABBOT OF FULDA, LIEBE-TRAUT *(a courtier), and* OLEARIUS *(a Doctor of Law). A suitable number of* SERVANTS *in attendance.*

BISHOP. Tell me, Dr Olearius, are there many law students from Germany at your University of Bologna?

OLEARIUS. A great many, my lord Bishop. Both from the merchant classes, and, I am happy to say, the aristocracy. They have acquired a prodigious report of themselves. Indeed, without exaggeration, there is already a pleasant proverb current from end to end of the University – 'He is as studious', they say, 'as one of the German noblemen.'

ABBOT. Aha.

OLEARIUS. Gratifying, is it not, to hear it?

LIEBETRAUT. Gratifying, maybe, but a trifle unexpected. You are quite sure, Doctor, that the application of this proverb is all that you think it is?

OLEARIUS. Of course I am sure, sir. The sons of our Princes are the admiration and ornament of the whole University. I have no doubt that the Emperor is only waiting for the formal bestowal of Doctorates to appoint many of them to the highest offices in his Government.

BISHOP. Is that so indeed?

OLEARIUS. I am convinced of it, my lord.

BISHOP. This interests me greatly. I am anxious to encourage expert jurists to Bamberg to assist me in my own administration. I take it that these young men are students of the Roman legal system rather than the traditional German common law?

OLEARIUS. Indeed yes, my lord, that goes without saying.

BISHOP. There is a book, is there not, called the *Corpus Juris*—

ABBOT. Doctor, a young fellow I once met, you know – oh, his father lost an eye, what was he called? He was a Hessian – you have Hessians at your University?

OLEARIUS. A great many, sir, yes.

ABBOT. Yes. You must have known this one, you must . . . His father had one eye, used to be an Imperial Marshal—

LIEBETRAUT. Von Wildenholz.

ABBOT. Eh, what? That's right. Von Wildenholz. A Hessian, of course . . . You do know him, Doctor?

OLEARIUS. Oh yes, indeed! He is very well renowned for his force in disputation.

ABBOT. Aha? He'll have got that from his mother. His father lost an eye, you know.

BISHOP. Doctor, this book I was alluding to. It was written by one of the Eastern Emperors, I believe.

OLEARIUS. Justinian, my lord.

BISHOP. Justinian it was. He deserves the highest praise. I drink to his health.

OLEARIUS (*drinks also*). To his imperial memory.

ABBOT. He is no longer with us? Oh dear.

BISHOP. No, my lord Abbot, he has the misfortune to be dead. But the book that he wrote is very far from dead. How would you describe it, Doctor?

OLEARIUS. It is the greatest book in the world. It comprehends every conceivable legal issue. The man who knows his *Corpus Juris* needs in effect no further authority.

ABBOT. Does he have the Ten Commandments?

OLEARIUS. I beg your pardon?

ABBOT. This Emperor, the dead one – I mean, the Ten Commandments – if his book is all that you claim, you know, he must have put them in.

OLEARIUS. They are there *implicite*, though hardly *explicite*.

ABBOT. Of course not; you wouldn't look for it. You don't want explication where Commandments are concerned. They go down in black and white and you do what you're told. That Emperor of yours clearly knew his business.

BISHOP. As far as *I* go, Doctor, his business is this: by the use of *Corpus Juris* and men like yourself who are trained to interpret it, we can at last set to work, utterly and finally, to eradicate the inconsequential and traditionalizing anarchy that has flattered itself for centuries with the name of common law! Today, Doctor, it sticks there and it balks, entirely balks, any sort of comprehensive administration throughout our principalities!

OLEARIUS. My lord, you say truly. The German common law is an overgrown, outgrown monster.

BISHOP. Every town, every village, has its own ridiculous list of precedent. A bedraggled one-and-a-half-ounce highwayman with a jacket of greasy leather and three unshaven horse-troopers to gallop at his arse can live in a rabbit-hole on top of a rock and call himself a Free Knight of the Empire, owing allegiance to no one but himself!

LIEBETRAUT. Somebody, I think somebody, feels his memory scratched by Berlichingen.

BISHOP. If you like, why not? Though when Weislingen comes home I hope there will be an end to *that* itch. But there are others, you know. The one with the wooden leg – what do they call him? – Selbitz. And then there's Franz von Sickingen – now *he's* a dangerous man. More names, as well; I forget them at the moment. . . . But they are protected, these bravos, by generation over generation of legalized absurdity, recorded upon goatskin and buried in their dungpiles as likely as not. Yet judges will listen to them and even give decisions in their favour, unless they can first be intimidated. And I very much dislike the intimidation of judges. It is a perilous symptom. Doctor Olearius, the whole legal framework needs to be changed and it needs to be changed quickly. I have already made some beginning in Bamberg. Please God we shall progress.

OLEARIUS. Please God we shall, my lord.

LIEBETRAUT. But we have to be careful, do we not? I mean, *lente, lente currite*, Doctor, if your Latinity will stretch so far?

OLEARIUS. I am not entirely with you.

LIEBETRAUT. You see, you drive one set of lawyers out and you replace them with another. What happens in between?

OLEARIUS. There *is* a period of transition, of course.

ABBOT. Of course.

LIEBETRAUT. Ah yes, transition . . . You come from Frankfurt, I believe?

OLEARIUS. I regret to say, yes.

BISHOP. Why should you regret it, Doctor?

OLEARIUS. I have suffered there, my lord, for my profession. I returned home recently to collect my deceased father's belongings, God rest his soul, and the population pelted me with stones when they heard I was a lawyer.

ABBOT. God preserve us, why?

OLEARIUS. The usual story, sir. The old common law holds force in Frankfurt. We who adhere to the rational and indeed more truly ancient system are regarded as conspirators against the ancestral freedoms of the city, which their ignorant and vulgar Tribunal continues to uphold.

LIEBETRAUT. Exactly.

OLEARIUS. Exactly *what*, if I may ask?

LIEBETRAUT. Exactly what happens. Your period of transition is a period of no law at all. Your existing Common Courts are declared no longer valid, and your new Roman jurists are hounded out by the mob. Whip she larey, tiddle-fol larey – good black puddings and the gulp of looted wine for Ironhand Berlichingen and all his bully boys, or else; and it's happening – did you know it was happening? Somebody who wants justice sets it up for himself! Ooh, I'm going to make your flesh creep, Doctor – secret courts in session in dark secret cellars by secret, terrified people determined to terrify. No lawyers' fees, Doctor, and not much in the way of pleading, but a Vigilante Tribunal at midnight, a melodramatic row of black masks, and the noose hanging ready at the fork of an oak tree. Me, I'm the Bishop's man, I don't need to worry, but I think it's worth while bearing it in mind: incompetent policemen and discredited procedures don't necessarily mean undetected crime.

OLEARIUS. I have heard nothing about any of this.

BISHOP. I have. It is quite unimportant. An elaborate way of carrying out blood feuds among some of the rural people, that is all. It cannot be attributed to any attempts at reform. I wish you would be good enough not to frighten my dinner-parties, Liebetraut. Shall we change the subject?

LIEBETRAUT. I beg my lord's pardon. Of course, Doctor, though I do appreciate how Frankfurt must have unpleasant associations for you, I have always found it a most delightful town. Why, I remember celebrating the Emperor's coronation there – years ago, simply . . . I don't recall any citizen of the name of Olearius.

OLEARIUS. No. Well, as a matter of fact, you wouldn't . . . You see, my father by his trade was a dealer in oil, and surnamed accordingly Oelmann. When I went to Bologna it was necessary to give one's thesis a Latinized superscription, and I felt that the name Oelmannus was perhaps not quite—

LIEBETRAUT. It does rather smell of the lamp.

OLEARIUS. That is not what I am trying to say! I meant that Olearius, being the name borne by one of the great jurists of history, as of course you are aware—

ABBOT. Of course.

OLEARIUS. Thank you, sir. Of course . . . You see what I mean?

LIEBETRAUT. Oh yes, I think so. A very old adage – honour and one's own country and prophets and so forth. Though I suspect that the impression you made on the Frankfurt men might have been improved had your name as well as your learning been a little less exotic.

OLEARIUS. You seem determined to make your jokes, sir, regardless of good manners! I assume that such is your function at my lord Bishop's table, but I would prefer to have been forewarned of it!

BISHOP. Gently, Doctor, gently: there is no need to take offence. Liebetraut, dear boy, behave.

LIEBETRAUT. I am as ever, my lord, your most faithful penitent.

BISHOP. Yes.

OLEARIUS. Ha h'm, my lord: have you heard any news of the projected expedition against the Turks?

BISHOP. It is the Emperor's dearest wish, Doctor, that it should be put in hand without delay. He is on fire with enthusiasm to liberate his frontier from the hereditary heathen foe. The funds are set aside and the troops can be levied whenever we want. But alas, while Swabia and

Franconia remain in such anarchy, how can anyone begin to march to the East? The appalling ravages of the Free Knights *must* be put down first. I have hopes, I have hopes. Weislingen is a fine soldier. If only he can take this abominable Goetz, we are half-way to achievement. I am expecting his good news any time now.

ABBOT. I hope it *is* good news. Otherwise, God help us, we'll all be carried off like pigs inside of pokes. It's a terrible state to be in.

LIEBETRAUT. It'll need a fair size of poke for one or two of us, I think.

ABBOT. Eh?

BISHOP. Liebetraut—

LIEBETRAUT. My lord.

BISHOP. I have great confidence in Weislingen.

> *A trumpet call, off.*
> *A* SERVANT *runs to the window.*

What's that, who is it?

SERVANT. It's one of Weislingen's men, my lord; he's just ridden into the courtyard.

BISHOP. Aha! Go and meet him, dear boy! Bring him up here.

> *Exit* LIEBETRAUT.

He'll have sent him on ahead to carry the dispatches. Gentlemen, our good fortune – a toast to ourselves!

> *They drink.*
> LIEBETRAUT *re-enters.*

Well, where's the rider?

LIEBETRAUT. He's wounded, collapsed.

BISHOP. What?

LIEBETRAUT. He's the only one left. Ironhand has ambushed them. Weislingen's a prisoner.

BISHOP. Holy St Peter, no.

LIEBETRAUT. Yes, my lord. I'm sorry; oh dear, I'm so sorry . . .

BISHOP. I'll go down and see him. Can he talk?

LIEBETRAUT. A little.

BISHOP (*to* SERVANT). Have him taken to my study. This is very unfortunate.

Exit BISHOP *with* SERVANT.

ABBOT. A messenger sent to Job.

OLEARIUS. I beg your pardon?

ABBOT. From the Bible – Job. Let's have another drink.

OLEARIUS. Perhaps, my lord Abbot, you would prefer a short turn in the garden – after dinner, after all, *post coenam stabis, seu passus mille meabis—*

to LIEBETRAUT.

Or does your Latinity stretch so far?

LIEBETRAUT. Oh yes, it gets there. . . . Besides, if the Abbot sits any longer, he might have an apoplexy, mightn't you, sir? *I'll* carry the wine, shall I? Oh dear, I'm so sorry. . . .

They go out, the ABBOT *supported by* OLEARIUS, *and* LIEBETRAUT *bringing up the rear with the bottle and glasses.*

SCENE FOUR

Jaxthausen.
A guardroom in Goetz's Castle.

GOETZ *enters and throws his helmet and sword down on a table.*

GOETZ. Well, here we are! Bring him in, Peter!

His two TROOPERS *enter with* WEISLINGEN, *in armour, but a prisoner.*

Adelbert von Weislingen, welcome once more to Jaxthausen!
It'd a good many years since we last had the pleasure, I think.
If you'd care to shift your harness, we'll leave it in the guard-
room here and we'll go up to the hall together, at our ease—
Does my wife know that we're back?

FIRST TROOPER. Johann's run on in to tell her, sir.

GOETZ. Good. That's his job. Notwithstanding, I've no doubt
she'll have heard the horses on the bridge and already she'll
be alarming the butler and beating the cook and the cook
beats the scullions and the scullions kick the dogs and the
master's come home and the whole lot's confusion! An alert
wife, oh yes, but you might call her intemperate with it. Ha
ha! I'll tell you this, Adelbert, if it *is* all confusion, it's not
without good reason – you certainly put us out of wind these
last five days round and round the forest!

To TROOPERS.

Help him to unbuckle, will you? Where are your clothes?
We *did* bring his bags, didn't we? Go and find his riders and
make sure they unpack for him. See there's nothing missing.
If there is, we'll make it good.

Exit FIRST TROOPER.

WEISLINGEN. It is not of importance.

GOETZ. Oh yes, it is, though. You see, we don't want your
dunnage, Adelbert: all we want is *you*! To save time you
might as well borrow something of mine – I can find you an
excellent tunic and I'd like you to put it on. It seems to have
shrunk, or I've grown, I can't get into it now – I obtained it,
if that's the word, to wear at the County Palatine's marriage –
how many years ago? Eight? Go and fetch it, Peter, sharp.

Exit SECOND TROOPER.

That was the first time, now, that your Bishop – oho, yes,

your Bishop, he was there at the wedding as well. Y'see, two weeks before I'd sunk a pair of his ships on the river, one of them being loaded with bales of cloth of gold – I told you, an excellent tunic. Anyway, here was the wedding breakfast laid out in the upper room of the best inn in Heidelberg. Half-way up the stairs you had a kind of a landing with one of these wrought-iron banisters, and there stands me Lord-in-Christ, as if he was the bridegroom himself or the father of the bride, offering out his hand to every guest who comes up. I was with Franz von Sickingen, and Franz was walking first, and the Bishop shakes his hand, and then along comes me, and begod he shakes mine, too! This one, you see . . .

He shows his left hand.

So I said to the Margrave of Anhalt, who was standing just behind, I said, 'Well, he shook the hand,' I said, 'but I'll lay any wager he didn't know whose it was!' Your Bishop's thick neck goes as red as a lobster; he spins round on both heels: 'No, sir, I did not know whose it was. Pray, sir, inform me!' So I offered him the other one. Ho ho, he knew! I said, 'If you didn't like my handshake, you can have it back directly!' But he wouldn't, you know – he just pranced away upstairs and complained to the bridegroom. That was the first time we ever met. I've had a deal more to do with him since. If it hadn't been for an informer, I'd have kidnapped him last month. But I dare say on consideration, *you'll* do as well.

WEISLINGEN. I don't know why you imagine I should be interested in your boasting.

GOETZ. I only thought to make you feel a little more easy. You may be in my power, but I'd rather be a host than a gaoler – why not take it the way that I give it? It's only common sense.

WEISLINGEN. Your treatment of me is prescribed by the code of knighthood. It is not very probable you are going to abuse it. But I *would* like some privacy – or is that too exorbitant?

GOETZ. Very well: but, you know, you ought to think how your Bishop would handle *me* if I was in *his* castle.

The SECOND TROOPER *returns with a tunic which he assists* WEISLINGEN *to put on.* KARL, GOETZ'S *son, aged about* 7, *accompanies him in.*

KARL. Good morning, father.

GOETZ. Hallo, boy. Good morning. Have you behaved yourself while I've been away?

KARL. Yes, father. My aunt says that my conduct has been very good.

GOETZ. And what does your mother say?

KARL. I didn't ask her, father.

GOETZ. Did you not? I hope her report will prove in agreement. Weislingen: my son Karl. Does he resemble me?

WEISLINGEN. A little. Not much, perhaps.

GOETZ. No.

KARL. Did you bring me a present?

GOETZ. We have not been to the toymakers, boy. We have had more serious business. I am sorry.

KARL. My aunt has been teaching me lessons.

GOETZ. Indeed? What have you learnt?

KARL. I learnt about Jaxthausen.

GOETZ. Tell me.

KARL. 'Jaxthausen is a village and a castle beside the River Jaxt, the sole property and heritage for two hundred years of the Lords of Berlichingen.'

GOETZ. Go on.

KARL. That's all, father. I learnt it.

GOETZ. And who *are* the Lords of Berlichingen?

KARL. Who are—

GOETZ. Would you know them if you met them? Who owns this Jaxthausen?

KARL. 'Jaxthausen is a village and a castle beside the River Jaxt—'

GOETZ. Never mind, never mind . . . With all his education, he doesn't know his own father. When I was his age I could follow every path, road, and ford in the district, long before anyone tried to teach me their names. Where is your mother?

KARL. She went to the kitchen to look after the dinner. There's roast lambs and white turnips and—

GOETZ. At any rate he knows the menu. One of these days we can see about getting you apprenticed to a cookshop.

KARL. I'm going to eat a baked apple.

GOETZ. Always has to have something different from everybody else. Why can't you eat them raw?

KARL. Isn't as nice. My aunt said she was going to bake it with—

GOETZ. Now you run along, boy. We'll be up for dinner shortly.

KARL. Yes, father, I'll tell them.

GOETZ. And pay your respects to the Lord Weislingen as you go. Here he is.

KARL. Yes, father. Welcome to this castle, sir. I hope you like your dinner.

WEISLINGEN (*kissing him*). Thank you, boy: I'm sure I will.

Exit KARL.

An intelligent child, Berlichingen. You might say, too intelligent. I doubt if he'll do much credit to you in the cattle-raiding line.

GOETZ. For heaven's sake, Adelbert, you're grunting and grumbling like a disfranchised alderman!

Enter FIRST TROOPER *with some bundles of clothes and a leather bottle.*

Have you got all his stuff? Good: well, he's wearing something else now – and I'll tell you, man, it suits you! So you keep it, d'you hear? Now have a drink, and be cheerful. I was talking to an odd sort of monk the other day about the restorative properties of wine— I'm of opinion you and he

would make an excellent pair. . . . Drink it down and stop
worrying!

WEISLINGEN *drinks, so does* GOETZ, *then passes bottle to
the* TROOPERS. *During the ensuing dialogue it circulates.*

Ah, it's a long long time, my friend, since we last sat side by
side and drained a flagon together. What in God's name
possessed you to sell yourself to the Princes?

WEISLINGEN. I have sold myself to nobody. And I see no
advantage in sentimental reminiscence. Those times are
finished and done, Goetz: they belong to a different age.

GOETZ. Do they? I hope not. Because if they do, the pleasure
and strength of life is falling from us all. Do you remember
when we lived as pages at the Court of the Margrave? God's
feet, Adelbert, they called us Castor and Pollux, the inseparable pugilists! Ha – ha – ha—

He indulges himself in some violent sparring motions.

WEISLINGEN. The Bishop of Wuerzburg gave us that name, I
think.

GOETZ (*breaking off the exercise*). Now, he was a *good* Bishop,
with gentle spirituality, which belongs to his trade, and in
those days *we* had a true comradeship, which is what belongs
to *ours*. D'you remember the day I quarrelled with the big
Polack, the one they called Brzezinsky – accidentally on-a-
purpose I knocked across his topknot with the edge of my
sleeve—

WEISLINGEN. Oh yes, I remember. You were waiting at table.
He wore these Polish ringlets all oiled and piled up, and you
made a terrible mess of them. He went for you with a knife.

GOETZ. But I beat him into wet parchment: and you yourself
had to have a fight with his friend – what was his name,
Ladislaw something, with the pockmarks on his jowl! Comradeship and brotherhood: that was our life! Do you never

think, even now, of returning to it, Adelbert? Don't try and pretend it doesn't attract you. I know you better than that.

WEISLINGEN. Of course it attracts me. Freedom from responsibility, living in your own castle, owing no allegiance—

GOETZ. Except directly to the Emperor. I am the Emperor's man, and I never forget it.

WEISLINGEN. He lives at a convenient distance, does he not?

GOETZ. You have grown very sardonic, Adelbert. It grieves me, I can tell you. And it would not have happened had you done what I asked and come with me that time on expedition to Brabant. But no, all the while you were lusting for the courts of the Princes, even as a boy: the ridiculous gossiping monkeys singing their sly songs on the back stairs of the palace, the adulterous sophisticated wives, and the young girls with their hot shaven armpits and their eyelids half-closed in a dream of dishonouring their fathers with fatherless progeny and themselves taking pleasure in the shame! Bad places, Adelbert, and I am afraid you are corrupted.

WEISLINGEN. I don't know about that, but I certainly *shall* be if I listen to you any longer.

GOETZ. What do you mean? All I am doing is to show you the truth! What possible value can this damned Bamberg Bishop and his overweening administration have for a man like you! You were born a Free Knight and you should live your life accordingly. Look, we have a league of noble friends in this country, independent gentlemen understanding their right! Hans von Selbitz, Franz von Sickingen, Ulrich von Hutten – the finest names in the Empire – and we ride proud for liberty! What have *we* to do with selfish malicious priests!

WEISLINGEN. Permit me to explain myself, Goetz.

GOETZ. Explain, how can you explain? The virtues of the matter are entirely self-evident.

WEISLINGEN. Oh, for heaven's sake. . . . The Bishop is a territorial Prince. Never mind his spirituality – I'll admit it is somewhat lacking. He is a territorial Prince and he looks to

his interests, and his interests are the establishment of peace
and prosperity and a clear flow of commerce between the
borders of his land. To do this, he is compelled to rationalize
justice, levy equitable taxes, and control all marauders. How
is this corrupt? You claim, I believe, to be the protector of
the poor. All I say is this: God help the peasant who sees the
Free Knights and the horse-troopers trampling down his
corn, burning his barns—

GOETZ. I do not burn barns, Weislingen! The men that I
plunder are the gross merchant oppressors from the vampire
cities that squat upon our fields and vineyards, destroying
our life! Take an example, take an example – bear witness,
you two men – one of your comrades is in Bamberg prison
this instant, isn't that so?

SECOND TROOPER. Yes, sir, it is.

GOETZ. And who was it betrayed him? The citizens of Nuremberg. Why is he there?

WEISLINGEN. This I do not know. I am sure there is a good
reason.

GOETZ. How can there be a good reason when all my previous
quarrels with the Bishop had been settled by arbitration? I
bowed to the judgement, and he takes my young man!

WEISLINGEN. I think it was the action of an impetuous
subordinate. The Bishop did not order it.

GOETZ. Then why is he not released?

WEISLINGEN. I am told he has not conducted himself properly
in confinement.

GOETZ. God's feet, man, you mean he has conducted himself
only too well! He has shown courage, hasn't he, and stood
firm by his master! I am proud of him, Weislingen; he lifts
up my heart!

WEISLINGEN. I have no doubt he does. My friend, has it ever
occurred to you to wonder what does the Emperor think?
His service, you would have us believe, dictates all your
allegiance. But for years he has been endeavouring to muster

his resources and drive back the Turks, and every single time he is ready to begin, what happens? His independent German gentlemen are once again shedding the blood of Germans within his own boundaries! And what justification can you give me for this? Simply you dislike the fact that intrigue and adultery are prevalent at court. Goetz, you are still a rude little page-boy damaging the hairstyles of cleverer men than yourself. I think it is time you thought rather carefully about your position.

GOETZ. *My* position, by God! What about yours?

WEISLINGEN. Oh yes, I have considered it. I am still your prisoner.

GOETZ. And as for the Emperor, whom you speak for so glibly, let me tell you this, Adelbert: I happen to know that that knightly courteous lord is the object and victim of continual slanders, always some new flag-waver flattering his gaudy rotten banner in front of the poor man's eyes to divert his attention, and to splinter the bright image he ought to have of his realm. I love him, but with pity, for I know how you delude him.

ELISABETH *enters*.

My dearest wife, we have returned!

ELISABETH. So I observe. I heard your bugle as you came. I said to myself, here he is, victorious, what shall he have for dinner? So the butcher is set to slaughtering three lambs, the cook to boiling turnips and stirring the sauce, and what does the master do? He sits in the guardhouse and soaks himself with wine.

She takes the bottle from the TROOPER, *and drinks.*

GOETZ. You see, my love, we became involved in something of an argument. I have had to be troubled by long explanations of no merit. Do I need to introduce this gentleman?

ELISABETH. No. I can see him: and the way he hangs together.

The great Lord Weislingen, is he? To whose treacheries and persecutions we have so long been indebted.

WEISLINGEN. Gracious lady, forgive me. I had not realized how deeply my corruption had ingrained itself in my features. I promise you I will make a determined effort to smooth them into a surface more befitting your own open honesty. And yours, Goetz, as well, if that is how you wish it. God knows I hold no personal quarrel with you or your family. We are, after all, gentlemen of the one class, and the better side of chivalry should be common to us both.

GOETZ. Embrace him, Elisabeth. He is my old friend and my guest. And as soon as we can negotiate an exchange, we'll send him back to his Bishop and our brave young man in Bamberg can come home to us. I think it should turn out very happily for all.

ELISABETH (as WEISLINGEN returns her embrace). Well, he has his manners, I can't gainsay those. And when all is said and done, perhaps the Bishop's malpractices have not completely contorted the lines of his body.

WEISLINGEN. The best leg in Germany, madam. Or it would be, if it didn't happen to be concealed in these unduly practical boots.

GOETZ. We'll give you some slippers directly and then you can show us. Come on up to the hall. You must be anxious to meet our household, my little sister Maria and the rest. You'll be with us some time, so enjoy it, man; live strongly, the world is turning backwards at last!

SCENE FIVE

Jaxthausen.
A room in Goetz's Castle. Evening.

MARIA *sewing*, KARL *playing on the floor.*

KARL. Aunt . . . Aunt . . .

MARIA. Yes, love, what is it ?

KARL. How long is the Lord Weislingen going to stay here with father ? He's been a whole week already.

MARIA. I don't exactly know, love. He's a prisoner, you see. That means your father isn't allowed to let him go away until he promises to be good and not quarrel with him any more.

KARL. Does he want to go away ?

MARIA. I suppose so. I think prisoners usually do.

KARL. Oh . . . Then why won't he promise ?

MARIA. I expect he will, soon.

KARL. I expect he will, yes. I expect father will make him frightened like he does the merchants before he takes their money.

MARIA. Oh, I don't think he'll do that, love.

KARL. He'll make him frightened. That's what he does . . . Will you tell me the story ?

MARIA. Which one ?

KARL. Same one as before. About the little boy.

MARIA. No, you tell it me. Let me see if you recollect it. How does it begin ? Once upon a time—

KARL. Once upon a time there was a little boy called Karl and his mother was poorly, so the little boy went—

MARIA. No, no— First, his mother said—

KARL. His mother said, 'I'm poorly; you'll have to go to the town and buy your own breakfast.' So he went to the town and the old man said to him—

MARIA. He *met* the old man first, and this old man was a beggarman—

KARL. A beggarman, yes— And the beggarman said, 'I can't walk, little boy, and I've had nothing to eat all day today and—

MARIA. 'Nor all day yesterday—'

KARL. 'Nor all day yesterday.' So the little boy gave him all his money, so he couldn't buy his breakfast, and the old man turned into a Saint of God and he said to the little boy, 'Every time you touch anybody with your right hand, because your right hand gave me all the money, you will cure their diseases.'

MARIA. That's right. And he went home and he touched his mother—

KARL. He touched his mother and he cured her and the old woman next door and he cured a sick dog and he went to the Emperor—

Enter ELISABETH.

—and there he cured the Emperor and he cured the Pope of Rome and cured everybody with his hand and he became so rich in the end that he went and built an enormous golden palace and he lived in it for ever— Why did he become so rich?

MARIA. Who told you he became rich?

ELISABETH. Of course he became rich, Maria. With a miraculous gift like that, what else would he become?

MARIA. Did you tell him he became rich?

ELISABETH. The child has to learn something of the necessities of life, my dear. If he wants to be a sort of sawbones when he grows up he ought at least to know how to set about it properly.

MARIA. Well, he didn't build a palace anyway, Karl. If he built anything at all it must have been a church and a monastery to the memory of the blessed Saint who gave him the gift. And I hope if anybody does that to you, you'll do the same.

KARL. Yes, aunt, I hope so.

ELISABETH. Goetz has gone to Nuremberg.

MARIA. To Nuremberg! What for?

ELISABETH. To find out about the movements of their traders on the roads. He has to know these things. In disguise, if you please – with that hand! I think the man is mad.

MARIA. But they hate him in Nuremberg. If they catch him, they'll—

ELISABETH. That is understood, Maria. That is the way we live. Karl, remember this: the danger that surrounds your father while he rides brings us food to our table and clothes to our backs and gold and silver to the strongbox. So it enables him to redress the injustice when he sees it in the world. If all that he did with his money was to build churches for a pack of miserable geldings to whine away their barren hours, a valuable man he would be, to be sure!

MARIA. I would prefer him none the less to live without the danger and without the violence that provokes it. I am sorry to differ from you, Elisabeth, but—

ELISABETH. It is necessary, Maria, for Karl to understand how brave his father is, and to build his own courage upon the example.

MARIA. Where is Weislingen this evening?

ELISABETH. Oh, him? In the courtyard, singing songs to the milkmaid, I dare say. Karl, go to your bed. It is time you were asleep.

KARL. Yes, mother, directly.

ELISABETH. Kiss your aunt.

KARL (*doing so*). Yes, mother. Good night, aunt.

MARIA. Good night, my sweetheart. Sleep well, happy dreams.

Exit KARL.

ELISABETH. If I permitted this irresistible Weislingen to follow his inclinations, we would not have a virtuous girl left in the castle by Tuesday. Furthermore, I told him so. I said, 'Air your compliments on me, by all means: but I decline to allow you to disrupt my domestics.' So he quoted some foolish poetry and ordered drinks for the horse-troopers.

Enter WEISLINGEN, *carrying a lute.*

Here he is now, the picture-book of fashion.

WEISLINGEN. From your husband's wardrobe, dear madam. If he doesn't want to wear the fruits of his plunder, surely you don't begrudge him adorning his friends? My lady Maria, I have been practising the song that you asked me to sing for you. Would you like to hear it now?

ELISABETH. A dress rehearsal with an audience has its advantages.

WEISLINGEN. If you can find me a place in a castle the size of this where a man can learn his music without being overheard by somebody, you will not only be opening untrodden paths in the study of rural architecture—you will also be bringing yourself perilously near an accusation of witchcraft. Well, am I to sing?

ELISABETH. I accept your polite hint in the spirit with which it is given. Enjoy your concert, my dear. If Goetz should return, tell him I'm down in the cattleyard. We are trying to breed from the Frisian bull we took on the last riding, and the cowman seems to think he shows a curious reluctance. I have no idea why.

WEISLINGEN. Ah, the poor creature. Oppressed by his captivity . . .

Exit ELISABETH.

WEISLINGEN *settles himself to play and sing.*

This song is supposed to be sung by the ghost of a Holy Cross Knight who has died fighting the Turks – after he dies, he comes back to Germany and sings it, of course, at midnight, beneath his mistress's window.

He sings.

> A thousand miles and a thousand miles
> Is the journey you must go.
> So call my name out along the road
> And they will let you know
> The way I went and the way I went,

Through the forest and the snow,
Until you do come to the Middlemost Sea,
And that is the way to go.

The Middlemost Sea and the Middlemost Sea,
A black ship stands into the bay.
Row out to her in her little waiting boat
And board her without delay.
But once she spins upon the wind
Your passage will cost you dear,
For the sailors' pay and the sailors' pay
Makes many a falling tear.

A falling tear and a falling tear
For every man on the deck.
Each man of them must serve you hard
But bow your pretty neck,
As one will come and the other will come
And the deed is done and done,
For that is the only fee they will take
To sail to the eastern sun.

And when you come into that sun
You must call my name once more:
My bones will rise from their burning grave
And walk upon the shore.
One hundred bones and a hundred bones
You shall see them grow together—
For the price you will have paid, my love,
They will hold you tight for ever.

MARIA. She must have loved him indeed to endure such a
    terrible journey.
WEISLINGEN. The song does not tell us whether she did or
    not. After all, she may not have taken the journey. It is not

everyone who would care to obey the instructions of a ghost. Rather I should say, he loved *her* so very greatly to believe that she might. It is from *his* point of view that I sing it, you see.

MARIA. Yes. I do see. And I think I believe it. I would like to believe it. To be happy with you and to make you happy also. And to pay any price and to travel any journey if necessary to complete it, as I believe a full happiness must be completed—

They kiss.

WEISLINGEN. Maria . . . Maria, it *is* completed. I am utterly your man.

MARIA (*putting him gently away from his proffered second kiss*). Not just yet again. One, I have given you: that was what we call God's Penny to seal the bargain. The rest of the payment by custom must come later.

WEISLINGEN. You have been brought up a little too strictly. There is no danger and no destruction in our love: indeed, how can God do other than rejoice at it when He knows both its sweetness and the truth of its sweetness?

MARIA. For myself I would not venture to speak on behalf of God: but I have been warned something of the dangers you so pleasantly deny. A few kisses, a few touches, a little trembling of the fingers:

And where was Samson when his lovely hair
Was scattered on the ground?
His eyes were burned and the millstone turned
And his feet till death went round and round and round.

WEISLINGEN. One song sung picks up its brother. Who taught you that one?

MARIA. The Prioress of the convent where I lived until this Easter – I was turned seventeen, you see, so *my* brother fetched me home: but before you came here I often wished I had stayed. She sang from experience, having known a great deal about love. I have learned rather more from her than perhaps you give me credit for. But you must wait: because danger and destruction are never so far distant that we should not take pains to avoid them. I mean it, my love: my breath comes very short just now, so I know I am speaking the truth.

WEISLINGEN. But what is going to happen when I have to go from you? You realize that your brother is trying for an exchange – when his soldier is released, I must return to Bamberg. The Bishop is waiting for me.

MARIA. Do you love him so much?

WEISLINGEN. Love who? The Bishop? What has that to do with it? I am his man.

MARIA. You told me you were mine.

WEISLINGEN. Yes, but that was – well, in a different meaning. The one way is politics, the other is – I suppose, when I consider it, they do both mean the same. Politics and personality are all in a net together. If I am to love you, then I ought to leave the Bishop . . . Supposing I did leave him?

MARIA. Then indeed and indeed you would be the true friend of my brother! Before he rode out to bring you in from Schwarzenberg, do you know what he said? 'I am going to set an ambush for the happiness of my youth!'

WEISLINGEN. He really said that? Well, *he* certainly keeps no distance between politics and personality, does he? . . . God's heart, though, God's heart, it *does* attract me: to live in one's castle, to owe no allegiance except to one's freedom and except to one's love— I *could* be the means of making permanent peace between Berlichingen and the Princes. Do you not think so?

MARIA. Oh, my dearest love – if only it might be possible—

GOETZ (*offstage*). Adelbert, Adelbert, where are you hiding—

Enter GOETZ. *He has disguised himself as a ragged peasant, and his iron hand is concealed in a dirty bandage and carried*

in a sling. As he talks he is unwrapping this and removing his
unpleasant outer garments.

Aha, here you are! Don't look so astonished, Maria, I am
back from my travels. I am still quite alive. I do this sort of
thing more regularly than you think. Adelbert, there's a
squire of yours just ridden in from Bamberg. He's half dead
from the bad roads and the hurry, so I've sent him down to
my wife to get him some supper. But his message is this: the
Bishop has refused to release my young man. Which is
entirely in keeping with his dishonourable character. *But,* he
has reluctantly allowed an Imperial Commission to examine
the whole affair, so I am confident all will be well. I have the
utmost trust in the justice and good sense of His Majesty. In
the meantime, you are free, and you can go home when you
like! But naturally you must give me your pledge you will not
take up arms against me until everything is settled. Will you
do so, directly?

WEISLINGEN. Yes, Goetz, I will. Here is my hand. And
furthermore, here is my other hand, and with it, I take this
noble lady. Now then: I swear eternal friendship and
alliance – on this side, man to man: and on this, man to wife.
What have you to say to it, sir?

GOETZ. Sir, I am overcome. Maria, was this expected?

MARIA. Not just yet expected: but it is true, and I agree.

GOETZ. Very well, so do I! Weislingen, you are now the friend
and the brother of Ironhand Berlichingen. Sir, once again the
strength of noble knighthood is renewed! And I knew that it
would be, because last night I had a dream: I gave you in
reconciliation the grasp of my hand, just as at this moment. I
dreamt it, and it happens! There was one curious circum-
stance, though – it was the iron hand I gave you in the dream,
which is a thing I never do, and you held it so hard it broke
off from my forearm. . . . I didn't understand that, but, of
course, now I can see it. It's my sister is pulled from me, and

I'm nothing but glad for it! I must call my wife and tell her—
Elisabeth!

He goes to the window and calls.

Where is my lady? Ask her to come up!

He turns back to the couple.

Of course, you will once again be living on your own estate
and good-bye, good-bye to Bamberg! It's a fair fine country,
Franconia, sister, and you'll find your man's castle in the
finest part of all. Look, here flows the River Main, you see,
and it loops around this high rock where the cornfields and
the vineyards climb right to the fortifications. You can stand
in the great hall: on the one side the cliff falls sheer to the
water, and on the other there's hills and there's woodland for
miles and miles rolling. I'd call it downright beautiful. And
you will be the lady of it, and your lord will be my friend!
Ah, we'll ride together, Adelbert, and our banners will sweep
through every corner of the forest!

Enter ELISABETH.

Elisabeth, do you see them? I am sending to the lawyers to
prepare a marriage contract at once! There's a great deal to
be discussed over the financial aspect, of course – the
dynastic advantages could be enormous! We shall need your
advice.

ELISABETH. Yes, I should think you will. . . . It *has* happened
very quickly, we cannot but admit it, but that is probably all
to the good. I felt it was inevitable. Only the time was
uncertain. . . . Maria, my dear girl, may I wish you every
happiness? And as for our new brother-in-law, how are we
going to express ourselves to *him*? I wonder, my Lord
Weislingen, what *are* you going to do next?

WEISLINGEN. Do next, gracious lady – I don't quite—

GOETZ. Before anything else, he'll have to go and have a look at his estates. God knows what sort of chaos your scoundrelly servants will have made there all these years since you sneaked away to Bamberg! There's one place for a knight to live, and that's in his castle – you'll have no excuse now for failing to do so.

Enter FRANZ, WEISLINGEN'S *squire – a dandified 17-year-old.*

Aha, here's your boy. Are you feeling recovered, boy? Good. Here's your master; we'll leave you to talk to him. You had better come with us, Maria: until the contract is drawn up your demeanour must be formal. I believe absolutely in traditional observance.

MARIA. Until the contract, dearest husband.

WEISLINGEN. We shall not have to wait very long.

He kisses her hand and she goes out with GOETZ *and* ELISABETH.

FRANZ. Sir, God be with you. I bring you greetings from so many different people that I hardly know how to begin. But from Bamberg itself and from ten miles around that city, all your friends say: God be with you.

WEISLINGEN. Thank you, Franz. I see you are developing a very pretty courtesy. Anything else?

FRANZ. It is difficult to express the concern and solicitude that has been felt for you at Court.

WEISLINGEN. H'm. I suppose that is possible.

FRANZ. Sir, you are in error. Men's tears were unfeigned when the news of your capture was brought.

WEISLINGEN. What about the Bishop?

FRANZ. He has been questioning everybody without rest concerning the details of the ambush. The unfortunate trooper who managed to escape with the tidings has practically expired in the hospital through the intensity of interrogation. 'Can you convince me, can you convince me,' reiterates the

Bishop, 'that my dear servant Weislingen is alive and un-hurt!'

WEISLINGEN. Why has he refused to release the Berlichingen soldier?

FRANZ. Oh, indeed, sir, to obtain your liberty, he would have released five hundred soldiers if necessary and paid any ransom demanded . . . except that he heard you were already on parole and that your relationship with Ironhand had become so very friendly – well, to be frank, sir, he thought that your liberty was as good as achieved. And if that should be so, sir, the Bishop has commanded me to give you this message: 'Weislingen is the heart and the soul of my state,' says he. 'I cannot live without him.'

WEISLINGEN. Can he not, hey? Then it's time he began to learn. We are not going back to the Court.

FRANZ. I see. Again, to be frank, sir, this is news I had expected. I have always been thought to have a good ear for a rumour. So – I have conveyed the Bishop's sentiments: I am once again your servant, and what you decide I shall follow with-out question. But we will, I assume, be paying at least one more visit to the city before we must resign ourselves to our rustic retirement?

WEISLINGEN. There is no need to be impertinent, my dear fellow, just because you are not partial to the smell of manure.

FRANZ. But the transfer of your furniture and your financial deposits will have to be seen about – you usually prefer to do that yourself. And surely you cannot wish to leave Bamberg for ever without taking some note of the present angelic visitation?

WEISLINGEN. Angelic visitation? Ah, you mean the Bishop has found himself a new one. Who is she this time?

FRANZ. Sir, sir, this is very different . . . you would call *me* sophisticated, but in the presence of *this* one – I was drunk, I was delirious, I sauntered up to my neck through a pool of golden honey and the bees that made the honey buzzed

inside my brain: I swam naked in the pool of it and luxuriated
in its richness – all she was doing was playing chess with the
Bishop and I had to be in attendance to take his message and
so forth. But still, she was there, and I was drunk with the
sight of her. So how much more yourself, sir?

WEISLINGEN. I asked you what her name was.

FRANZ. Adelheid von Walldorf.

→ widow visting the Bishop

WEISLINGEN. Ah yes, and widely reputed, too. What colour
would you say she is?

FRANZ. Indubitably black, as to her hair. Her eyes, a dark
brown. Her skin, not too white. I would call it more golden,
almost green where the shadows touch it underneath her
jawbone and between the precellent gradients of her paps.
Her mouth and her nipples – which a calculated corsage
permitted me to see – were nearly as brown as her eyes. I
think she had painted them to create a harmony, but the
basic colour cannot have been very far different – at all
events, they were not the crude carmine that has lately
become so wearisome. She wore gold in each golden earlobe,
and three massive chains of it, which I judge to have been
extremely heavy, were hanging round her neck. The Bishop
had given her five rings of various sizes, and one large silver
bracelet.

WEISLINGEN. And where was her husband?

FRANZ. Oh, the husband – he's been dead for four months. I
forgot to tell you that. She is, of course, wearing her widow's
weeds. I believe she finds the life at Court in some measure
diverting to her natural melancholy.

WEISLINGEN. Let us hope so, at any rate. Thank you, Franz,
for the description. And now perhaps you will be so good as
to pack up my luggage and we will leave for my castle first
thing in the morning. You do appreciate, of course, I am
about to get married?

FRANZ. Yes, sir: and I am sure all your friends will wish you
the very greatest felicity.

SCENE SIX

Bamberg.
A room in the Bishop's Palace.

> *The* BISHOP *and* ADELHEID *are at chess.* LADIES *and*
> GENTLEMEN *in attendance.* LIEBETRAUT *playing on a*
> *zither.*

LIEBETRAUT. Gentle ladies, we must never underrate the
merciless power of the God of Love, but, on the other hand,
remember, you, too, have your power and he *can* be controlled.

> *He sings, with satirical emphasis.*

> A-flaming and flashing
> Lord Eros came dashing
> With arrow and bow
> To fight for your life, man,
> In terrible strife, man,
> And never lie low.
> > Ho Ho!
> > No No!
> His weapons a-clanging,
> His brazen wings banging,
> His eyeballs aglow!

> He spies her bright bosom
> So naked so fair,
> He needs but one arrow,
> It hits the mark square!
> But alas for the victor,
> O weep ladies, weep,
> His sweet-willing victim
> Has rocked him to sleep.
> > Aye aye oh
> > Lullabye oh!

BISHOP. Engaged to be married . . . I can hardly believe it.

ADELHEID. You are not paying attention to the moves. Check.

BISHOP. Oh yes, I am. I am feeling my way into them, that is all.

ADELHEID. Unless you are more careful, there will be no way left you to feel. Check.

LIEBETRAUT. If I were Your Eminence instead of merely the blower of Your Eminence's majestical nose, I would not only decline to play this game myself, but I would forbid it altogether throughout my dominions.

ADELHEID. Why?

LIEBETRAUT. It doesn't suit me, that's why.

ADELHEID. You're quite right; it does need a keen brain for its accomplishment.

LIEBETRAUT. That is not my reason. How can a great Prince, who is given power and commandment over his fellow men, endure to sit at a little table and listen without trembling to this continual biting cry— Check, check, check! For who is it who is checked? His Majesty himself. And who is it who checks him? Knights, squires, fortified castles, inferior clergy – it is the most subversive game under heaven.

ADELHEID. Check and checkmate.

They rise from the game.

You should write a book of political theory, Liebetraut, you are wasted in singing love songs.

LIEBETRAUT. Political practice I think would be more valuable. That way we could *include* the love songs, could we not?

BISHOP. He refuses to return because he is getting married – or is he getting married because he refuses to return? It is altogether incomprehensible.

ADELHEID. Put him out of your head. He is gone and that is all.

LIEBETRAUT. I do not think so. If you really want him back, I believe he could be fetched.

BISHOP. Of course I want him back. He was the only good

soldier and the only administrator with a brain between his ears in the whole of this Court!

LIEBETRAUT. Then send me to talk to him.

BISHOP. You? But, dear boy, what could you tell him that he does not know already?

LIEBETRAUT. If the lady would permit it, I could tell him quite a lot.

ADELHEID. The lady might well, Liebetraut: but what about her lord?

BISHOP. When the interests of my state are concerned, I am a man of very broad accommodation. Reassure me, my sweetheart, that this does not insult you? My greatness and my wealth should remove all offence from my words. . . . You may consider yourself quite free as regards my side of the question, dear boy: all that I require is you bring Weislingen home.

LIEBETRAUT. Yet still, I should have my lady's permission. May I, just once, mention your name to him?

ADELHEID. Yes, if you do so with all due propriety.

LIEBETRAUT. That is rather a sweeping condition. Could you not give it a more accurate limit?

ADELHEID. Are you so inexperienced that you cannot look upon me and know without asking how you should refer to me in the presence of an unknown nobleman?

LIEBETRAUT. Gracious lady, I *am* looking: and what I see tells me there is but one way to handle your name – it must be blown into his ear with the fury of a clarion! Check, Weislingen, check!

BISHOP. That will do, thank you very much. Now waste no more time: you can have the best horse in my stable and as many men as you want – but see you bring him home!

LIEBETRAUT. My lord, I take my leave! He is once more your servant.

ADELHEID. God go with you, Liebetraut.

LIEBETRAUT. Dear lady, dear ladies, adieu!

He goes.

BISHOP. Does it make you feel happy to be used as a butterfly net?

ADELHEID. I have heard so many wonderful things about the splendour and the rarity of this particular butterfly that the palms of my hands are already damp at the thought of his flutterings. I think we *both* know the virtues of a broad accommodation, my lord. Let me prove to you how your manifest generosity can be matched by my own. . . .

she is anxious to meet W —

SCENE SEVEN

Jaxthausen.
A room in Goetz's Castle.

Enter GOETZ *and* SELBITZ (*a knight with a wooden leg, which is designed to fit into the stirrup of his horse*).

GOETZ. The Nuremberg merchants are sending a full convoy of goods to the Frankfurt Fair next week. I was in the town only three hours and I heard the whole thing – how many wagons, what time they'll set out, what company of militiamen is being ordered for the escort – Jesus, Mary, and Joseph, Hans, I was all but hired myself to ride alongside 'em! Except I had a bad arm, you see, and couldn't hold a spear. Now, are you with us in this?

SELBITZ. I am.

GOETZ. That's the good word! So we have Berlichingen and Selbitz; between us we should make up fifty riders at least. What about Sickingen – do you think he could come?

SELBITZ. I doubt it. Not this time. That lad's involving himself in a sight higher politics than raiding wagon-trains at present. I hope he knows what he's up to.

GOETZ. Higher politics! This *is* higher politics! I have declared

revenge ?

formal feud against the city of Nuremberg. They betrayed my young trooper into the hands of the Bamberg men, and, God's feet, they must be taught! What is it with Sickingen, though – what's he trying to do?

SELBITZ. He's forming a sort of indefinite league between one or two of the big Princes – wiser not to name them just yet, but you'll no doubt guess who they are. If he succeeds, there could be grand advantage to all of us. If not – well, like my old timber leg, it'll be a bit of a stumbling-block, but a man can still walk. Now then, this Weislingen of yours – have we got him, or haven't we?

GOETZ. Not quite at once, no. He has to play rather delicate till his finances are sorted out. But he's no longer against us, and that's a marvellous thing. The fat priest without him is what the Holy Mass would be without the fat priest, and I talk in no riddles. I sent him a message to tell him what we're going to do and to warn him to stand clear—

Enter GEORG, *from riding.*

Hello, here's the boy that took it. Well, did you tell him?

GEORG. No, sir; he wasn't there.

GOETZ. What d'you mean – wasn't there? He rode home five days ago; he must have been there.

GEORG. He'd been and he'd gone. I spoke to his steward. I said, 'Where's the Lord Weislingen?' He looked back at me with eyes like two oysters; he said, 'Bamberg, of course. Where else would he be?'

GOETZ. When did he go there?

GEORG. Only the day before. There's a fellow called Liebetraut came and stayed the night; then they rode off together, and that's about the lot. I came straight here to tell you. Should I have gone to Bamberg? They say it's a lively town. . . .

GOETZ. No, no, you did right. . . .

SELBITZ. Look, I've heard of Liebetraut. Goetz, ten to one your new brother-in-law's a lost man already.

GOETZ. No. I'll not believe it. But we'd better find out. Georg, *go* to Bamberg. But do it discreetly. There's some of their soldiers' coats we captured at different times; choose one small enough to fit you, put it on, get some dinner, and take yourself off. Don't come back here till you know the full story. Now, this is the first time I've sent you on a proper expedition. So do yourself credit . . . Of course, he has all the arranging of his money and so forth to consider; it could easily be that . . . go on, boy – stop gaping!

plan.

GEORG. Sir, I'll follow him down through every mousehole in that palace!

GOETZ. I told you to go!

Exit GEORG.

It's highly improbable there's anything wrong. I'm refusing to worry about it till we've dealt with the Nuremberg men – so don't mention him to me. I mean that, man, *don't*!

SELBITZ. Whatever you say . . . When do we ride?

GOETZ. Day after tomorrow, if you can make it so soon. We'll meet at your castle. I'm aiming to catch them where the road narrows in, at the bottom of the forest. Do you think that's a fit place?

waiting to trap Nuremberg men.

SELBITZ. I most certainly do. And good God being with us, we'll have a most prosperous enterprise. Cross your heart and count a prayer.

They both sign themselves with the cross.

BOTH. Holy Jesus . . . Amen!

SCENE EIGHT

Bamberg.
The Bishop's Palace: a Room in Adelheid's Apartments.

ADELHEID *and* MARGARET, *her Lady-in-Waiting.*

ADELHEID. Already?

MARGARET. Already, already – I didn't think it possible it could be him so soon, but no, here he was, high a-cock horse into Bamberg, and I saw him first!

ADELHEID. Then you deserve to go to bed with him first, but I think we won't let you. What a remarkable little Liebetraut! However has he done it!

MARGARET. And what does *he* deserve?

ADELHEID. Oh no, not Liebetraut – altogether too small. *You* can have him, if you wish – if I was the Bishop, I would melt myself down and coin myself into gold to reward such insidious diplomacy. But I don't suppose he will. So there you are, Margaret, I grant you the pleasant duty of saying 'thank you' to the gentleman.

MARGARET. Perhaps . . . and perhaps not, my lady . . . Though they do say, don't they, the smaller, the sharper. Perhaps, after all . . .

ADELHEID. Tell me about Weislingen.

MARGARET. He came in on a grey horse – oh, as tall as a towering falcon. At the bridge, for some reason, the horse took shy; he stopped dead for two minutes. All the people ran to him, cheering and throwing their hats—

ADELHEID. He is popular with the Bamberg men?

MARGARET. Oh, very easy, very easy indeed with all the ragged world – *that* sort of a lord he is, throwing out his money like a prince in a fairy tale; at least, his squire held the purse, but his own long white fingers dipped among the gold and tossed it left and right like the leaves of a salad. He looks like the Emperor.

ADELHEID. The Emperor? How old is he?

MARGARET. I mean, the Emperor as he would have been twenty years ago – golden hair, my lady, and a proud soldier's nose like the stride of a warhorse, and inside his grey eyes, such crouching sadness, I could see it and I wept – comfort him, comfort him.

ADELHEID. But will *he* comfort *me*?

MARGARET. Can anyone, ever? I am sure he will try.

Enter LIEBETRAUT.

LIEBETRAUT. Gracious ladies, I stand before you puffed up with accomplishment! The butterfly is caught. What does the catcher deserve?

MARGARET. That question is already under consideration, sir.

ADELHEID. Though we could think of nothing to give you you are not quite capable of taking without desert. How did you persuade him?

LIEBETRAUT. No difficulty at all. As easy as this—

He takes MARGARET'S *hand.*

Or as easy as this—

He strokes her neck.

MARGARET (*as his hand comes down a little more*). Don't be too confident.

She breaks away.

LIEBETRAUT. Nor was I, my sweetheart. *He* hesitated, too, but not for very long. I approached him with three voices. One: the voice of sentiment. His old friends in Bamberg, his loyalty to the Bishop, the delights of the city, etcetera . . . Two: the voice of materialism. His office in the Government was one of great profit, how very unwise to relinquish it so hurriedly . . . And finally, three: the strongest voice. Of his own personal obsession. He is a man who cannot leave off from telling other men how to live. Deprived of the responsibilities of administration, deprived of the respect accorded his undoubted intellect, existing from day to day instinctively, like a violent wild-wood swine, instead of ennobling creation like a rational, financial, political human being, how could such a man do anything but die?

ADELHEID. But what about me, Liebetraut? I was under the impression my name was to be used?

LIEBETRAUT. Oh yes, it was. Forgive me, I had to put you into my third, my administrative category. You see, it was evident he had heard of you already and that all he desired was some practical justification for his clearly abundant physical impulse. So I told him what is true: that since the death of your husband you have been involved in tedious legal battles over the ownership of his fortune, and that you were anxious for a man of experience to advise you and if possible put in a word for you at the Imperial Court . . . Well, he is now in Bamberg, and I expect in due time the Bishop will be only too happy to present him to your divinity. Will you excuse me, dear lady, if I take my humble leave?

ADELHEID. With pleasure and with gratitude. Margaret will show you out. I think you will find she knows a way to place that gratitude in a fuller perspective than my own poor talents are able to encompass. In the meantime, I will wait. . . . Comfort yourselves, both of you – make sure that you do . . .

LIEBETRAUT *and* MARGARET *go out together.*

SCENE NINE

Bamberg.
The Bishop's Palace – his study.

BISHOP *and* WEISLINGEN. FRANZ *in attendance.*

BISHOP. But you are no sooner arrived than you inform me you are going! Why? Tell me why!

WEISLINGEN. My lord, I have told you. I have sworn an oath to Berlichingen. I am in Bamberg now merely to – to settle my affairs. Nothing further. These are the terms by which I am bound. Can you not understand?

BISHOP. What is all this archaic nonsense about oaths? Do you imagine I have no credit whatever with His Holiness the Pope? My dear fellow, in two months I can obtain from him a dispensation which—

WEISLINGEN. It is absurd: but it is done. I am sorry.

BISHOP. So am I. So am I! Holy St Peter, if only I had known! Why, I could have released his trooper, I could have paid any amount of ransom – all you had to do was send me one letter! Anything, anything, to have prevented your giving *oaths*. One does not give *oaths* to criminal bandits! . . . Nor does one engage oneself in marriage to their sisters. I had forgotten about that. I suppose the next time I see you, you will be leading an army against the walls of my city.

angry at W

WEISLINGEN. Really, my lord, there is no need to—

BISHOP. Tell me it is not true. Tell me that all the years you have served me so faithfully as the most trusted of my officers are not to be ground away to nothing by the blood-stained grip of this lunatic's iron hand. Weislingen, I need you. Pull yourself together. You are my man! . . . I could hold you here a prisoner, you know: I could force you, I could!

MB

WEISLINGEN. I'll offer no comment on that remark, my lord. It is unworthy of your intelligence. Now please listen to me: I am retiring from political life: I am *not* your declared enemy. I have made alliance with Goetz for only one purpose, to bring peace to the country, which I think I can do. Will you not permit me to go home and do it?

BISHOP. Very well then: go! I am no longer interested in you, your name, your history, your capabilities, your prospective family, or anything else. I have forgotten you, sir. Good day.

Exit BISHOP.

WEISLINGEN. Not good. Not good at all. But how else could I put it?

FRANZ. It is nearly time for your evening's assignation with the lady – are you going to tell *her* you are leaving tomorrow?

WEISLINGEN. That is nothing to do with you. I shall tell her what seems most appropriate to her mood and the occasion. I am not without some practice in boudoir excuses.

SCENE TEN

Bamberg.
The Bishop's Palace. Adelheid's bedroom. Evening.

ADELHEID *being prepared for bed by* MARGARET.

MARGARET. He has said good-bye to the Bishop – or the Bishop has said it to *him*. It must be true, then; he really *has* only come here to wind up his business.

ADELHEID. Which is what he tried to make me believe this morning. It is perhaps just as well. He does not measure up to your description, I am afraid.

MARGARET. No?

ADELHEID. No. He went to sleep two hours after midnight, and would not be woken till the page brought in my breakfast. What am I to think of a man who does that?

MARGARET. He'd had a hard day's riding.

ADELHEID. Not hard enough.

MARGARET. I meant the road to Bamberg. At all events, Liebetraut was suffering from saddle-sores.

ADELHEID. Indeed? Did you cure them?

MARGARET. If I did it was at my own expense. They seem to have been transferred.

ADELHEID. I am not going to marry Weislingen, however often he asks me.

MARGARET. Oh, I don't believe it! He *can't* have proposed so soon! *Can* he?

ADELHEID. I proposed to him. He didn't take it seriously: but someone has to put the idea into his mind. He is rich enough, isn't he? Under no vow of celibacy? And, moreover, the sooner he forgets his languishing princess in her dark tower of Jaxthausen, the sooner he is likely to return to the Bishop. Which is where he ought to be. I am paying the rent of this very splendid episcopal apartment by performing these services – I must be conscientious.

    Enter WEISLINGEN.

MARGARET. Here he is now.

WEISLINGEN. Good evening, dear ladies. . . . My love, what is the matter – are you not well?

ADELHEID. No. I don't think I am.

WEISLINGEN. Why not? What is wrong?

ADELHEID. I have a headache, that is all: it is too hot, it is too confined in this room – do *not* open the windows – do you want to give me muscular contractions in the back of my neck? Margaret, my child, will you leave me alone, please!

MARGARET (*who is anxiously feeling* ADELHEID'S *neck*). I thought just to massage—

ADELHEID. Out, get away, stupid girl. I hate you – *there*!

    She smacks MARGARET'S *face.* MARGARET *jumps back a pace and looks at her for an instant in surprise, then smiles a long, slow smile, purring like a cat, turns the smile to* WEISLINGEN, *and slips out of the room.*

I shall do the same to you in a moment, Master Peacock! Sit down.

WEISLINGEN (*obeying*). Am I responsible for all this – or has it been rehearsed?

ADELHEID. I told you already it is the heat of the evening. And I am like the Italian actors – no rehearsals, only improvisations. You may undress me if you wish.

WEISLINGEN. As you have dismissed the girl, there is no alternative, is there? Unless you had intended to go to bed in your clothes.

ADELHEID. It is none of your business how I go to bed. You will not be here to see.

WEISLINGEN. No?

ADELHEID. Why do you imagine I sent for you tonight?

WEISLINGEN (*ironical*). No doubt to discuss the safeguarding of your estates. Does this unhook here?

ADELHEID. No. Leave it fastened. Take away your hand! Yes, I *do* want to discuss the safeguarding of my estates. Open that box and bring me the papers you will find inside it.

   He obeys.

They are transcripts of the deeds to a small castle and two manors belonging to the late Lord Walldorf, God rest his soul.

WEISLINGEN. God rest it.

ADELHEID. Read them through, if you please, and tell me if you can discover any loopholes in my title. The Landgrave of Hesse is laying claim to the property, and I should like to know why.

WEISLINGEN (*looking through the papers*). At a cursory glance only, I should say that your inheritance appears to be based on some ancestral transactions as obscure as they are remote. A skilled common lawyer could easily invalidate them by producing contradictory conveyances from someone else's family archives. This needs both time and patience – I don't know why I'm supposed to be looking at it now. It would be much more convenient to postpone it till tomorrow . . . Yes, it would, and I will. In the morning and not before I will give it my full attention.

ADELHEID. No, you will not! Now, I said, *now*! I *must* have your opinion. My entire fortune is in danger. How *can* you be so selfish as not to help me when I ask you! All you ever think of is the satisfaction of your disgusting body. Up, down, out, away, like a boatrace on the Rhine – and the minute you're told you've won, you fling yourself over the thwarts and sleep for five hours. Bargemaster. Barbarian.

WEISLINGEN. Now sleep, is it – sleep! Don't you call *that* sleep! I was ridden last night for two hundred miles on the bare back of nightmare. You know it, lady, you drove it, you *were* it, by God's Mother! Forest, mire, and quickset hedge-row. I woke this morning like a damned sweating murderer with the hue-and-cry behind. Look at me now: would you call me rested, would you call me in repose?

ADELHEID. The Landgrave of Hesse is robbing me of my life.

WEISLINGEN. Let it wait till tomorrow—

ADELHEID. Supposing he should occupy the estates with his soldiers – he may act this very night!

WEISLINGEN. I know only one man who is going to act tonight—

ADELHEID. Very well, here's the bed. Climb up, sir, and show me. You must do better than before, though; or this is the last time.

WEISLINGEN. Oh ho-ho, no: it is *not*!

ADELHEID. Not? How is that? I understood you were leaving for your castle in the morning.

WEISLINGEN. Eh? Well, yes, I was . . .

ADELHEID. Then there can be neither a repetition of our love-making, nor an opportunity for you to look through my papers. The Bishop has told me you have sworn an oath to Berlichingen.

WEISLINGEN. Certainly, that is true.

ADELHEID. Of course it is true. You are nothing but a chameleon. You take a different colour from every stone that you perch on. In Berlichingen's hall you are a savage, un-washed bandit, in the Bishop's private study a twisting politician, and in my bedroom, God help us—

WEISLINGEN. Go on, describe me.

ADELHEID. You are faithless, inconsistent, hysterical; and moved by such a depth of lechery that I marvel you can stand upright on your two shaking knees. You are exactly the mirror of my own qualities, Weislingen; and you are not going to steer me tonight!

A knocking on the door.

66   IRONHAND

FRANZ (*off*). Sir, sir, my lord Weislingen, sir—

    WEISLINGEN *opens the door and* FRANZ *blunders in.*

WEISLINGEN. What the devil is it – damn you, boy, damn you, what do *you* want *here*!

FRANZ. I am sorry, sir – I *had* to. It's the Bishop, he's calling for you!

WEISLINGEN. The Bishop!

FRANZ. He says you have left his administration in disgraceful disorder. That as an honest servant you owe it to your successor to tidy up your documents before you leave the Palace. He says you must call the secretaries and see to it at once. Lady Adelheid, my apologies—

WEISLINGEN. Absolute tomfoolery at this time of night! Tell him—

ADELHEID. Tell him, in the morning. You will do it in the morning. Do it all in the morning! Go out of here, go! Margaret! Margaret!

    MARGARET *comes running in.*

I will not have you admitting all these unmannerly ruffians whenever you think fit! Send them out at once!

MARGARET. I don't think she feels very well tonight – I am sorry, my lords: it would be better if you went . . .

WEISLINGEN. This is not the last time, lady, no! You may humiliate me now, but I have words for you, and by God you're going to hear them! Franz, come along.

    He goes out with FRANZ.

MARGARET. Is he still going?

ADELHEID. Oh, I dare say . . . The day after tomorrow, or the day after that, or maybe the year after next – who knows, little sweetheart, little swallow, little dove? . . . I love him. He makes me quite sick to my stomach in an ecstasy for him. Wipe my temples, sweetheart; that's right, gently, oh ever so gently . . .

Act Two

SCENE ONE

The forest near Nuremberg.
The courtyard of a small farm.

A peasant wedding is in progress of celebration. A bagpiper is playing and PEASANTS *are dancing in the yard, together with* TROOPERS *wearing* GOETZ'S *and* SELBITZ'S *badges. At the table at the head of the yard the* BRIDE *and* BRIDEGROOM *with the* BRIDE'S FATHER *are seated with the principal guests, who include* GOETZ *and* SELBITZ (*in armour*). *All eating and drinking with gusto. The peasant* METZLER *is in the crowd, talking intermittently with various of the men. A* BOY *is on the roof.*

BRIDE'S FATHER (*beats on table for silence*): Hallo there! Everybody, all and sundry! Give attention, lug-oyles, *if you* please! I'd just like to say one word, two words, afore we get on wi' the good cheer. It's not every day I give out my daughter to be wed to a rare young man of my own fair choice, nor it's not every day neither as we can lay claim at a local bridal to guests of such honour as the Lords of Berlichingen and Selbitz. Sirs, for gracing our festivities, we one and all are made both free and happy, likewise to all your jolly lads, who ride along of you, and to whom we all declare: 'Good fortune in your enterprise against the Nuremberg wagons, and may you knock their wheels off!' Drink!

Health drunk amid cheers.

GOETZ (*rising*). Sir, if you're glad to have us at your table, it gives all the greater delight to us to be set here with *you*. I hope you won't think it an impertinence if I take it upon myself to propose the health of the bride. May she and her good man live many happy years together and may they be blessed with the increasing happiness of continual increase – a process, which, I hear with satisfaction, has already begun!

Cheers and ribald laughter. BRIDE *registers giggling bashfulness.* BRIDEGROOM *slapped on his back by friends, etc.*

Ladies and gentlemen: drink to the bride!

Health drunk.

SELBITZ. And while you're on your feet, Goetz, it might be a good notion if you said a few words about how this marriage came into being in the first place.

GOETZ. And that's a fair point, and all. Ladies and gentlemen, for those of you who didn't know it already: this wedding began with a quarrel and a lawsuit. A young man and an old man at odds over an acre of land. So they go to the Judge, and what did the Judge say?

BRIDE'S FATHER. He said: 'Twenty gold guilders to be paid for this decision.' I said, 'Is it a fee or is it a bribe?' He said, 'Never mind which.' He said, 'Pay.' I'd to sell just about all that I owned – cattle and pigs, household goods, the lot. Didn't I, daughter?

BRIDE. Aye, father, you did.

BRIDE'S FATHER. By the finish, I raised eighteen. He took it and that was all. No decision.

BRIDEGROOM. In *nobody's* favour. I gave him fifteen, and he gave *me* nowt neither.

BRIDE. Bribed by both sides – that's justice in this country.

GOETZ. But as it so chanced, you turned out to be fortunate after all. Because this young man one day met the old man's daughter at the back side of a hayrick and they fell into talking about the lawsuit and the Judge, and there betwixt the both of them they managed to discover a new sort of justice that these damned dishonest lawyers never heard of in their lives! And I say, good people, I say more power to them! The

honest country folk in this part of Germany have been
trampled on too long!

Cheers.

Various cries.
That's right.
Hear hear.
Down wi' the lawyers.
Down wi' the citizens.
Kill all the Princes.

METZLER (*taking the last one up*). Kill all the Princes, hang up
the lawyers, burn out the merchants—

GOETZ. Hey, no, now wait – wait – that's not what I said. The
virtues of our country life are fixed in a framework of due
harmony and order and we break it at peril. Live honest on
your land, good friends; till it, in fit season, like your fathers
did before you, and leave it to *us* to give you your protection!
Because we can and we will – so long as we ride, we shall keep
the townsmen out!

METZLER. What about some of us going *in* to those towns,
maister? We walk in on foot, and we come out again on horse,
and he who sees us come will see the blood running after,
down the threshold of the gate.

SELBITZ *comes down and confronts him.*

SELBITZ. I don't know you. Who are you? You don't belong to
this country?

METZLER. No, maister, I don't. I'm a Swabian man; they call
me Klaus Metzler.

In a snatch of song.

And every man into this place, they will avow the same:
I never thought to do a crime, that I should deny my name.

SELBITZ. What do you want here?

METZLER. I'm a guest at a wedding. I've got kinsmen in this village. You ask 'em, go on.

SELBITZ (*seizes a* PEASANT). All right – hey, you: I'm asking *you*.

PEASANT. That's right, maister. He's our brother.

ANOTHER PEASANT. Aye aye, our brother.

A THIRD PEASANT. Brother Klaus, out of Swabia.

SELBITZ (*baffled*). Aye, aye, is that it? . . .

BRIDE'S FATHER (*to break the tension*). Come on now. Who was dancing? Stir it up there, piper—

GOETZ. To be free and to be merry, boys, I'm going to dance with the bride!

> *He takes the* BRIDE *by the hand and dances with her as the music starts.*

BRIDE'S FATHER. Come on, come on, everyone, dance—

> *The dancing generally begins again.* SELBITZ *takes* METZLER *into a corner.*

SELBITZ. Now sithee here, Brother Klaus: I'm warning thee, baht laiking. Thee get back to thy own thorpe, sharp! Because let me just catch you in any part of Franconia after this day, and I'll splice my wooden leg wi' the top of your backbone!

> *Tapping* METZLER'S *ear.*

Is that heard?

METZLER. Aye, maister, it's heard.

SELBITZ. Good. Then let it bide.

> GEORG *has come in, in a Bamberg coat. He pushes through the dancers and speaks to* GOETZ, *who breaks off dancing with a cry.*

GOETZ. *What!*

GEORG. Sir, it's all true.

GOETZ. On with the dancing, carry it on, take no note of me—

> *He comes down to* SELBITZ.

Hans, listen to this. Go on, boy, say it.

GEORG. I put on this coat and I got into Bamberg. Couldn't have been easier. And the first thing I see as I set my feet on that street is Weislingen, and the Bishop, and a tall dark jingling queen: and they all walk out of church. So I asked who she was. They call her the von Walldorf. And they're going to get married.

GOETZ. Married. Weislingen.

SELBITZ. What did I tell you?

GEORG. All the old wives in Bamberg were crying: 'They *do* make a lovely couple.' I went to see him next day. I met him on his road to early mass with only one squire. I whispered to him: 'Berlichingen.' He said: 'God's sake – come tomorrow', and he went flying past me with his head turned round to the doorposts. So tomorrow I was there: two hours in his anteroom waiting, and all the sneery little pages looking on and laughing in silk jackets and gold braid all over their cod-pieces. And then when he *does* see me – 'We are not exactly accustomed to receiving messages at the hand of stable-boys. Tell Berlichingen we see no reason to implement promises made under constraint of captivity. And be out of Bamberg yourself within less than an hour!'

GOETZ. Jesus, Mary, Joseph . . . Jesus . . . Mary . . . The next time I take that man there will be no code of knighthood. I am in bloodfeud with him now and he had better be aware of it. My sister, Hans; Maria – what can I tell her?

SELBITZ. Nothing you can tell her – except that she's forfeited her name. If you *do* take him, do you know how I'd serve him? I'd pike out both his eyes with blackthorn and put a garland of it on his head, then a white rope round his neck, and give the other end to her, and let her lead him out and lead him in for as long as she likes. By God, Goetz, I had rather lose my second leg than be a man of such dishonour.

THE BOY ON THE ROOF. Hey-ey – the wagons! I can see them on the road!

SELBITZ (*calling his men*). Aha, ready! Selbitz, to me, Selbitz!

GOETZ (*likewise*). Berlichingen, Berlichingen! Every man! To your horses. We're riding at once! Good people – we're away! God rest with you and help you!

BRIDE'S FATHER. And with you, sir, God be praised!

> *Confusion as the* TROOPERS *all pick up their gear and hurry out. Bugles and shouting.* GOETZ *and* SELBITZ *go out with them.*

BRIDEGROOM. Ironhand and Wooden-leg for ever! Razor the tripes of the Nuremberg bastards!

BRIDE. Why don't we all go and give 'em a hand—

BRIDEGROOM. Come on, boys, come on—

A TROOPER (*turning round and holding the* PEASANTS *back*). Hey, no – not for you! Didn't you hear him say no?

ANOTHER TROOPER. Let 'em come if they want to. They live beside this road, don't they? Let 'em take their own shares.

PEASANTS. Come on, boys, come on – there's wagons are on the road!

> *They hurry out after the* TROOPERS, *with pitchforks and billhooks, etc.*

SCENE TWO

Augsburg.
Garden of the Imperial Palace.

> *Two* MERCHANTS *enter.*

FIRST MERCHANT. I think we had better stand just here, sir. His Majesty is bound to pass us here. Look, here he comes, down the Long Avenue.

SECOND MERCHANT. Who is it with him? Can you see?

FIRST MERCHANT. I am not entirely sure—

SECOND MERCHANT. Adelbert von Weislingen!

FIRST MERCHANT. No! Oho, how very lucky – he is the Bishop of Bamberg's very good friend, you know.

SECOND MERCHANT. Yes, yes, I know—

FIRST MERCHANT. Now, sir, I think the best thing for us to do is to fall flat at the Emperor's feet.

SECOND MERCHANT. You do?

FIRST MERCHANT. Yes. With an appearance of the extremity of distress. We must move his royal heart, sir. Let me do the talking.

SECOND MERCHANT. I'd be obliged if you would, sir. Ssh, here they are.

The EMPEROR *walks in, talking to* WEISLINGEN. *The* SECOND MERCHANT *steps forward, but his companion pulls him back.*

FIRST MERCHANT. Wait till we catch his eye.

EMPEROR. No, sir, I said no . . . The fact of the matter is that the older I grow, the more disappointed I become. For how many years now have I been under vow to lead my chivalry against the Paynim Turk? Twenty at least. I am sorely afraid, Weislingen, that I must go to my grave foresworn. And see, how many other projects have I had, for the benefit of my people, indeed for the common weal of Christendom, that have met their frustration, turn in, turn out, through jealousy and suspicion, apathy and sloth?

His eye falls on the MERCHANTS. *They fall to their knees and prostrate themselves.*

MERCHANTS. Almighty Sovereign! Most Illustrious Majesty!

EMPEROR. Who are these gentlemen? And what do they think they are doing?

FIRST MERCHANT. We are poor merchants, Your Majesty, from the city of—

EMPEROR. Stand up, sir, if you please. This is not Constantinople!

They stand.

Now then: where do you say you are from?

FIRST MERCHANT. Nuremberg, Your Majesty. We are Your Majesty's most loyal servants and we implore Your Majesty's help! Thirty loaded wagons, on the road to Frankfurt Fair, were attacked, overthrown, and robbed, by Goetz von Berlichingen and Hans von Selbitz at the head of an enormous troop of men!

WEISLINGEN. You had provided no escort?

FIRST MERCHANT. Indeed we had, my lord – a company of the civic militia reinforced by several horsemen from the Bishop of Bamberg. But, sire, they were outnumbered and they could do nothing! We beg you, Your Majesty, grant us your royal aid, for otherwise we shall be broken men, Your Majesty, forced to beg for bread in the streets of our own city!

EMPEROR. Goetz von Berlichingen . . . Hans von Selbitz . . . One leg on the one and one arm on the other! Tell me, sirs, what would have happened if you'd met two men riding with *all* of their bones in place!

FIRST MERCHANT. But, Your Majesty—

EMPEROR. No, sir: no! You are insufficient, both of you. You imagine, it seems, that every time you find a robber's knife-blade stuck into one of your sacks of pepper the whole of Germany must fly to arms! But if your Emperor, to whom you so readily appeal, should have his *own* small problems, for which he may require perhaps some soldiers here, some taxes there, the occasional loan from his wealthier citizens, in order, it may be, to prevent his few domains from being completely overrun by the trifling hordes of heathendom – well, gentlemen, what then? These oriental prostrations of yours are not quite so evident, are they?

He turns away. WEISLINGEN *speaks confidentially to the* MERCHANTS.

WEISLINGEN. I am afraid you have chosen an unsuitable time.

His Majesty is rather disturbed this morning. But don't go home just yet. Stay here in Augsburg for a few more days, and I will see what can be done for you.

FIRST MERCHANT. We are most grateful to your lordship.

SECOND MERCHANT. Yes, indeed, my lord. Thank you, sir, thank you.

The MERCHANTS *withdraw.*

EMPEROR. Hydra-heads, Weislingen, hydra-heads. How many more of them?

WEISLINGEN. The only policy of any use to Your Majesty is a policy of strength.

EMPEROR. Very probably, sir: but how am I to find one? . . . You have yourself of late been associated with this Berlichingen, have you not?

WEISLINGEN. I was temporarily seduced by the memory of an old friendship. I had hopes that by entering into personal alliance with the man I might succeed in bringing some sort of sanity to bear upon his conduct. I discovered only too quickly that he regarded me as just one more recruit to his band of mountain wolves. There was even talk of a betrothal to his sister. I regretted having to repudiate that: but this latest development truly proves to me how well clear I am from any such connexion.

EMPEROR. Yes, I think it does. Though I do not like to hear of these broken espousals. They have little to do with the ancient courtesy of knighthood . . . Which reminds me, Weislingen: I have failed to congratulate you upon your other betrothal – indeed, I think by now it is an achieved marriage, is it not? The lady Adelheid is both beautiful and debonair. May you find good fortune in your partnership together.

WEISLINGEN. I am deeply grateful for Your Majesty's kind wishes. My wife, I am sure, will be ravished by your remembrance.

EMPEROR. And you would have us set our Holy Roman sword to walk against our own free liegemen, would you? Yet pay good note, young man, it is these brawling mountain wolves, as you describe them, who will be the bravest and most whole-hearted of my army when the onfall of the infidel is heard!

WEISLINGEN. Yes, indeed – the more heads they can cut off, the happier they will be . . .

EMPEROR. Ah, sir, delight of war is dead for us, I think . . . What must be done, then, must. Let their formal condemnation be approved by the Diet of Princes, and afterwards – whom shall we make commander of the punitive force? You?

WEISLINGEN. I had rather not, Your Majesty. My personal feelings toward Berlichingen are still extremely complex. You would do better to appoint some uninvolved officer . . .

The EMPEROR *turns to go.*

Your Majesty, there is one other matter, if I may have Your Majesty's ear. Will you grant me permission to take up arms against the Landgrave of Hesse?

EMPEROR. In God's name, whatever for?

WEISLINGEN. He has wrongfully seized a castle belonging to my wife's inheritance from her first husband, has filled it with his men, and is in posture of defence.

EMPEROR. So now appears the reason for all the dutiful solicitude you have been showing me this morning! You want to levy private war upon your *own* account, sir, do you! Not content with condemning the Berlichingens and the Selbitzes—

WEISLINGEN. Your Majesty, the ownership of this castle is in legal dispute. The Landgrave has anticipated the judgement of Your Majesty's courts. This is not a private war. It is the enforcement of Imperial justice. It is essential that I have

Your Majesty's permission. The alternative is yet one more
of your provinces reduced into anarchy!

EMPEROR. Very well, very well . . . I suppose I must sign you
a paper. I am out of touch with the times, Weislingen. All of
my sympathies run stirrup-to-stirrup with men like Goetz
Ironhand: yet I cannot but recognize that they will bring my
life's work into ruin if I am not able to stand and cry:
Check. . . Check. . .

WEISLINGEN. Checkmate would be better.

EMPEROR. Eh? . . . No, it is no good . . . I find *you* insufficient as well, sir. I find you *all* insufficient. . . .

He walks away, leaving WEISLINGEN to follow him.

SCENE THREE

Jaxthausen.
A room in Goetz's Castle.   letter from Emperor.

GOETZ, *holding a parchment, in conversation with* SICKINGEN.
MARIA *sitting at a little distance with her back to them.*

SICKINGEN. This is bad news, Goetz, bad: and we can't
pretend other. What are you going to do?

GOETZ. I shall have to forget my hospitality and turn you out of
my castle, Sickingen. Selbitz and myself have been laid
under the Imperial Ban. We are no better than outlaws: the
carrion birds and the wild swine of the forest can take their
dinners off our bodies and the world is forbidden to offer
them hindrance. If you hold my friendship, you are a felon
yourself, so go, ride away, leave our ankles in the trap, man –
we can bide it alone!

SICKINGEN. Indeed I will not.

GOETZ. Look at this summons; it has the Emperor's Seal. My
master's commandment. Look at it, Sickingen.

SICKINGEN. Evil scorpions at the Court made this writing, friend. Maximilian himself could never have dreamed—

GOETZ. My master's commandment . . .

SICKINGEN. Goetz: I will join you! I will bring you—

GOETZ. No. Follow your own work. If your policies succeed among the great Princes who trust you, you will be able to do me ten times the service that any rash battle could produce. This is not self-sacrifice: it is intelligent self-interest. Let us think what Weislingen would do, and do the same ourselves. God's feet, they are teaching us how to live in this creeping world of theirs!

SICKINGEN. Ah, yes, you see, politics – they *do* have their value. But let me at any rate send you some troopers. They need not wear my badge: and they will serve as a reminder I am still your good friend.

GOETZ. For that, sir, I thank you.

SICKINGEN. And let me offer something else while I am here. My hand and my heart to my lady your sister.

GOETZ. What? Do you not realize she has forfeited her name? She was tokened to Weislingen while he stayed in this castle, and now that he has flown clear away peering out for his concubines in the brambles and ditches she carries the mark of a forsaken creature. How can I hand her now into the bed of my friend?

SICKINGEN. Goetz, it is not her fault.

GOETZ. Did I say that it was? But you know very well that such a misfortune can only lead her to the cloister. We must follow the customs, Franz, however heavy they may be.

SICKINGEN. No, no, no despairings. She is young enough to be comforted: and I am the man to do it.

He goes over to MARIA.

My lady Maria, have you heard what we were saying?

GOETZ. Franz von Sickingen is a noble gentleman and my

friend, sister. Whatever should happen now, we are greatly
beholden to him.

MARIA (*to* SICKINGEN). I will speak to you later, sir. You have
a generous heart.

She goes out.

SICKINGEN. She will agree. And so will you, won't you? Of
course you will. Now listen: as you say, it would be foolish
for me personally to join you in your war. But can you wage
it without me? How many men have you got?

GOETZ. Not very many. But they have ridden with me for
years and they won't leave me now. By God, they'd better
not! I have sent Georg to find Selbitz. We will join our
troops together. And if we *are* to be outlaws, we're going to
fight with due ferocity! I know these Imperial Executions –
they look impressive on the muster: but when you meet them
in the field you find a hireling rabble with neither order-of-
march nor proper command. I bear in mind once, to oblige
the County Palatine, I had to lead one of 'em myself against
that fellow Konrad Schotten. They gave me a long screed
from the Imperial Chancellery and said, 'Here's your commission; see you follow it precisely.' I threw the damn thing
back into their bureaucratic faces, and I told them this
straight: 'I fight from no paper, but by eyesight and brain. If
you want Schotten, I'll get him: but I'll get him my own
gate!' And so I did, by God's feet.

SICKINGEN. Ah, you'll spring up again: you'll destroy them
all yet!

GOETZ. I will! I will so! Now you send me these troopers, and
before you leave Jaxthausen, we'll have a word with my good
women and we'll clear up this business about Maria and her
fortune. Because she's got one, you know, and I'm happy to
say that devil of a Weislingen never touched a penny of it!
Come along, let's be hearty: we only live the one life!

SCENE FOUR

Bamberg.
A room in Weislingen's house.

ADELHEID *and* FRANZ.

ADELHEID. So His Majesty has at last been persuaded to act, has he? The highroads are to be made safe for our lawful occasions – shall we take advantage then, and visit our good husband at the Augsburg Court?

FRANZ. He will not be there if you do, madam. Even as I carry his true-loving greetings to your adorable bosom, he himself rides against the Landgrave to redress your long sufferings.

ADELHEID. Indeed, sir, so soon! We have but to petition him, and clap! It is done! How wonderful to have a husband who loses no opportunity of putting himself in danger in the service of his wife. And of absenting himself several hundred miles in order to do so. I suppose when the Landgrave has been crushed, your master will then set out immediately in the opposite direction, for Berlichingen and Selbitz to be crushed in their turn. Is there any chance at all he may turn aside to Bamberg between his expeditions? Or does he find his marital bed to be like the fabulous Upas Tree that scatters out its poisonous miasma five days' journey all around it, and which he must avoid at the cost of his life?

FRANZ. He has refused to concern himself in the Berlichingen business, madam. The Baron von Sirau has command of that Execution. I am certain my lord will fly home to your arms as rapidly as—

ADELHEID. Have you eaten since you rode from Augsburg, Franz?

FRANZ. Eaten? Food or drink – no. I stand here. You are there. That is sufficient.

ADELHEID. Come here. Nearer.

FRANZ. How near is near enough? Nearer still, lady?

ADELHEID. Stop. You are very well trained in Court compliments, Franz: which do not necessarily carry with them sincerity. To prove you we must look into your eyes, not listen to your words . . . Here is my hand. Kiss it.

FRANZ. Like this, madam?

ADELHEID. Like that . . . Good . . .

She puts him back from her a little.

You have warm lips, very warm. That is as it should be. I shall bear it in mind . . . Thank you, Franz, you may go. You have carried out your errand with courtesy and dispatch.

SCENE FIVE

The camp of the Imperial Execution.

A CAPTAIN *and* OFFICERS (*all wearing the* EMPEROR'S *badge*) *in a council-of-war.*

CAPTAIN. It is without question we have a very difficult task, gentlemen. The Emperor has expressly forbidden us to kill either Selbitz or Berlichingen. But to take such men alive – well, we must be cautious, that is all!

FIRST OFFICER. A Fabian strategy, in fact.

CAPTAIN. If that is what you insist on calling it, yes.

SECOND OFFICER. Frankly, sir, I take no pleasure in this campaign. I have nothing but admiration for these knights and their courage. I should prefer to be with them.

CAPTAIN. But you are not, sir: you are with us! So frame your duties accordingly, if you please.

FIRST OFFICER. Ah, Fabius was wise indeed: but Hannibal was *great*! Why cannot we make a sudden and glorious onfall and seize the smoking dragons by the throat!

CAPTAIN. The mouths of the dragons may not be quite as wide

as yours, young sir: but they are very full of teeth, and you
will find so soon enough.

FIRST OFFICER. H'm.

CAPTAIN. I have begun by sending a letter to Berlichingen to
order him to surrender. If he refuses, as he certainly will, I
shall set forward a small force of an exploratory nature and
test his dispositions.

FIRST OFFICER. Sir, let me lead it!

CAPTAIN. Are you acquainted with the country? It is not quite
as open as the Plains of Philippi, you know.

FIRST OFFICER. One of my troopers was raised here, I am
told. No doubt he will be able to guide me.

CAPTAIN. No doubt . . . As you wish, then. But make sure
you have an intelligent Serjeant-Major: and in the name of
the Sacrament, sir, I beg you to be careful!

SCENE SIX

Jaxthausen.
Guardroom in Goetz's Castle.

GOETZ. *To him,* GEORG.

GEORG. Wouldn't tell me his name, but he's clearly a soldier. A
right strong-set man with fiery dark eyes.

GOETZ. Bring him in, boy.

> GEORG *beckons in* LERSE, *a flamboyantly-equipped mer-
> cenary.*

God be with you, sir. I don't think I know you.

LERSE. Probably not, Berlichingen. But I know *you* all right.

GOETZ. What do you want?

LERSE. I've brought you a present.

GOETZ. A present?

LERSE. Me . . . Don't look so surprised: I'm told you're wanting men.

GOETZ. By God, sir, I am! But I confess I see nothing attractive in the work I have to offer. This is about to become a beleaguered castle: and everybody in it is under the Emperor's Ban. Be very clear in your mind what it is you are joining.

LERSE. I know all about it. I make my choice of service by the sight of *men*, and not their fortunes.

GOETZ. What do they call you?

LERSE. Lerse. Fritz Lerse.

GOETZ. And your experience, Lerse?

LERSE. Do you remember when the Palatine asked you to bring in Konrad Schotten a few years ago?

GOETZ. Of course I do. Well?

LERSE. A small village on the Hassfurt road. Half a hundred horsemen lying in wait. You rode into the middle with no more than sixteen.

GOETZ. That's right. So we did. And they all ran away from us except two. One of them was Erhard Truchss – a grand fighter, but a fool of a captain. I put a bullet through his eyeball.

LERSE. What about the other?

GOETZ. By God – *you*.

LERSE. Yes, sir, me. You're quite right about Erhard – if they'd given *me* the setting of that little ambush, we'd have had all of your heads strung from the village maypole in less than ten minutes. But as you say, they ran. And being no belted knight with standards to live up to, I fired all my barrels empty and turned and ran after. But I made myself remembered.

GOETZ. You did, Lerse: God's feet, yes, you did!

He opens his shirt and shows one of the scars on his body.

Look, this one was yours. It took six weeks to heal. And I can tell you I'm damn glad to have you come and join us. What length of engagement?

LERSE. One year. And seeing you're on the run at present, I'll serve you without pay and take it out in plunder. Is that agreeable?

GOETZ. Certainly not. Whatever my circumstances, I always pay my men. Besides, I doubt very much if there's going to be any plunder – any more, for any of us . . .

LERSE. Aye . . . aye . . . the profession of arms is a sinking trade these days, it seems. All the Princes can ever think of is what they're pleased to call pacification. What this country needs is something like a big outbreak of heresy to burn up men's hearts and put a bit of oil of hatred into our matchlocks! Then there'd be good work for us and good advantage from it!

A TROOPER *wearing* SELBITZ'S *badge enters.*

SELBITZ TROOPER. Berlichingen, my master Hans von Selbitz sends you his greeting. He'll be here with fifty men first thing in the morning.

GOETZ. Good. Very good.

SELBITZ TROOPER. There's another fifty men, and all, wandering in the forest. They have the appearance of a gang of burgess-wives pricing fruit from stall to stall of the market, and it's coming on to rain – the poor bastards, they've not even brought their greatcoats! Selbitz reckons they're the advance party of the Imperial Execution – have we to go out and do 'em?

GOETZ. Why not? Tonight. Tell your master he can bring his riders round their rear and *we'll* take 'em from the front. You've got a good horse with you, Lerse?

LERSE. I have.

GOETZ. Right. Then we'll ride!

SCENE SEVEN

Forest and marsh.
A dark night and raining.

Enter two TROOPERS *with the* EMPEROR'S *badge. Both very bedraggled.*

FIRST IMPERIALIST TROOPER (*he carries a dilapidated parcel*). Hey-up! Hey-ey, you, Trooper! What d'you think you're on! Why aren't you with your Squadron?

SECOND IMPERIALIST TROOPER. By Christ, I thought you wor the Troop-Sarnt. Don't play jokes like that, boy. I can tell you I'm in no condition. It's this bloody pouring rain; I'm fair bloody saturated. I've had the running squitters in me guts all the last six hours – had to get down and squat behind a bush about every half a mile! And I can't take it no longer. I thought I'd just nip back into that village over there and see if I can't scrounge summat dry to put on— Hey, you won't let on that you've seen me, will you? They'd spread-eagle me to a gun-carriage if I'm caught.

FIRST IMPERIALIST TROOPER. They would, boy, and all . . . Where did you leave the Squadron, then?

SECOND IMPERIALIST TROOPER. The other side of this forest. It'll take you about an hour – you'll have to walk; you can't ride, it's all bog and bloody marsh. Where ha' *you* been sliding off to, any road?

FIRST IMPERIALIST TROOPER. The officer wanted his dinner, that's where! I had to knock up an old fool of a pig-herder and commandeer it off his wife!

He shows his parcel.

Hot sausages and kraut, begod – leastroads, they *were* . . . Like, they've deteriorated a bit on the transit . . . I'll tell you, have you ever seen such a ramshackle bloody shambles as this night's bloody effort, eh? Soldiering? They call it

soldiering – I'd call it the woodchoppers' harvest home, none
but bloody mugginses invited, please come dressed as frogs
and toads on account of the weather—

   Horse-hoofs heard.

SECOND IMPERIALIST TROOPER. Ss-sst – listen!

FIRST IMPERIALIST TROOPER. My God, there's someone
coming! Horses through the thicket. It can't be our lot—
Here, me for the tree-tops, boy—

   He climbs a tree.

SECOND IMPERIALIST TROOPER. I'm getting in the bull-
rushes – they'll see you up there, you know—

   He jumps into the marsh.
   GOETZ, LERSE, GEORG, *and* GOETZ TROOPERS, *wrapped
in heavy cloaks over their harness, run in.*

GOETZ. We'll have to leave the horses here and get through on
foot – we ought to cut them off at the charcoal-burners'
crossing. Come on!

   They hurry off into the forest.
   FIRST IMPERIALIST TROOPER *descends.*

FIRST IMPERIALIST TROOPER. Aye aye, I'm still alive; they
didn't see me! But it looks bad for the Squadron, though,
dunnit? Hey, Michel, they've gone – Michel—

   SECOND IMPERIALIST TROOPER *gives a choking cry
from the marsh.*

Michel, what's happened? Michel! By Christ, he's stuck in
the mud! Pull yourself out, man – get hold of a branch – I
can't get in to help you—

   While he is stooping into the reeds, two TROOPERS *in*
SELBITZ'S *badge come in behind him.*

FIRST SELBITZ TROOPER. Turn around, you! Out, out, out!

The FIRST IMPERIALIST TROOPER *turns round and holds his hands up.*

Drop your sword-belt, *quick!*

He obeys. The SECOND SELBITZ TROOPER *picks it up.*

SECOND SELBITZ TROOPER. Where's the other one? Through here?

FIRST IMPERIALIST TROOPER (*the cry from the marsh has died away into gurgles*). He was, but he's not now: he's sunk in, he's gone under, he's smothered in all that shit – . . . Who are you? Berlichingen?

FIRST SELBITZ TROOPER. Selbitz, us. Berlichingen's gone forward.

FIRST IMPERIALIST TROOPER. What you going to do to me?

FIRST SELBITZ TROOPER. You'll find. Come on. Get moving. On, on, on—

They drive him out with them.

SCENE EIGHT

The camp of the Imperial Execution.

CAPTAIN *and* OFFICER (*the* SECOND OFFICER *of Scene Five*).

CAPTAIN. Thank God at least it's left off raining for a while; let the sun get up a quarter of an hour over these damned tree-tops and we'll see where we've got to. Any reliable news out of the advance party yet?

SECOND OFFICER. They're still coming in, in twos and threes. I get the impression they've been entirely broken. Thrown their guns away, half of them. Weeping and sobbing.

CAPTAIN. No officers back?

SECOND OFFICER. They could all be dead. If that roaring Lancelot you put in command – if *he's* dead, there'll be no loss to any of us.

CAPTAIN. I did not ask for your commentary, sir. Your own capabilities have yet to be proved. Hello, here he is now—

The FIRST OFFICER, *wounded, is helped in by a* TROOPER – *both filthy and exhausted.*

And how is Gnaius Pompeius Magnus this morning, hey? A little the worse for the weather? Your report, sir, at once!

FIRST OFFICER. We got lost, that's all.

CAPTAIN. Lost.

FIRST OFFICER. I defy any officer to lead cavalry through there the way it was last night. Round and round in circles, tripping and tangling, horses breaking their legs in the bog before we even *heard* the enemy – and he came in on foot every side of us like watersnakes!

CAPTAIN. This famous trooper of yours with all his local knowledge – what happened to *him*?

FIRST OFFICER. How should I know? I think he went home. I think most of 'em went home. . . . Look, I've got two broken ribs – do I have to talk all morning? Can I not have the surgeon!

CAPTAIN. Take him away. Useless young idiot.

The FIRST OFFICER *is helped out. Another* OFFICER *enters.*

THIRD OFFICER. We're getting a clearer view now of what's happened. Berlichingen and Selbitz have combined their forces in the night, sir. They surrounded the advance party, broke it up, and they're coming on through the forest towards the rest of us.

CAPTAIN. How many are they?

THIRD OFFICER. Can't be more than a hundred. I don't believe their commanders have them very well under control; they're all mad excited with what they've done

already, and I think a good many of 'em are drunk. They've
left their horses behind.

CAPTAIN. Now, that's a good point. They're all basically
riders, not foot-soldiers at all. So what we'll do is this: take
back our cavalry behind the high ground, scatter the infantry
on the open heath in front, let the enemy think we are all in
disorder – which we too damn nearly *are* – and when he
comes out at us, ride him down with the horses! What's the
ground like up there?

SECOND OFFICER. On the heath? It's wet, but it's not *too* wet.
It's possible to ride.

CAPTAIN. Good. So: to your commands, gentlemen! And any
repetition of last night's disgraceful nonsense, I shall hang
the man in charge, whatever his rank!

SCENE NINE

The edge of the forest, looking out on to the heath.

TROOPERS *of* SELBITZ'S *Force run across the stage, cheering
and shouting,* GOETZ, LERSE, *and* GEORG, *trying to hold them
back. Small-arms fire. Bugle calls.*

GOETZ. Call them back, call them back, for God's sake, Georg—
Find my trumpeter; tell him to sound the recall. Where the
devil's Johann? Get hold of Peter; tell him to fetch those
fellows back!

GEORG *runs off.*

Jesus, Mary, and Joseph – I said bide within the trees. Have
they all of them gone mad! What's happened to Selbitz! Has
anyone seen Johann?

LERSE. If that's your squire you mean, he's dead; he caught a
bullet in the pursuit and fell down in a bog-hole. These are

Selbitz's stupid clowns running all over the wilderness like
the ten tribes of Israel! Come back, come back, and let's have
some order! I've got all ours in hand and they are formed up
behind. . . . Now listen to me, Berlichingen, the next time
you reckon to put horsemen on foot and let them run wild to
the four winds of heaven, you ought to make sure that your
confederate commander isn't an old man with a wooden leg,
that's all!

GOETZ. Don't you talk to me like that— You've been in my
service twenty-four hours; I've known Hans von Selbitz for
thirty-three *years*!

LERSE. There's only one standard to work by in this game, and
that's the highest professional standard, and that's how I
fight! I led a squadron at the Battle of Marignano, I'd have
you know!

GOETZ. That will do, that will do, Lerse! God's feet, if you
forgot yourself in that battle the same as you are today, it's
not a surprising thing that the Emperor lost it! Here comes
Selbitz at last – he's the bravest knight in Franconia, so you
mind your manners!

SELBITZ *hobbles in.*

SELBITZ. Goetz, we've let you down. We're entirely responsible. I shall take every tenth man and flog him within an
inch of his life and then I shall take every fifth man and—

GOETZ. Never mind, never mind, we've pulled them all back.
No damage done.

SELBITZ. Too many men killed last night in the forest. We
drove 'em off, fair enough, but we can't do it again wi' that
like of casualties.

LERSE. He's got horsemen over that hill. He's going to taunt us
to come out and then he'll ride down on us. What are we
going to do? We're in the smaller numbers; we've got to
keep the initiative.

Re-enter GEORG.

GEORG. Sir, sir, Berlichingen! There's three fresh companies coming up the southern road behind of us! They're carrying no banners, but I recognize their Captain. They're Sickingen's men!

SELBITZ. Sickingen, by God! Is he with them himself?

GEORG. No.

GOETZ. I should hope he damn well isn't. What sort of soldiers are they, boy? Horse-troopers?

GEORG. Pikemen.

SELBITZ. I'd heard of it, I'd heard of it! He's been hiring himself Switzers! The best foot-soldiers in Europe—

GOETZ. They ran away at Marignano – didn't they, Lerse?

LERSE. Never mind that now. They're here and that's enough. Sirs, will you take my advice? We'll dispute this clever enemy according to his own rules. Let the Selbitz men run on forward just like they *were* doing – when he sends down his cavalry, you lure 'em back toward the forest, then we face 'em with the Switzers drawn up in phalanx. If they know a quarter of what they've been trained, they can keep these horsemen playing for hours like a salmon on a line – in the meantime our young lads behind can have brought up our remounts; we get on 'em refreshed, we're once more in our own trade, and with any luck at all we can hoick them on the gaff!

GOETZ. It sounds good, sir. We'll do it. Georg, fetch the trumpeter. Then run to the Switzers and tell them the word. God's feet, that man Sickingen, he's a friend to be proud of!

SCENE TEN

Camp of the Imperial Execution.

CAPTAIN *dictating a letter to the* THIRD OFFICER.

CAPTAIN. Address it to His Majesty and the Commissioners of the Diet at Augsburg with the correct formality of heading, and continue as follows:

> The Baron von Sirau has the honour to report upon his command of the Imperial Execution against the knights of Berlichingen and Selbitz, both under Your Majesty's Ban. After unsuccessful preliminary night operations, as described in my last report, I withdrew my advance party and was thereby enabled to entice the enemy to attack us upon the open heath: where my mounted counter-attack was met unexpectedly—

Underline 'unexpectedly'.

> —by a force of Swiss pikemen, assessed as at least five companies. These troops displayed no colours, but interrogation of prisoners has revealed that they are in the pay of the so-called Free Knight Franz von Sickingen, which information I commend to Your Majesty's notice. Two hours' severe fighting ensued, with heavy losses upon both sides. The enemy has withdrawn once again into the forest . . . The enemy has withdrawn once again into the forest, but it is as yet too early to regard this engagement as in any way victorious.

I do *not* propose to tell the Emperor we have been completely outwitted: but I suppose I must make *some* reference to the truth.

> Your Majesty's Imperial Execution has suffered heavily from casualties, and, I regret to say, even more heavily from desertions. I cannot emphasize too strongly—

More underlining, if you please.

> I cannot emphasize too strongly the vital importance in campaigns of this nature, of appointing subordinate commanders who are acquainted very fully, not only with their Captain, but also with the men under their charge. In both instances has the composition of this force been in default. Our original muster was five hundred; we are now reduced

to one hundred and fifty. I am awaiting reinforcements, which I trust—

Underline.

—which I trust will include an adequate siege-train. Upon their arrival I shall march directly to Berlichingen's castle of Jaxthausen and prepare to invest it. I am informed that his own losses have been such as to prevent him molesting me on my way thither. His confederate Selbitz was wounded and in all probability killed in this morning's fighting. I regret this, as being contrary to Your Majesty's instructions: but I would point out that once open conflict has been joined, it is not easy to ensure that a hostile commander remains uninjured. The soldiers in Selbitz's pay have largely dispersed, and indeed, their presence in the battle did little service to the enemy's operations, as they showed throughout a fortunate lack of discipline – matched only, I may say, by that prevalent among certain squadrons of this, Your Majesty's, force. I deeply regret this: but feel unable to excuse it.

Conclude the report in the usual fashion and bring it to me for signature. I expect it will mean my professional ruin.

SCENE ELEVEN

Jaxthausen.
Guardroom in Goetz's Castle.

Noise and bustle. Two TROOPERS (*one of* GOETZ'S *men, and one of* SELBITZ'S) *carry in* SELBITZ, *wounded, on an improvised stretcher, and lay him on the floor.* GOETZ *comes in after. All the men in this scene are out of breath and bear marks of hard fighting. Other of* GOETZ'S TROOPERS *run in and out on various urgent military errands.*

GOETZ. Carry him up to the main building, put him in my bedroom. Peter, go and find my wife; tell her—

SELBITZ. No, no. I'll stay here. I want to see what's going on begod; you'll not box me up to die in a stinking bedroom – flannels and hot water, and pisspots and physic – at my time o' life! Take your hands off me, Trooper: and do what you're told. That's the way, boy, yes. Just on account I'm laid out cold and flat like a threshold flagstone, don't you be thinking I've not got teeth to bite you if you come too near—

GOETZ. Leave him be, then: leave him . . . What about the rest of the wounded?

GOETZ TROOPER. They're clearing the floor of the big barn in the inner bailey. I told them to get more straw from the cattleyard if they hadn't enough . . .

GOETZ. Good. We'll leave the women to attend to them – they know what they're to do. I'll have a walk round there myself in a few minutes when things have got settled.

Enter GEORG.

GEORG. We're all over the bridge and inside, sir. Shall I—

GOETZ. Yes, do. Bridge up, gates closed, portcullis down – pass the word directly.

GEORG. Yes sir.

Calls to someone off:

Bridge up, gates closed, portcullis down – all right?

The order is repeated by a voice offstage.

GOETZ. They're some way behind us; we've got time to take breath. How many are we? Did you check the numbers?

GEORG. Thirty-two wounded disabled, of walking wounded and fit men there's twenty-four of ours, forty-eight of Sickingen's Switzers, and—

SELBITZ. How many of mine?

GEORG. Six.

SELBITZ. What's that? . . . How many?

GEORG. Six.

SELBITZ. God. Jesus God, is that all I've got left? Goetz, they all ran away. Why, they all ran to buggery— *deserters*

GOETZ. Take it quiet now, take it steady; they thought you were dead, that's all—

SELBITZ. I am not dead.

GOETZ. They believed their service was finished; it's their right to be off. Besides, this isn't their castle; they're not bound to defend it. *excusing them.*

GEORG. Sickingen's here, you know.

GOETZ. He isn't . . . How?

GEORG. Came before we did. He's reviewing his pikemen now, in the base-court.

GOETZ. The fool, the interfering fool – I told him to— Has Lerse come back yet?

GEORG. No, sir.

GOETZ. Has nobody seen him?

SELBITZ TROOPER. Not since last afternoon. Dietrich said he was knocked off his horse in the mellay at the waterfall; there's no one seen him since.

GOETZ. Jesus, Mary, and Joseph – I made sure *he'd* still be with us.

GEORG. He can't have deserted – he must have been killed.

GOETZ. Not Lerse, no – too crafty by far, that lad, to get himself *killed*. I'll offer a wager he's in command of an Imperial Squadron at this very moment. That's what you'd call the Professional Approach, boy: bear it in mind. If you come out of this alive, you might as well learn it.

Enter SICKINGEN.

Ah, the smart politician, in his gay silk coat and all – though perhaps not *too* smart? What are *you* doing here?

Enter ELISABETH *and* MARIA.

ELISABETH. He came to marry his wife, Goetz, before it was too late.

GOETZ. Oho, he did so? And have you married her?

SICKINGEN. Oh yes, I've married her. In your castle chapel. We caught the village priest on the point of scuttering off with the rest of your peasants, and one, two, three: he read the Book on us – oh, quite correctly done, Goetz: all the holy words of God.

MARRIED

GOETZ. You might have waited.

SICKINGEN. Too quick an emergency. I wanted her out of this before the siege began. I'm sending her home with a guard of my horsemen now.

MARIA. No, you are not. I am staying in this castle.

SICKINGEN. I am sending you home . . . Her girl's packing up the luggage, and as soon as its ready— Look, Goetz, of course I'd far rather you'd have been here with us to have given her away and done it all properly, but as things were standing, we had to make do with Elisabeth and a pair of my servants.

GOETZ. But what about the contract?

SICKINGEN. My God, he thinks I'm cheating him! We can write it out later! Besides, if you like, and if we survive for it, we can always have another wedding: in a big church with choir-boys and a good breakfast after, and make everything regular. Time mendeth all . . .

He goes over to SELBITZ.

Hello, Hans, how are you? The leg that isn't there still itching at the toe, is it?

SELBITZ. I want no man to talk no more to me . . . They all ran to buggery . . .

SICKINGEN (*aside, to* GOETZ). Did they?

GOETZ (*aside*). Some o' them. Not good . . .

SICKINGEN (*aloud*). At all events, what's left of my Switzer boys seem to be in good shape. I reckon we'll find them useful enough when it starts.

GOETZ. You are not proposing to *stay* here, are you?

SICKINGEN. Naturally. Have you any objections?

GOETZ. I thought we agreed this was none of your war.

SICKINGEN. Oh well, that was last week. We're supposed to be in a League, you and I – to help one another at need.

GOETZ. I'm telling you: go home, Sickingen. You have half an hour to do it. The postern gate's still open. Take your wife and make her happy. And while you're about it, you'd better take my boy. What's happened to Karl?

ELISABETH. He's sick.

GOETZ. What with?

ELISABETH. Caught a fever of some sort. I've got him in his bed.

GOETZ. All the more reason why he ought to be away. Harness a horse-litter and carry him in that. Maria will look after him; she's used to it, isn't she?

MARIA. Goetz, I want to stay—

GOETZ. No, no, no! I have not got heart any more to argue. I am giving you orders: I am the lord of this castle. Maria, you will take my boy with you and you will go. Sickingen, you will go, too. And so will your Switzers.

SICKINGEN. Those men are in *your* service now – it is ridiculous to—

GOETZ. There is no value for pikemen in a beleaguered fortification and I don't want to have to feed them. For God's sake, you stupid blockhead, will you do what I ask?

SICKINGEN. Very well, I will . . . It is not good in adversity, Goetz, to give offence to *all* your friends. Good-bye to you, sir.

MARIA. Goetz, good-bye.

SICKINGEN. Selbitz, live well. Put blood on your banner, man, and fly it from the roof! You'll destroy them all yet . . . Come on, wife; we're superfluous here. Come!

He takes MARIA *out.*

GOETZ. Better for a bride to weep on her wedding day than a year or two after . . . Is Karl going to die?

ELISABETH. I don't know. It is possible.

GOETZ. I expect Franz von Sickingen keeps a doctor in his house. He is rich enough for it.

LERSE (*shouts from a distance*). Hi hi hi – Berlichingen!

GOETZ. Who's that—

GEORG (*at the window*). Lerse!

GOETZ. God's feet, he's come back to us!

He goes to the window and calls.

Lerse, you're late! Go round by the postern; there's some men coming out, so you can come in. Make it sharp, though: we're pressed!

Comes back into room.

What did I tell you? Too crafty by far . . . Ha ha.

SELBITZ. Is that that dog-faced mercenary of yours?

GOETZ. That's right, he's with us again.

SELBITZ. I don't like that man. He's lacking in respect. A new man. I don't like him.

GOETZ. Now quieten down, Hans, or you'll do your wound some damage. There's none of us likes new things, but we sometimes have to take them. Do you want some more water?

SELBITZ. No . . . Goetz, come here, come here. I'm going to tell you summat. You think you're not going to live beyond after this siege. You think your enemies out there, Princes, and the Bishops, men of the cities, all the like o' that – your enemies, eh?

GOETZ. They're barely my *friends*, any road.

SELBITZ. No, no. You watch the men with the dung on their boots and the patches on their jackets. The countryside these last years, someone's been there . . . someone's been telling 'em things they've no right to know about. Falsehoods, the bad falsehoods, the lying words of Christ. Goetz, they think they want to take the world!

GOETZ. I don't know what you're talking about – his mind must be wandering . . .

SELBITZ. No, I can see it. I can see it, and I *know*. The world, Goetz, the world: someone's turned it upside down. Up . . . side . . . down . . .

Enter LERSE.

I don't like that man. He has the face of a dog.

SELBITZ *falls back on to his stretcher.* ꓹ*DEAD*

LERSE. Me? So they say, but I still survive 'em all . . . Is he dead?

ELISABETH. Yes, soldier, he's dead. How comes it you're not?

LERSE. Because I watch where I'm going and I look for no one to follow me . . . You know, I shouldn't have thought he had a very serious wound. Of course, he was old . . .

GOETZ (*to* LERSE). How long before they get here?

LERSE. How long? They're here already. I saw them fording the river. There's more than two hundred; they must have been reinforced. *enemy near now*

GOETZ. Do they have any cannon?

LERSE. Not yet.

GOETZ. That's good. If they've not got their ordnance, they can bide out there and whistle until the angels fetch them home. I'm not over-certain about the strength of these barbican walls – we may have to withdraw into the inner bailey and the keep. What do you think?

LERSE. Hold 'em here as long as we can first, then move back in fighting. The harder we hurt 'em, the less happy they'll be – good professional logic.

A trumpet outside.

Hear that? They're beginning their business in an orderly style. They want a word through the window before they start throwing things.

GOETZ. We might as well hear what they have to tell us, I suppose.

He opens the window shutter, and calls.

Hallo! Who blows his trumpet at Berlichingen's gate? Take off your hat, young man, before you talk to *me*! Dandy red coat he's got on, a white staff in his hand, and a great roll of parchment – where does he imagine he is, for God's sake – opening a session of the Imperial Diet?

The voice of the HERALD, *blown on the wind, is dimly heard.*

I can't hear a word – why doesn't he realize, if he calls into the wind, he's going to need a bit of *voice*? . . . Ah, I heard *that* all right. 'Unconditional surrender.' We know what to say about *that*. So I'll tell him my answer, and duck your heads when I've finished.

He calls through the window again.

D'you hear me, d'you hear me! This is Ironhand Berlichingen here, and you can listen to *me*! If His Majesty the Emperor comes before my walls, I shall yield him due obedience, as indeed I always have! But any man else can come and lick my arsehole, *if* he can get to it, and that's all I've got to tell you! Hah!

He slams the shutter to, and there is a volley of small-arms fire from outside.

And now, me boys, it starts . . .

SCENE TWELVE

Jaxthausen.
Kitchen of Goetz's Castle.

ELISABETH *is preparing soup in a cauldron over the fire.* GOETZ *enters. Intermittent shooting, off.*

ELISABETH. Three more days only, at the present level of eating. If we cut down the rations we could call it another week, maybe a fortnight. Then we butcher the horses. After that—

running out of food

GOETZ. Catching rats and boiling boots. It's been done, you know.

ELISABETH. All right for us. What about the wounded? There are more of them every day.

GOETZ. Came on me too quickly altogether, this affair. Forty-eight hours further warning, I could have rounded up cattle, got in loads of grain – I was counting on my peasants to send up supplies while we were out in the forest. They didn't do it. Why?

ELISABETH. They did the reverse. They took themselves clear off and took their stock with them.

GOETZ. But why *should* they, Elisabeth? I don't understand it. I have protected them all of these years . . . We're pulling in back from the outward walls this morning. We haven't enough soldiers left to man them. I told Lerse to start exploding the breeches of the great cannon on the barbican: they're too heavy to bring in and in any case the inner bastions aren't strong enough built.

A dull explosion heard.

There's the first gone, now.

A second explosion.

And that's for number two. It's a pity to hear it, Elisabeth: I had a love for those guns. I gave them both good names and engraved them on their muzzles. 'Wake-up' I called the one, and 'Danger' was the other. Ah, pity, pity, great pity . . . If we hold out long enough and frighten them enough, it's conceivable, you know, we may get advantageous terms. But 'Unconditional surrender' – oh no, no, no . . .

A TROOPER *enters with a brazier and tongs.*

TROOPER. Hot coals from the fire.

He starts filling his brazier.

We're running out of bullets for the hand-guns. Lerse's bringing down the moulding tools to make some more. He's had the boys ripping off lead-guttering and that from the roof.

GOETZ. How much powder left?

TROOPER. Powder, still plenty. But we need to go easy.

Enter LERSE *with bullet mould and some strips of lead. Another* TROOPER *to help him.*

LERSE (*setting to work*). I'm using this leading out of the windows to make a start – good glazier's work here – craftsmanship, time and labour spent: and it all goes into death . . . Bellows, boy: that's right . . . Time and labour spent on *me*, and all; there was a father and a mother, they had pleasure, what's more, and an education they gave me, and a portion of money to go out into the world: and how do I spend it? Converting love and craftsmanship into implements of death – and I *like* to do it, too; there's a bloody beauty in this work. Now, if you were a philosopher, Berlichingen, instead of a belted knight with standards to live up to, you could no doubt find a moral? . . . Is she soft enough yet? Get ready to pour when I tell you.

GEORG *enters with a chunk of lead.*

GEORG. Here's a length of rainspout. Any good?

LERSE. Very good. Put it down, son.

ELISABETH *is pouring the soup into bowls.*

GOETZ. We'll have our soup in here, Elisabeth. Georg, take the pot out and let the men on the watch serve themselves where they are.

GEORG *obeys.*

It all seems very quiet on a sudden, doesn't it? I'm surprised they made no move at all when we drew back from the walls.

LERSE. They're a sight shy of us be now, that's what. They'll be coming soon enough, though.

GEORG *runs back in.*

GEORG. Summat funny in the camp down there. Running about and shouting. And what looked like draught-oxen on the road. I couldn't see it clearly, but I think he's bringing up guns.

GOETZ. At last. I knew it. He's been waiting for this. It'll take him some hours to dig 'em in position – but once he does . . . These walls were never made to hold the shock of ordnance.

ELISABETH. Could you not make a sortie?

GOETZ. What do you think, Lerse?

LERSE. We haven't enough men. We've done all we can already, fighting in the open. It seems to me, speaking purely from the craftsman's side of the business and leave honour and such-like severely apart, that this is the moment we negotiate terms. They don't know our losses, they don't know about our supplies, and I doubt furthermore if they have much acquaintance with the state of our architecture. Would you like me to stroll out with a trumpet-of-parley and see what I can see?

GOETZ. I don't know . . . Elisabeth?

ELISABETH. If you don't do it now, you'll get no chance later. You *could* save the lives of all of your men.

GOETZ. It might be best to have a try . . . Off you go, Lerse. But remember: nothing dishonourable. No humiliation. Talk to them from strength: that's the only way I'll tolerate.

LERSE. Strength is the word! Cross your heart and count a prayer.

They all cross themselves.

ALL. Holy Jesus . . . Amen.

LERSE. Right: I'm away.

He swallows his soup in a gulp and goes.

GOETZ (*calling after him*). And if there's any o' those lads outside who aren't on their duty, send 'em in to me – I want to have a word. While he's doing his talking we're all going to enjoy a drink. The last of my cellar and it could very well be the last we'll ever need.

He has taken a bottle from a shelf.

Have we no more than only this bottle?

ELISABETH (*aside to him*). There's one more in the cupboard – I was keeping it for you and me.

GOETZ. No, no, we'll have it round.

She fetches the wine.
A number of TROOPERS *come in.*

Come in to the kitchen, men, come in, set yourselves down. I'm going to give you a toast and I want you to drink it!

GEORG *and* ELISABETH *serve the drinks.*

To the health of the Emperor! Go on, men, drink! Because he is our lord and we are his servants. Drink!

They drink.

I say it is of no importance he is in arms against us now. Knighthood and freedom are the truth of this Empire – whatever else you see, or men tell you that you *should* see, shut your eyes, blind eyes, blind walking, do *not* ask the questions! I ride for what I always rode for and what my father rode and all our house before him. One path to follow, one speed to travel it, certain places to rest upon the way: and that is *all* of your duty. The Emperor used to understand it: some of us still do.

He holds up the bottle and pours out the last drops.

Look at this: the last few drops run out. That's all of us here, that's what *we* are, and why I gave this toast. Now that we've drunk it, there'll be nobody left to drink it any more. The country falls under the rule of the Princes and the Aldermen of the great cities. They have destroyed the rhythm of life, because they will not be content – they say all the time: 'Make it new, make it new, improve it!' They say, 'We are not afraid to be in error, and to create injustice, because we are tearing down the old injustice, and that is our only work!' But *I* say I am not afraid to be in error and to preserve that old injustice, if that is what it was, if by so doing I can also preserve the order of rank and hereditary truth that was given us from the beginning, and which, rightly looked at, is the only framework of a life of freedom. How can you be free unless you know where you can't go? Otherwise, don't you see, we shall all of us be lost!

GEORG. But the Princes are hereditary, I don't quite understand—

GOETZ. The Princes have corrupted themselves, boy, by endeavouring to control men who know how to control themselves. In the old days it was different. I remember how the Margrave of Anhalt, when I was his page, how he used to make these hunting-parties for his people, and how, under God's beautiful heaven, we all sat round him on the grass, and there we ate our dinners, in our due order, and every man had his place, from the Margrave at the top and the Free Knights beside him, to the soldiers and the servants and the countrymen, with their honest round heads and their pretty sunburnt girls, whom they'd tumble in the ditches after, I can tell you! But there they were, and they rejoiced every one in the pleasure of their master! This could have continued; it was the golden age: but no, it has been broken into pieces. Broken.

ELISABETH. Greed and ingratitude and irreverence have broken it. Useless destruction, that is all I can see.

FIRST TROOPER. It's argued, you know, we've done violence to the order ourselves, on account of our ridings – but surely all we were doing was to fight for our right!

GOETZ. True, true. But in an honest world there should be no need of fighting.

GEORG. Oh no, no need – what would we do! How would we live?

GOETZ. How? Why, by living. In our castles, controlling our land, and judging among our people. Of course, there would be hunting, ridding the forest of wolves and so forth, and we could ride against the Turk! Plenty of warfare there, boy, but honest Christian warfare that a good knight could believe in! How can anyone believe in *this* – in arms against the Emperor and our people grow to hate us! I do not understand what has gone wrong with the world.

SECOND TROOPER. That Hans von Selbitz, he thought he understood – upside-down *he* called it.

ELISABETH. He was a good lord to his people.

GOETZ. But, you see, they forsook him in the battle: it broke his heart, Elisabeth.

FIRST TROOPER. That's the truth, Berlichingen: it did indeed. Peter made a song.

GOETZ. A song?

SECOND TROOPER. Like a little lament, you might say – one of these with his own last words in it, or that's what we suppose. Do you want me to sing it?

He sings.

> They called me Hans von Selbitz
> And I rode through many a war:
> A gunstone cut my leg in two
> And that did pain me sore.
>
> Lay me now in the dark forest
> Where the brown pine-needles fall.
> For my people ran away from me
> And that was the worst of all.

Stand upright then my timber leg
And plant it on my grave
And write one word to say I died
Being neither a coward nor knave.

But my people ran away from me
For why I do not know:
They were not worthy of my trust
And they melted like the snow.

GOETZ. That's a good song, Peter: it carries the spirit of the
man – why, he might have written it himself! It all comes
down to this: No one can live without he trusts in his people.
God gave us the power of knighthood. What adversity can
take it away or what words can deny it? Only those of the
Devil: for it is he that asks the questions. We should pay
heed, every one of us, that we don't dare try to answer them.

LERSE *runs in.*

LERSE. I've done it, I've done it, I've frightened him silly!
Berlichingen, he's giving us marvellous terms – we can all of
us go – men, weapons, horses, and armour! We have to leave
the castle as it is and all the food and fittings in it: but we
ourselves can ride free men to wherever we want to go!
GOETZ. Lerse, you know your trade! Shake me by the hand!
Elisabeth, all the valuables in the castle, silver plate and so
forth, bury them under the dungeon, there'll be little enough
food for 'em to find, never mind about *that* – we can live off
the country once we get clear. Bring every hand-gun we can
lift, powder, bullets, swords, lances – banners, bring all the
banners! Well, this the end of my Jaxthausen, soldiers. By
the entitlement of your service, I should grant you all your
release. Any man who wishes it can have it directly. But I
would rather you didn't. Who wants to bide?

TROOPERS. We all do, Berlichingen! We're all your men yet!
Ironhand for ever!

GOETZ. Ironhand for ever! And long live the Emperor!

SCENE THIRTEEN

Augsburg.
Weislingen's lodging.

WEISLINGEN, ADELHEID, *and* MARGARET. FRANZ *in attendance.*

ADELHEID. You are a dutiful servant, my lord. You are so kind
and so loving. You have defeated Hesse and my property is
restored. You do everything I ask you – I have never been so
spoiled, ever – have I, Margaret?

MARGARET. No.

WEISLINGEN. I am altogether too good for you.

ADELHEID. Why, yes, you are. Truly you are, I think. You
make me ashamed sometimes. Now, is not that a confession?
Adelbert, I do love you: but do you know how long for?

WEISLINGEN. I am not a credulous man.

ADELHEID. That is very sensible; we should always love without promises and without hopes, otherwise . . . What did
you say to the architect who is to build our new house here in
Augsburg? You have seen him, haven't you?

WEISLINGEN. A letter. I wrote to him.

ADELHEID. No, you ought to *see* him – these people will not do
what you want unless you talk to them personally and bind
them down fast! Are you sure he understands about the
Italian loggia?

WEISLINGEN. Every single detail.

ADELHEID. I am very doubtful about that loggia. I do not
believe anyone in Germany has any experience of such
designs; we should have sent to Milan. And the fountains as

well – they must be *real* fountains, cornucopias of water sounding in my ears like woodwind in consort as I walk upon the terrace – I do not think you appreciate the importance of sumptuousness, display. We are at the Emperor's Court! How can you carry sufficient style as you go up and down among your clients if they know that all you have in your garden is a series of stultified birdbaths ?

WEISLINGEN. I am not aware I have ever lacked style or display. I wish you would occasionally leave these things to me.

MARGARET. Real fountains are so full, so vital, so much exuberance – it is impossible to live without the continual music of falling water—

WEISLINGEN. Can you not be content for one half of one week ? Is it not sufficient that I have obtained high office in the Imperial Secretariat ? I have my work for His Majesty, I have my work still for the Bishop advancing his causes at Court, I have the multitudes of details hung over from the Hessian dispute, every one to be settled and registered in the Archives or else the Walldorf estates will once again slide from you – and all you can think of is your damned Italian loggia! I should like to know the day when *I* shall be able to sit and listen to these fountains. Sometime in the seventeenth century, as likely as not . . . Did you hear about Berlichingen ?

ADELHEID. Ah, that. Yes, we did.

MARGARET. We were disgusted, my lord.

ADELHEID. The Baron von Sirau ought to be impeached.

MARGARET. Dance around that castle for more than a month and then let them ride out as though nothing had happened.

ADELHEID. I expect if the truth were known, precisely the same slovenly indulgence has been paid to the Landgrave of Hesse. This property of mine is not yet mine at all!

WEISLINGEN. I refuse to be beleaguered by the tongues of two rapacious women! You resemble the horse-leech, both of

B. is a prisoner of w's.

you – 'Give' and 'Give' are the only words you know. Stand back, leave me room, I desire to walk, ladies, across my own floorboards. I am a man of some authority in this Empire now – and as it so chances, my informations are commonly more up to date than yours. You will be interested to hear that von Sirau has acted upon *my* instructions. And as a result, we hold Berlichingen a prisoner in the city of Heilbronn. He is awaiting his trial before an Imperial Commission. You can go to the devil: I am now on my way to an expensive brothel-house for relaxation and entertainment. What a pity, isn't it, I can no longer obtain it at home?

N?

He goes out. FRANZ *is about to follow him, then stops irresolutely, looks at* ADELHEID, *and puts out his hand towards her. She ignores it.* MARGARET *touches his elbow and signs him to the door. He goes.*

SCENE FOURTEEN

Heilbronn.
A room in an inn.

GOETZ *is walking restlessly up and down.*

GOETZ. I bear in my mind a story about a learned monk who conjured an evil spirit into a sack and tied the string at the top and carried him about with him from monastery to monastery. Just the same with me. Up and down, up and down, fastened in by treachery . . .

ELISABETH *enters.*

Well, did they tell you yet?

ELISABETH. No certain news, Goetz. Some of your men they seem to have executed already, some are in prison, but which ones and where—

GOETZ. I could have released them all from my service before we rode out . . . He waited, he only waited, till we got clear of the drawbridge and into his lines, and then – we had one and a half dozen, he had two hundred. I had said to myself, no, not to release them; I may not have my castle but at least I have my troopers – too proud, you see, too stubborn. Well, I am humiliated.

ELISABETH. Never say that. That is not a word that should be used outside of the doors of churches. They would still have arrested them, whatever you had done.

GOETZ. Do you think so? I don't know . . . But the treachery, the safe-conduct, the word of the Emperor! Dishonoured, Elisabeth! Where are my friends? What has happened to Sickingen?

ELISABETH. Sickingen is no use to us. He is reaching out for land within the bounds of the Palatinate. He would have helped you once, but you turned him away. Now he is mounting on a stone tower of politics – too high up to see you, and if he were to look down, he is afraid he might be *pulled* down.

GOETZ. Yes, so he would. All the old voices, 'Improve it, improve it': and it breaks good men to pieces.

Enter a SERJEANT-AT-ARMS.

SERJEANT. Goetz von Berlichingen: the Imperial Commissioners have taken their seats in the Council House. They have sent me to summon you.

GOETZ. And who are *you*? The donkey of false justice, to carry the grain to the mill and the muck to the meadow, are you? I will come.

SERJEANT. Your lady must stay behind.

GOETZ. Indeed?

To ELISABETH.

I will see you later then. It's Friday, isn't it? Order me some

good fish for my dinner. I do not expect to be long . . .
Which way do I go?

SERJEANT. I am to escort you. You may wear your sword if
you wish.

GOETZ. You do me too much honour.

SERJEANT. I would recommend you, sir, to moderate yourself
before we go in.

GOETZ. I am sure it would be wiser.

He goes out with the SERJEANT.

SCENE FIFTEEN

Heilbronn.
A hall in the Council House, arranged for a Court of Justice.

The two Imperial COMMISSIONERS *are on the Bench, attended
by the* BURGOMASTER *and* ALDERMEN *in their robes of office.*
CLERK OF THE COURT *and* OFFICERS *complete the assembly.*

BURGOMASTER. Everything has been done according to your
orders, my lord. We have collected a force of the sturdiest
and bravest citizens to stand armed in the anteroom.

FIRST COMMISSIONER. Thank you, Mr Burgomaster. What
sort of men are they? Good, solid working lads, I hope?

BURGOMASTER. Hard-handed men, my lord – blacksmiths,
coopers, carpenters: not easily put down, you'll find.

FIRST COMMISSIONER. That is as it should be. I would have
preferred soldiers, but as they are not available—

Enter SERJEANT-AT-ARMS.

SERJEANT. My lords, Goetz von Berlichingen is waiting at the
door.

FIRST COMMISSIONER. Let him be admitted.

SERJEANT. You may enter the Court.

GOETZ *comes in.*

GOETZ. God be with you, sirs. And what is your pleasure with *me*?

FIRST COMMISSIONER. I think first you had better bear in mind what place and before whom you are standing.

GOETZ. I am very well aware of it.

FIRST COMMISSIONER. We are glad to hear you say so. Be seated, if you please.

GOETZ. Where? At your feet? No, sir, I will stand.

FIRST COMMISSIONER. As you wish.

GOETZ. May we get to business?

FIRST COMMISSIONER. We are doing so, sir, but in the proper order.

GOETZ. Good to know *somebody* has heard of the proper order around here. It has not been very evident up to now, has it?

FIRST COMMISSIONER. You realize that you are unconditionally in our power, and that your fate is entirely at our discretion?

GOETZ. Jesus, Mary, and Joseph – do you imagine I've *forgotten* it!

SECOND COMMISSIONER. You have certainly forgotten your manners, it seems.

GOETZ. And who'll help me remember them – you?

CLERK. Am I supposed to be taking all this down, my lord?

SECOND COMMISSIONER. Only what is relevant to the proceedings of the Court.

GOETZ. Oh, write it *all* down, boy; we'll make it into a ballad and we'll sing it in the streets—

SECOND COMMISSIONER. Berlichingen!

FIRST COMMISSIONER. We will continue from where we left off. Your fate is entirely at our discretion, and at the mercy of the Emperor – through whose paternal goodness, I may say, you have already been permitted to retain your sword and to await your trial under open arrest in a public inn, instead of joining your various confederates in prison.

GOETZ. Thank you very much.

FIRST COMMISSIONER. His Majesty has instructed me to intimate to you the vast extent to which his clemency has prevailed upon strict justice, and to inform you that he is prepared to forgive you your transgressions and even to release you from his Imperial Ban and its consequent penalties – provided that you in your turn are prepared to accept his royal bounty with true suppliant humility, and to subscribe your name to certain articles which are to be read to you forthwith.

GOETZ. I see. I am, and always have been, His Majesty's loyal servant. . . . What about my men?

FIRST COMMISSIONER. That is no concern of yours just now.

GOETZ. Is it not, sir, is it not? I hope one day when *you're* in trouble for your bribes and peculations or whatever other vices you care to commit up there, *you* won't find your master being told you're no concern of his! What have you done with my men?

SECOND COMMISSIONER. Our commission goes no further than to lay the articles before you and ask if you are willing to subscribe your name.

FIRST COMMISSIONER. I would point out to you, Berlichingen, that if you want to help your associates, you would be well advised to assist this Court first.

GOETZ. Let me see the paper.

FIRST COMMISSIONER. Will you read, please, Mr Clerk.

CLERK (*reads*).

I, Goetz von Berlichingen, make open acknowledgement of all my offences committed against His Imperial Majesty. First, that I have risen in armed rebellion against his lawful jurisdiction—

GOETZ. That's a lie to start with!

FIRST COMMISSIONER. Read, please, Mr Clerk.

CLERK (*reads*).

Second, that after receipt of the Imperial Summons, I—

GOETZ. I said that was a lie to start with.

FIRST COMMISSIONER. Are you going to be quiet and listen or are you not!

GOETZ. No, I am not! Everyone here, citizens, Judges, Serjeant-at-arms, bear witness to me! Have I, at any time in all of my life in any one of my feuds and honourable quarrels, ever, I say ever, conducted myself other than with all due respect and obedience towards my liege lord the Emperor and the noble House of Austria? Of course I have not – and you know it very well! If I sign that paper, I make my whole life a lie!

FIRST COMMISSIONER. I am sorry to hear you say so. Because, you see, we have orders that if we cannot by free persuasion obtain your signature today, you are to be thrown into close confinement in the dungeon of a fortress until such time as you decide—

GOETZ. In the dungeon of a fortress . . . Close confinement . . . *Me*!

FIRST COMMISSIONER. That is our commission, sir.

GOETZ. But I am a knight of hereditary status. I am a free feudatory of the Imperial power – I was taken by treachery! I am not the servile henchman of one of your Princes – I am the brother of the Emperor – look at my hand! Lost in *his* service – lost in *his* service, sirs—

> The FIRST COMMISSIONER *has made a sign to an* OFFICER, *who has slipped to the door during* GOETZ'S *shouting, and beckoned in a squad of* CITIZENS *armed with swords and halberds.*

Who are these men? More treachery, is it?

FIRST COMMISSIONER. The word 'treachery' is not applicable to the treatment of Outlaws under Ban. These are the citizens of Heilbronn and His Majesty's subjects. Take away his sword.

GOETZ (*drawing and standing on guard*). Aha, no, no, you don't, sirs, no . . . You promise me to allow me my knightly parole as I have had it before and I will consider your paper. Otherwise . . .

SECOND COMMISSIONER. Do you bandy words with your Sovereign, holding a sword at his throat?

GOETZ (*pointing his blade at the* COMMISSIONER). Not his throat – *yours!*

FIRST COMMISSIONER (*to* CITIZENS). Take him. Go on, take him.

GOETZ (*threatening the* COMMISSIONERS). Will you? Will you?

An OFFICER *comes running in from outside.*

OFFICER. My lords, my lords – oh, my God, what's happening?

GOETZ. Tell us the news, friend. What do you want?

OFFICER. There are two hundred soldiers coming into the market-place; there was no guard at the gate. What shall we do?

BURGOMASTER. Soldiers, what soldiers?

OFFICER. Franz von Sickingen's men!

GOETZ gives a great yell.

He says he's come to burn the town unless you stop this trial!

FIRST COMMISSIONER. We are not to be intimidated. Continue the proceedings.

BURGOMASTER. My lord, my lord – how?

FIRST COMMISSIONER. How? . . .

OFFICER. Listen: here he comes.

A drum coming nearer. The Hall suddenly fills with SICKINGEN'S SWITZERS, *led by their* CAPTAIN, *a* DRUMMER-BOY, *and* STANDARD-BEARERS.

SWISS CAPTAIN. Stand back, clear the room, clear the room – here comes the Lord of Sickingen with a petition for the Court!

A SWITZER. Silence in Court!

The SOLDIERS *all laugh. They stand clear of the door, holding back the frightened* CITIZENS *with their pikes, to allow space for* SICKINGEN *to make his entry. The drum stops.*

SICKINGEN. Good morning. My Lords Commissioners, Mr Burgomaster, gentlemen . . . ah my dear Goetz . . . I have come to offer bail on behalf of this prisoner. I trust it will be accepted.

FIRST COMMISSIONER. What sort of bail?

SICKINGEN. Your lives, and your property, and the continued virginity of the young ladies of Heilbronn. I have two hundred Switzers at my back this morning. It's quite a long time since they last had a city to sack. Yes or no?

FIRST COMMISSIONER. We have no choice. Take him.

SICKINGEN. Thank you . . . Some breathing-space, Captain. Chase them out.

The SOLDIERS *chase all the* CITIZENS, COMMISSIONERS, *etc., out of the hall.*

SWITZERS. Everybody, out – you sir, out – never mind your papers, we'll send them on after you – out you go, out—

ELISABETH *pushes through the crowd towards* GOETZ.

GOETZ. Elisabeth, Elisabeth—

To SICKINGEN.

I was told *you* were in the Palatinate. However did you—

SICKINGEN. I thought it would be better if I called in, in passing . . . I've let your men out of gaol, they're mostly still alive, though they've hurt them considerably. Now understand this, Goetz; I can't do this always, you know. My affairs are getting too great to be prejudiced now: the Emperor is still my friend, but if—

GOETZ. You mean he *was* your friend.

SICKINGEN. Oh, he still will be. You see, he finds himself standing in between me and Weislingen: but he prefers me of the two, most of the time. I fancy I can persuade him to forgive without difficulty. Go back to Jaxthausen.

GOETZ. But he has confiscated Jaxthausen—

SICKINGEN. He has not installed a garrison. I saw to that. So no one can stop you. Maria sends her love.

GOETZ. How is my son?

SICKINGEN. Still poorly, I am afraid, but we hope he may mend.

GOETZ (*to* ELISABETH). Shall we go home, then? Or what shall we do?

She shakes her head hopelessly.

SICKINGEN. You could join with me on expedition to the Palatinate. I have a sort of permission to – take over the city of Trier. Would you care to lead a company?

GOETZ. No . . . I am too old these days to accept subordinate commands, particularly from my friends . . . Good-bye and good fortune, Franz. May you win your war.

SICKINGEN. I will, Goetz, I will! The next time we meet I shall be a Prince Elector! Captain, call the assembly; we march out at once!

The CAPTAIN *signs to the* DRUMMER-BOY, *who beats out a call, and the* SOLDIERS *file from the stage.*

Come this way, Goetz – are you tired? Take my arm, then; up the steps, that's right . . .

He helps him out and ELISABETH *follows.*

SCENE SIXTEEN

Jaxthausen.
A room in Goetz's Castle. Evening.

GOETZ *is sitting writing at a table by the light of a candle.* ELISABETH *is sewing.*

GOETZ. I am wasting my time at this work.

ELISABETH. No, you are not.

GOETZ. Wasting time, wasting candlelight. Damaging my eyes. I would do better to employ a clerk and dictate it to him.

ELISABETH. Can you afford to pay one?

GOETZ. There was a time when I could afford to pay one hundred horse-troopers and they were all as fat as cock-pheasants.

ELISABETH. Slanders. Accusations. Secret enemies. It is they have brought you down and they will drag you yet further. You must finish your book, tell the truth in pen and ink, Goetz, only the power of the word on the paper can vindicate your name.

GOETZ. What will be the good? The favour of the Emperor has been turned from me for ever.

ELISABETH. No. It is not true.

GOETZ. You are talking foolishness, Elisabeth.

ELISABETH. No, Goetz, your book, you must finish your book! Pen and ink and write it down. The Emperor will read it.

GOETZ. Not he.

ELISABETH. He will read it, Goetz, and when he has read it, the black clear truth of the word on the paper will pierce his heart like an arrow. He will call you to Court, he will hang up that Weislingen in chains, the old wicked weasel on the game-keeper's gallows, and we shall walk round him and laugh at him and spit! You will wear his robes and a gold collar at your neck and you will stand in his place at Maximilian's door and you will say who is to come in and who is to stay out, and your wife will be beside you and our honour will be restored!

GOETZ. You must keep some sense of proportion. He will not read my book.

ELISABETH. What have you written today?

GOETZ. I have been remembering the first time I was ever put in prison some years ago in Heilbronn.

ELISABETH. That unlucky city.

GOETZ. Yes . . .

He reads.

> It was said to me at this time by a representative of these Princes, 'We marvel, Goetz von Berlichingen, that you should have espoused this ill cause, for with many other that do hold by it you have aforetime been at feud. Nevertheless, be of good cheer, declare yourself with us, and you shall find a right fortunate delivery.'

ELISABETH. To which you replied?

GOETZ (*reads*).

> 'Have I so often risked my life for the good and gold of others, and should I not now do so for the sake of my knightly word?' And they were dumbfounded by my steadfastness and spoke no more to me that day.

ELISABETH. Why, so it was, and so it has been with you always, the claws of your iron hand have gone deep into your brain, Goetz, and turned that, too, as hard and as stupid as iron! Never, never, never have you known how to fight for your right with any wisdom! And your house is dead and gone and your wife left in poverty—

GOETZ. Elisabeth—

ELISABETH. Where is Karl? Your son and your successor who should be riding for you with his hand on your banner – you gave him away and he is dead and gone beneath a stranger's roof!

GOETZ. Sickingen and Maria looked after him as well as they could. He was never in good health. He would have died anyway.

ELISABETH. Beneath a stranger's roof. And even this Jaxthausen is forfeited to the stranger. We have to pay rent for our own castle now . . .

GOETZ. Oh, my love, my dear heart, have courage, Elisabeth . . .

Enter GEORG *and* LERSE *from hunting, carrying some small game.* LERSE *is lame and broken and has lost all his soldierly panache.*

How did the hunting go, Lerse?

LERSE. Not so good as it should. Useless as a huntsman, useless as a soldier, look at me . . . God! *He* can run and ride well enough. What we found *he* killed. I was no help to him.

GEORG. I wish begod we could be after two-legged game again – can we not make just one more riding, Berlichingen?

GOETZ. You know it is forbidden – this castle is mortgaged on condition of my behaviour – do you want to deprive me of the only good I have left!

GEORG. I didn't mean to mention it.

GOETZ. What news have you heard?

LERSE. The comet is still in the sky.

GOETZ. I know. The eighth day of it now. What do they say that it means?

GEORG. The death of the Emperor.

GOETZ. What? Is he ill?

LERSE. So it seems. Sudden and bad, they tell me.

GOETZ. Have they thought of his successor?

LERSE. Almost decided. The Electors are looking at Prince Karl.

GOETZ. Seventeen years old. They will tell him what to do. He will never be permitted to even open my book.

LERSE. And there's bad news out of Swabia. An insurrection of the peasants.

GOETZ. Insurrection against who?

LERSE. Against everyone, I think. Traditions, old customs, the whole conception of the world. They say the changes in the law have deprived them of their rights and they'll murder everyone in Germany until they get them back. They've hoisted a banner with the crucified Christ and a ploughman's boot upon it and a word wrote under – it says: Naught but the Justice of God.

GOETZ. How can they think to murder everyone in Germany and yet hope for the Justice of God! We ought to go out and meet them and tell them to go home. They used to listen to me once—

ELISABETH. Ingratitude, irreverence, slanders and accusation – the Emperor's soldiers, they broke his safe-conduct, look what has happened—

GOETZ. Elisabeth, will you please—

ELISABETH. I saw two fiery swords in the sky on either side of the comet and they pointed towards Swabia. God's mark over Germany, Goetz, God's mark of His damnation!

Act Three

SCENE ONE

The Peasants' War.
A village: tumult and plundering.

A crowd of frightened people run across the stage.

AN OLD MAN. Hurry, hurry, the murdering devils are catching us up!

A WOMAN. Holy God, Holy God, look at the colour of the sky!

A MOTHER WITH A BABY. Red blood, red fire, all the houses are on fire—

WOMAN. My husband, where's my husband? He went back to fetch his—

OLD MAN. No, no, this way, run to the forest, girl, run—

> *They all flee.*
> *Enter* SIEVERS *and other* PEASANTS, *carrying various weapons, most of them farm implements and some rusty old swords and spears, etc.*

SIEVERS. All right, me boys, come on, we're through, we've turned 'em all out; now grab what we can and we burn up what's left; any man to stop you, chop out his throat!

> *Enter* METZLER *with a bloodstained pitchfork.*

METZLER. How does it go, brother?

SIEVERS. Upstairs and downstairs and out at all the windows! You're just in time for the last dance o' this town – where have you been?

METZLER. Weinsberg, and begod we crammed our wames there!

SIEVERS. What did you do?

METZLER (*showing his fork*). Look at him, brother: he's been through five and thirty in one half an hour!

SIEVERS. Who were they then?

METZLER. Dietrich von Weiler, he wor the first – oh, he jumped like a jackanapes! We wor all around the church, y'see, and we shut 'em all in, and we let out a roar – and he had his head through the tower window; he reckoned on to *talk* to us – he called us 'reasonable men, good people,' he called us. One knock from a hand-gun, he turns a right wryneck – up we go, and out they all tipple, bodies first and roof-tiles after!

SIEVERS. Ha!

METZLER. Now what are we waiting on here – there's five hundred gentry houses in Swabia to be burnt, or are you expecting all the white ladies to come without the asking, wi' cool drinks and green garlands? Move!

SIEVERS. Keep your banner up and keep your feet on forward; we've not done working yet, me boys!

METZLER. Knives out, staves up, and *move*! And we take the road west – there's not a soldier in Heilbronn; that city stands empty; through the gates and fill it!

The PEASANTS *hurry across the stage and away, leaving* METZLER *and* SIEVERS *alone.*

Strength of good hot brandy to a good man's hot heart, this is!

Come night come day, the day comes now
The sword of God shall overthrow—

All the names we've counted from winter to winter, I'm notching 'em off at last—

He shows a row of notches on the pitchfork handle.

Helfenstein, Eltershosen, all the lords of power and cruelty – we stood 'em in a row; nigh eighty they stood there and they shook at the knees, and the spikes of our long forks looked in at their bowels. D'you remember the great Rexinger, wi' the

plume in his hat and the high spread of his nostrils, how he
rode to his hunting and drove the people afore him like
hounds with his hounds at their heels? And he laughed and
he drank and he cheered? He came another laugh, brother,
when he smelt the faggots round his house and he knew the
teeth of his own dogs in the meat of his body. . . . Have you
seen the comet yet?

SIEVERS. We have, we have! Every night it still walks on!

METZLER. Our sign, brother, our victory there – you can call it
an arm holding a sword, there's three stars at the hilt o' the
sword and three at the point, and a thousand and a thousand
of streamers of light, all like lances of victory against the
black cloud—

SIEVERS. I saw men in the cloud.

METZLER. Men?

SIEVERS. Shaggy hair and beards and they ran round, they ran
round, all over hair like the wildmen of the forest, and clogged
black with old blood. I don't like to see men when no man
can live—

METZLER. We've had to live *our* lives where no man can live –
any such that we see we can call 'em our brothers – all they
mean is victory! Greet them, give them praise.

SIEVERS. I don't know about victory.

METZLER. What!

SIEVERS. Suppose we take Heilbronn. It's a big city there;
you've got to rule a big city—

METZLER. We shall rule it as brothers. Every man under Christ
and the Justice of God!

SIEVERS. Some o' the people are talking that we ought to
choose a captain.

METZLER. We *have* chose a captain. Me and you are captains.
What more do they want—

SIEVERS. A captain by rank. That he could know how to rule –
don't you see this, Metzler: someone's going to have to talk
to the Emperor.

METZLER. Let God and the people talk to the Emperor. There's not a better tongue nor that in the whole of Christianity! . . . Who do they want?

SIEVERS. Like, one o' the Free Knights maybe, who's stood out hissen again the Princes – Goetz Ironhand, for an instance?

METZLER. He's an inherited lord.

SIEVERS. He could talk to the Emperor and tell him who we are and all that we've suffered. Have I or you got words to use in a palace – only *this* word, brother Metzler—

He indicates his own weapon.

And we're going to need more.

METZLER. Heilbronn's the next city. I told you it stands empty. We have to go there and fill it. Then'll be the day we can give a mind to the Emperor.

They follow the others.

SCENE TWO

Augsburg.
Weislingen's house.

WEISLINGEN *and* ADELHEID.

WEISLINGEN. A dying man, that's all, and he refuses to die, and yet he will not rule. The news out of Swabia gets worse every day – we can't even move troops because of the weather, high winds, flooded roads, and how much blood filling up beyond them nobody can guess. Still, the Princes are combining: some efforts are being made. I have been granted a partial commission. As soon as I possibly can, I shall ride out with the army and do what may be done. I have never heard of a rebellion so dangerous as this – but the logical conclusion, you see – you give way to men like Sickingen, you give way to men like Berlichingen, and drop by drop in your hands your whole snowball falls to nothing.

ADELHEID. Is there no hope at all that Maximilian might die?

WEISLINGEN. Oh, he will die – but he takes his time doing it, and he does it in character. He can think of nothing more urgent than the enormity of the Turk! I told him: with all their enormity, and with all their false gods, the Infidels at least have their Empire well controlled. In this country we have people who believe in the true God, and moreover we have people who believe that the true God was hung upon His Cross by the nobility and clergy, and is not yet revenged . . . I told him, we all told him, he shook his head, said his prayers, and he gave us no answer.

ADELHEID. Is it not possible to anticipate his death? Prince Karl should be amenable. Why not work on *him*?

WEISLINGEN. How can he be amenable when he is not yet elected? There is no provision in law for it; we can do nothing without law; it is because we have no law that all this is on top of us!

ADELHEID. You should spend less time by Maximilian's bedside and pay more attention to Karl.

WEISLINGEN. I prefer to leave that to *you*. You are only too good at it.

ADELHEID. What do you mean?

WEISLINGEN. You might well ask what I mean. Have you slept with him yet?

ADELHEID. I most certainly have not.

WEISLINGEN. Astonishing. How did I manage to obtain my commission, then? I know Maximilian was unwilling to grant it – he thought he ought to send it to Sickingen, God help us.

ADELHEID. I did indeed speak to Prince Karl about you, I don't deny that – I was looking for some gratitude rather than hysteria—

WEISLINGEN. I have already been foisted off with the old cast clout of the Bishop of Bamberg: I will not accept advancement through the Holy Roman genitals of a half-elected Habsburg schoolboy. Leave him alone, madam: you are no longer sufficient. My policy will thrive by its own virtues and intellect, and if you think otherwise I shall banish you to my castle. There is terrifying anarchy enough in this Empire: I stand by the rule of law. I will not have it plunged into a swamp of aphrodisiac.

ADELHEID. If you wish to disconnect your head from your loins, by all means do, my dear. But I would not like to hazard which will suffer the worse from it. I suppose you did have a mother?

WEISLINGEN. Of course I had a mother – what is that to the purpose?

ADELHEID. Who killed the meat she ate to build your body, who milked the cows to fill her breasts to feed you? Whoever it was, I expect at this moment, they are marching across Swabia, looking out for the Justice of God. Go away and give it them. I don't want to see you ever again.

WEISLINGEN. I am married to you. You are part of my government, as is this rebellion. All one together. I shall follow my commission and I shall do so with diligence. Bear it in mind.

He goes out.

ADELHEID. You can come in now if you like.

FRANZ *enters by another door.*

The gentleman has left us. Did you bring me the letter?

He gives her a letter.

Prince Karl gave it you himself?

He nods.

In private, no one saw you?

He nods. She opens the letter and studies it.

Good . . . very good . . . he knows all about the rules of
true love, this excellent Prince, although he is so young . . .
Franz, what is the matter? You look very sulky. Have I
offended you?

FRANZ. Certainly you have offended me. How many letters
have I carried between you and the Prince?

ADELHEID. A great many, Franz; it has been very loving and
considerate of you to do so.

FRANZ. It has not occurred to you, has it, that I myself have a
heart to be wounded, as well as your husband?

ADELHEID. Why, Franz, Franz, my faithful sweetheart, I
thought you took pleasure in doing me these services—

FRANZ. You began this, you know. Oh yes, you did; you gave
me your hand and I kissed it and you told me I had hot lips
and you told me I—

ADELHEID. Why, yes – but Franz, these are the moves on the
chessboard, you know – this is how Court ladies calculate
their chances. I thought surely you were old enough, you
have lived in the Bamberg Palace long enough to understand
it . . . Oh my poor boy, you were so debonair, how could I
have believed—

FRANZ. It is one thing absolutely to deceive my own master
with messages and so forth, all the young squires they play
that game and laugh at it – but yourself and Prince Karl! He
is no older than I am, and look at the size of his jaw!

ADELHEID. He has the face of his family, that I will agree. But
after all, Franz, he *is* our next Emperor!

FRANZ. He can be the next Pope for all that *I* care! I am not
going to take him any more of your letters. I love you, I love
you, I am a better man than him!

ADELHEID (*taking him in her arms*). Franz, Franz, you are, I
know that you are. Forgive me. I have treated you so
wickedly. I treat them all wickedly. Never again, never again.
I shall reward you as you wish, everything you wish – sst,
he's coming back!

They break apart and FRANZ *is quick enough to be standing deferentially at the door as* WEISLINGEN *re-enters.*

WEISLINGEN (*ignoring his wife*). Franz! Ah, you're here. I am leaving for Swabia tonight. However bad the weather, we dare not put it off any more. I shall take what men are ready and let the rest follow. Now, you stay in Augsburg: the minute the Emperor dies and the Election is concluded, you are to ride like a red-hot gunstone and bring the news to me. Is that understood?

FRANZ. Yes, sir, it is.

WEISLINGEN. I am relying on you, Franz. This is very important.

He goes out again.

ADELHEID. As soon as he has gone; nothing else now; wait until he goes . . .

SCENE THREE

The open country.
In the distance two villages and a monastery are seen on fire.

METZLER, SIEVERS, KOHL, WILD *and other* PEASANTS.

SIEVERS. Have you got him? Is he fixed? Let's have a look at him!

Several PEASANTS, *armed, thrust* GOETZ, LERSE, *and* GEORG, *whose hands are tied behind them, on to the stage.*

GOETZ. What do you want, men – what are you doing?

SIEVERS. Goetz Ironhand, ent it? Stand him out here. Right, Goetz: they call me Wilhelm Sievers. God be with you, brother. Unfasten his hands.

This is done.

GOETZ. The worse deeds you do, you know, the worse will be done to you.

SIEVERS. That's not how *we* look at it. D'you know what we're fighting for?

GOETZ. I have been afraid to ask myself that.

SIEVERS. I'm going to tell you. We used to be free men in this part of Germany, farm our own land, raise our own flocks, fish our own rivers, cut our own timber where we wanted in the forest. And we had our own old laws, and all, to tell us we could do it. But the whole lot's been changed. They've brought in their new laws, and what do we find? My field, I called it *mine*, it belongs to a man in a gentry house t'other side o'the valley: the man in the gentry house, he called it *his*, it belongs to a lord in a castle at back end o'the forest: the lord in the castle, he called it *his*, it belongs to a man in a counting-house in the city of Nuremberg. They told us i' kirk when we wor little lads that Christ walked in the vine-yards in the heat of the day and He swinked and He sweated along of His poor people. We want to know where He's gone to now, and to bring Him back here to His own honest home. Will you be our captain?

GOETZ. Me? How can I be? Look, I know about your in-justices and I've known them for years, but – murdering, burning, raping and torturing, what kind of service is *that* for the Lord Jesus Christ!

> METZLER *gives a prolonged harsh laugh.* GOETZ *looks at him and their eyes meet for a time. Then* METZLER *gets up and goes out, waving his hand in a scornful dismissive gesture to them all.*
> *There is an uncomfortable pause.*

KOHL. There wor some of us did get over-wild, like, the first days we began – we're done with it now; we're fighting for right and we're fighting for honesty, just same as you wor when you rode down on the merchant wagons.

GOETZ. I see no kind of likeness.

WILD. *We* do. It's all fit warfare – there's some fight by the rule because they're called knights and they wear the great armour, there's others wi' no armour has to fight as best we can.

SIEVERS. Pitchforks and threshing-flails, that's how we stand. But happen we're going to finish, and happen on that day we're going to have to look to a right man to stand up for us to the Emperor, and talk to his face. He has to be told we obey no Princes now. He has to be told we're all of us free men. And he has to be told it so well he'll let us bide free for ever. Ironhand, what about it? Can you reckon on to do that thing for us?

GOETZ. But do you not realize my castle is held surety for my own good behaviour? I am nothing but the Emperor's bondman now. I cannot—

They all laugh a little.

SIEVERS. That's right, your castle's held. But who by, do you know?

GOETZ. What! Do you mean—

SIEVERS. Aye aye, we've surrounded it. And your good lady wife, she's still inside, and all . . . You'd do best to think on; it's a fair choice we're offering.

GOETZ. You could call it that, I suppose. . . . The murdering must finish! You want to be free men, then behave like free men. I will not help you otherwise. I'll get you out a writing and you'll put your marks underneath it; there is to be not one man killed except in fair battle.

SIEVERS. All right, we'll put our marks. Shake hands, brother Goetz. Unfasten his two lads.

LERSE *and* GEORG *are released. They stumble forward.*

Tell me your names.

LERSE. Lerse. Fritz Lerse.

GOETZ (*as* GEORG *hesitates*). His name is Georg.

SIEVERS. Brother Fritz. Brother Georg. You still wear your hireling's coats, aye, aye: but there's hearts of men inside 'em. Fair fixed and firm in the hope of our new Commonwealth, and our hope is the hope of the Passion of Christ!

SCENE FOUR

Wild country.
A burnt-out mill.

IMPERIAL TROOPERS *taking up positions*. WEISLINGEN *and an* OFFICER, *both wearing the* EMPEROR'S *badge on their armour*.

WEISLINGEN. All over the country, they are moving their hundreds along every road and through the valleys; if they were all joined together I dare not attack them – but as it is, we have this chance: discover from our scouts which gangs of them are where, what place they're going to, wait till they've got to it, wait till they've *burnt* it even – then, they're all drunk, they're all raping, they're all rolling in their plunder – and we take them by surprise! Five or six hundred killed in less than an hour. Then off we go away, find out the next town, wait till they've burnt that, and the same work at the same speed repeated and repeated—

OFFICER. But according to this tactic, all the towns will be laid waste – are we not to attempt to defend them?

WEISLINGEN. Not until we have a complete force behind us. In anything like a pitched battle at our present strength we are bound to be the losers. These peasants are fighting for victory or death and that is a concept that our nobility and our Princes know nothing about. You have not here a war over a heraldic dispute or the ownership of a castle, my dear sir: if we do not win it, all the government, all the law, the entire order of state will be utterly concluded!

OFFICER. I can hardly believe it is as radical as that – I am told they have appointed knights and gentlemen to be their commanders – surely if that is so—

WEISLINGEN. *If* that is so, it means they are becoming frightened of the extremity of their own demands; it indicates weakness, and it may be encouraging. But do not be deceived by it. Their real leaders are inflexible and possessed by a vision of God. We in our turn must therefore be possessed by a vision of Order, and we must allow no sacrifice to deter us from achieving it. One of their bands is marching towards Heilbronn. They have to go through Miltenberg. So let us make our first attack there. The squadrons had better be disposed as follows— Franz!

Enter FRANZ, *flustered with riding.*

FRANZ. Sir, sir, the Emperor—

WEISLINGEN. Karl, is it Karl!

FRANZ. Yes, sir, Prince Karl. The decision of the Electors was unanimous and immediate. Maximilian died more than a week ago – I am sorry, it was impossible for me to get here any quicker; the rivers are all in spate and the roads blocked by landslides. I had to—

WEISLINGEN. Yes, yes, I know . . . This means there will be no more procrastination; by the end of the month I shall have all the soldiers I asked for!

OFFICER. Are you so certain? The new Emperor may be as daunted as the old one by any thought of strong policy—

WEISLINGEN. Oh no, he won't – I have his most secure word for it! . . . Franz, it is conceivable that His Majesty, when he confirms me in my commission, may expect some sort of personal service in return. I shall be only happy to render him what I am able . . . except in one particular. So go back to Augsburg and give this letter to my wife. Make yourself

familiar with the instructions it contains, and see that she
obeys them. When she has done so, find me again and tell
me. I hope, my dear fellow, I am not exhausting you with all
these journeys. I am afraid I have no choice.

FRANZ. There is nothing for me to complain about, sir; it is all
part of my service.

WEISLINGEN. Very philosophical. Are you short of expenses?
Here you are—

He gives him money.

Good-bye and ride safely.

FRANZ. Yes, sir. I will.

He goes.

WEISLINGEN. Miltenberg. I think we ought to go and examine
the map. The better we know the topography, the fewer men
we shall lose.

He and the OFFICER *go into the mill.*

SCENE FIVE

A hill near Miltenberg.
The camp of the Peasant Army.

The Banner of the Insurrection (as described by LERSE *in the
last scene of Act Two), with its legend 'Naught but the Justice of
God' and the Crucifixion, etc., is hanging from a pole among the
tents.* GOETZ, LERSE, *and* GEORG. *A hymn being sung in the
distance, and men's voices shouting slogans and hallelujahs
through the music.*

LERSE. The first time o' my life I've had to march with an army
that knew why it was marching. Comes as a kind of a startler
to a man like me, I can tell you. When you hear hymns of

religion sung in the middle of the killing, and the killing twice as cruel as even Spanishers would fight, that day's the day an old journeyman soldier goes out a-walking. But *I'm* not to be called by any such name any longer, I suppose, so I dare say there's nowt to do but to bide it to the end. This has shrivelled up my heart, Berlichingen, like that dungeon in Heilbronn it shrivelled up my body, and when it comes the real battle, I'm fair sick terrified to think how it'll be.

GOETZ. You are not fit to soldier.

LERSE. No, I am not, and that's by God's truth. Look at my arm; it shakes like that standard pole on a day of north wind. I cursed the old man Selbitz because he couldn't keep up with his troopers – go on, you curse *me*. I've failed in my trade.

GOETZ. No, Lerse, I don't think so. It's the trade that has failed . . . But I will not keep you with me, if you say you are unfit. I have no money, you know that? You will have to go to my wife in Jaxthausen, if the peasants will let you, and ask *her* for your wages.

LERSE. It might well be thought that by reason of my loyalty I ought not to leave you. But I take a practical view. I say a useless man's useless and does damage to a campaign. How does that stand with your notions of knighthood?

GOETZ. Such notions are apparently no longer appropriate. You may go, sir, and I give you hearty thanks for all your good service. Greet my wife with my love and tell her – tell her not to be afraid. My purpose with these people is to speak for them to the Emperor. No doubt in the same interview I shall be able to speak for myself. Good-bye to you, Lerse.

LERSE. Berlichingen.

He hobbles away.

GEORG. When it does come the real battle, are we going to win it?

GOETZ. I hope so. Why should we not?

GEORG. And when we do win it, what happens then?

GOETZ *shakes his head.*

When I first joined wi' your service, d'you know what I believed? First, I'd be a horse-boy, then I'd be your page, then I'd ride as a trooper, maybe a squire, then I'd capture a castle, set in a garrison, and there I would live a Free Knight like yourself. Do it all on my own, you see, and nothing would change.

GOETZ. I thought the same for you, boy. When my son was born, that's what I said *he'd* do. But he was not of that spirit. So I cast my eyes on you. It is of little pleasure, after all, to follow a way of life and not to know that when you die there are men to continue it. You began well. Very well. I don't think it is my fault that your future will be different.

GEORG. How much different, that's the point. Do you credit these peasants, Berlichingen?

GOETZ. Why, yes, I do, now. I understand their cause. But beforehand they were not seeking it with justice. If they keep faith with me, they may even succeed . . . But truly, I myself am become like Lerse; I am a man with a shrivelled heart.

A PEASANT *enters.*

PEASANT. Ironhand?

GOETZ *shows his right hand without speaking.*

What wor your last orders to the captains of the bands?

GOETZ. Who are you?

PEASANT. I'm just one of the brothers. Like, there wor a question rose, what wor your orders this morning, Captain?

GOETZ. To send a party into Miltenberg, buy food in the town, and to secure any weapons that might be discovered there.

PEASANT. This question being rose, on account of one trouble

– why did you tell them to *buy* the food and forbid them force the houses?

GOETZ. Because that was the agreement I made with your brothers. It was written and it was signed.

PEASANT. Aye, so it wor . . . Like, some of 'em disputed it, you see. There are men living in Miltenberg whose names had been counted off.

GOETZ. That does not interest me. That business is finished.

PEASANT. Aye, so it is . . . Klaus Metzler reckons he's going to burn the town.

GOETZ. What did you say!

PEASANT. Klaus Metzler reckons he's going to burn the town, and then when he's burnt it, he's going to kill *you*.

GOETZ. But I deposed that vindictive lunatic from the leadership of his band. How has he come back!

PEASANT. He came back to his brothers because his brothers set to bring him. And because you deposed him. The day you did that they remembered who you are. They made you captain through their own unforced voices and by the same token they can take it back off you. Now they've finished wi' your agreement: and they've finished wi' Miltenberg . . . My wife has a cousin keeps a shop in Miltenberg; that's why I've warned you. You don't know my name – don't ask it neither.

He slips away.

GOETZ. Georg, get the horses.

He hitches on his sword-belt, which he had loosed when talking to GEORG *and they go.*

SCENE SIX

The same.

METZLER *comes in. He is wearing a woman's skirt, torn and*

bloody, and a feathered helmet that does not fit him. Round his neck is hung a firkin of liquor. At the end of his pitchfork is what appears to be the remains of a woman's headdress with jewels. He sings and dances, with heavy-booted stamps to emphasize the rhythm.

METZLER (*singing*).

> I saw a red eagle
> A-riding a swine
> Through Miltenberg market
> And the gentry so fine.

> There perched that red eagle
> On Miltenberg tower
> And fire from his wing-tips
> Ran down in a shower.

> There was fire through their window
> And smoke through their door
> The nails of their fingers
> Are scrabbling on the floor.

GOETZ comes in and kills him.
The PEASANTS *all come in, in ones and twos, and stand round about him, looking at him.*

GOETZ. My treaty was broken. You have destroyed your own cause. I am Goetz von Berlichingen, I am a hereditary nobleman and a Free Knight of the Empire and I came to believe in your cause. Tear down that banner – your Redeemer is dishonoured and His wounds are smeared with filth – tear it down; you are no men, you are nothing, you are like a spit of dirty water and Weislingen when he comes will wipe you away like spit—

He tears at the banner.
They all fall upon him.

Trumpets sound from one side of the stage.

A PEASANT. Watch out, we're attacked!

Trumpets from the other side.

A VOICE (*off*). Horsemen from the north!
ANOTHER VOICE (*off*). More from the west!
CONFUSED SHOUTING. We're attacked, we're attacked! Stand
  to your arms, brothers, stand and destroy them—

> *Etcetera.*
> *Trumpets and gunfire and shouts.*
> *They all run off, leaving* GOETZ *alone. He pulls himself pain-*
> *fully off the stage.*

SCENE SEVEN

The same. Evening.

WEISLINGEN *and the* OFFICER *walk through the camp.*

WEISLINGEN. We can call this our first victory. A dozen more
  battles as conclusive as this and the insurrection is wiped out.
  Do you know who was leading them?
OFFICER. I heard talk of Goetz von Berlichingen.
WEISLINGEN. Has he been taken?
OFFICER. Not yet.
WEISLINGEN. His body not found?
OFFICER. No.
WEISLINGEN. He must be taken. All their leaders must be
  taken. The Emperor's justice shall be fulfilled with complete
  severity and no exceptions. Muster our soldiers and we will
  prepare the next onfall. One dozen more, my dear sir – as
  conclusive as this.

SCENE EIGHT

Mountain and forest. A Gipsy encampment. Night.

An OLD WOMAN *sitting by a fire under a rough shelter of branches and thatch. Beside her a* GIRL.

OLD WOMAN. Raining and thunder, girly; put more straw on the roof, girly; cold, cold for the old woman's bones—

A BOY *comes in.*

What have you caught, boy?

BOY. A hamster and two fieldmice.

OLD WOMAN. Where did you catch them?

BOY. Hedges and the ditches.

OLD WOMAN. Ah, skin them and roast them and chew their little limbs. Make a cap of their fur and wear it on your curly head and then we can call you the King of the People. Oh, cold, cold, put some thorns on the fire; make it crackle and roar for your father when he comes—

BOY. Hamster bit my thumb, he did.

OLD WOMAN. Lick it, boy, lick it, with your tongue – that's right – huntsman's blood – good—

A WOMAN *with a baby on her back enters.*

WOMAN. We shall have to go from here – go; they're still burning houses, the pitchfork-men fighting and the iron-men are killing them—

OLD WOMAN. Let them all kill, pitchfork and iron; all the cruelty kill each other, then the People will be safe!

Some GIPSIES *enter with their* CAPTAIN.

GIPSY CAPTAIN. Are we still all with us, none of the iron-men come yet?

WOMAN. They're over the next valley. I could hear them before the rain. Trumpets and laughing and the smell of the battle.

CAPTAIN. I heard one thing more. I heard the wild huntsman.

OLD WOMAN. Oh no, not this night—

CAPTAIN. Oh yes, old woman, with his white-tailed hounds and the clang of his whip in the sky—

BOY (*howls like a hound*). Ow – ow – ow—

CAPTAIN. Holloo, holloo, holloo, he went.

> Who hears the midnight huntsman's horn
> Comes back that night to the day he was born.
> Who hears his twelve dogs, be he never so brave,
> Let him steal a spade and dig his—

OLD WOMAN. No, no, son, no, no, it was the thunder you heard.

CAPTAIN. What's to roast, boy?

BOY. Hamster, two dormice.

CAPTAIN. Three little creatures the size of a fist for to feed the whole people. Since the pitchfork-men started their war there's been neither pig nor cow nor cockerel nor goose—

FIRST GIPSY. I got a woollen jacket, and a pan of cold porridge; there was a dead man in a ditch and they lay beside him.

SECOND GIPSY. Bundle of linen, socks, boots, and a tinderbox.

CAPTAIN. What's left of a hare and a bit of a chicken. I found it in their camp, but we don't go there again. The iron-men have got there.

GOETZ'S VOICE (*off*). Hello there! Whose fire? Hello there! Help me—

CAPTAIN. Who is it?

FIRST GIPSY. It's one of the iron-men.

OLD WOMAN. Iron-men, oh oh—

CAPTAIN. Back from the fire!

They all step back into the shadows.

Is he alone?

FIRST GIPSY. I can see no one with him.

CAPTAIN. Horse, has he got?

FIRST GIPSY. No.
CAPTAIN. Sword?
FIRST GIPSY. No. Not in his hand.
CAPTAIN. Let him come in.

GOETZ staggers into the firelight.

GOETZ. Who are you? I heard you. I can't see you. Where have
you gone? Don't be afraid. I want help; I don't want
plunder—

*They come slowly up to him. When they see his condition they
begin to take off bits of his equipment.*

CAPTAIN. Iron-man.
FIRST GIPSY. Alone.
SECOND GIPSY. He's lost his sword, look.
CAPTAIN. Does he have a dagger?
FIRST GIPSY. Here.
SECOND GIPSY. Good iron, strong: but not of the best; it
ought to have jewels on it—
GOETZ. Leave that alone!

He frightens them for a moment and they crouch back.

Who are you? You're not peasants?
CAPTAIN. Romany people, we are, neither pitchfork nor iron.
You can call us the naked-men. We live in no one's land . . .
Leg of a chicken, eat it. You carry all your iron, but inside of
it, there's nothing.
SECOND GIPSY. Inside of it he's got blood. I think he's been
wounded.
GOETZ. Yes, that's right, wounded. Catching cold to the
wound. Let me sit by your fire.
OLD WOMAN. Come in under the roof, iron-man, come in and
be warm.

BOY. I know who he is. He fought *with* the pitchfork-men, this one. He's the iron-man with the iron hand. He's running from his brothers.

GOETZ. Can you shelter me – just an hour, one hour? I can't walk any more . . .

He faints.

WOMAN. Old woman, have we got some blood-wort and linen to tie him up? He's bleeding too fast; look at this here—

OLD WOMAN (*attending to his wound*). Here we are, here we are, lay it down, over and over—

> Blood come down and blood come up
> Blood to fill a little cup
> Blood lie still beside the bone
> Dry, blood, dry, and leave him to his own.

There we are, girly; that ought to save him.

Trumpets in the distance.
Another GIPSY *runs in.*

THIRD GIPSY. Horses, Captain, horses; they're chasing through the trees—

CAPTAIN. They're coming after this one.

FIRST GIPSY. What shall we do? They'll kill the whole people—

SECOND GIPSY. Who is he? He's an iron-man, that's all; give him back to his brothers—

OLD WOMAN. No, boy, no – we don't do that; he's sat beside our fire—

GOETZ (*starting up*). Trumpets, I hear trumpets – I'm putting you in danger, I must go, I must go – Georg, where's Georg—

More trumpets very near. Shouting.
WEISLINGEN'S TROOPERS *rush in from all sides.*
They capture GOETZ *and they kill all the* GIPSIES.

SCENE NINE

Augsburg.
Weislingen's house. The antechamber to Adelheid's bedroom.
Night.

FRANZ *hurries in in his riding-clothes and knocks on the inner door. Behind comes* MARGARET, *just awakened, in her nightgown.*

FRANZ. Adelheid, Adelheid—

MARGARET. Franz, what are you doing here? Have you gone insane, roaring at her door in the middle of the night—

FRANZ. Where is she? I must talk to her. I don't care what time it is—

ADELHEID, *in her nightgown, comes out of the bedroom.*

ADELHEID. Has Weislingen come back?

FRANZ (*embracing her*). No. Not come back.

ADELHEID. What do you want, Franz? Who saw you come to my room? If the servants find out—

MARGARET. Some of them are paid to tell him who she talks to – you ought to know that by now; be a lover or a fool, Franz, but not both together!

FRANZ (*gives* ADELHEID *the letter*). He gave me this to give you. Do you know what it says? You are to go to his castle, in the wildest part of Franconia, at once; you must write no letters, you must take no servants, and *I* have to see that you *don't*!

ADELHEID. But Franconia is full of the rebellion.

FRANZ. Right, right, just so it is – at the best you're a prisoner, at the worst you might be murdered.

ADELHEID. And he has left it to *you* to enforce his orders, has he?

FRANZ. Yes. He's my master. How can I disobey him?

MARGARET. What sort of conscience have you got, Franz? You have already cuckolded him.

FRANZ. Yes. Yes, I know.

ADELHEID. Do you feel guilt for it?

FRANZ. When I am two hundred miles away, yes . . . Not at any other time.

MARGARET. Not at any other time. She has to be rescued. If you do not do it, then she must throw herself on the protection of the Emperor. Do you dare do it?

FRANZ. Yes.

ADELHEID. Franz, my darling Franz, in the few nights that you loved me, you had to come to me in secret after it got dark, and you had to leave me in secret before it was light. Bring up the sun, Franz, bring up the sun, and we will lie in it together and let it stroke its living heat over every slope and crevice of our two golden bodies. You must kill the darkness, my sweetheart; you must kill it for both of us: or else we shall be drowned in it, separately, for ever, and cold.

FRANZ. I will put my sword to his throat.

ADELHEID. No, not like that. That would be too well known and the world would punish us for it. It will have to be done more shamefully than that, I am afraid.

She goes back into the bedroom.

FRANZ. What does she mean?

MARGARET. I don't know. I don't want to know. If you find out, don't tell me . . . Go on, silly boy; she's gone into her bedroom and she's left the door open. Enjoy it while you can.

He goes in after ADELHEID.
MARGARET *shudders and goes back to her own room.*

SCENE TEN

Jaxthausen.
A Room in Goetz's Castle.

LERSE *and* ELISABETH.

LERSE. He is a new man now, is Weislingen; he is a terrifying
man; he's got only one word between his teeth, lady –
'Justice'. That's what the peasants were after and all, and by
God now they've got it. I took myself off while time was still
open – d'you know they've given Weislingen more power
than they say any Imperial officer had since the days of
Charlemagne – every leader of a rebel band he's captured,
he's burnt him alive: two hundred others he's broken on the
wheel: there's heads cut off and there's quarters: there's men
stuck on stakes on every damned hill-top – he says 'Justice'. I
turned my back quick; I set one foot afore the other. I'm too
old, you see: and Berlichingen told me you could pay me my
wages; it comes to fifty-five gold pieces.

ELISABETH. Where have they taken him?

LERSE. Back to Heilbronn – ah, we've been there afore . . .
This time not so easy to find a deliverance.

ELISABETH. You are a coward and a renegade, Lerse; you are a
traitor and a thief.

LERSE. Not a thief, just a creditor. I make it fifty-five, but I'd
settle for forty. I signed articles with Berlichingen; it's all in
pen and ink. . . . No Sickingen *this* time. Do you know
what's happened to him? His Palatinate venture's collapsed;
he's a disgraced man himself.

ELISABETH. You have the face of a dog and the stink of a
grunting brock: go and find my steward and ask him for your
money.

LERSE.   Franz von Sickingen went riding out
                And high and gaily was his life
                But slowly slowly rode he home
                And slowly rides his sorrowful wife.

ELISABETH. If you do not leave me this instant I will have you
beaten by the stable-boys.

LERSE. I have written to her already; she is on her way to
Weislingen. I do not believe there is much she can do: I told
you, he is a new man. But I've heard him called a butterfly, a

chameleon, and so forth . . . She may remind him of something; he could change once again. If you want to go to Heilbronn, I don't mind riding with you. By rights that should put the bill up to fifty-eight or sixty, but . . .

She goes out without an answer.
He stands aside to let her, then follows, still talking.

SCENE ELEVEN

The end of the Peasants' War.
Weislingen's tent in the camp of the Punitive Army. Night.

Around the camp the landscape is made horrible by gallows and torture wheels. WEISLINGEN *is in his tent with his* OFFICER *and* FRANZ *in attendance.*

WEISLINGEN (*to* OFFICER). You have had the report from Heilbronn? Are you certain he is still there? In double chains, in the bottom dungeon, fastened to the wall? It is by no degree possible he can have escaped?

OFFICER. My lord, I have assured you already—

WEISLINGEN. Then how is it I saw him this evening, at the edge of the forest? I was walking through the camp and he stood just inside the trees. He was holding up a sword – like this, d'you see? Then he waved it once or twice in front of his face. He looked away from me, down at his iron hand, as if he didn't know why it was there, and he struck it against a tree, heavily: then he walked back into the wood. It was too dark after that to see him any more . . . Oh, just a minute, I – Franz—

He is gripped by a spasm of pain. FRANZ *quickly passes him a cup of wine, which he swallows urgently and seems to recover.*

OFFICER. Let me send you the doctor, my lord. You have been ill like this for nearly a week now.

WEISLINGEN. Fatigue, overwork; all any doctor could do is to tell me to rest. And that is impossible, isn't it? The country is not yet at peace. When it is at peace, then I can rest.

OFFICER. I have today's list of death-sentences for your ratification.

WEISLINGEN. What is the number?

OFFICER. One hundred and seven.

WEISLINGEN. Sacrament, Sacrament, how many more?

OFFICER. You have the power to reduce them if you wish.

WEISLINGEN. I am the instrument of the law, sir, not its creator . . . I ask myself this: what will be the effect of all these executions upon the young men who have to carry them out? I am afraid they may come to take pleasure in their work: and then what will happen? But with the help of God, order and peace will be here before that . . . Any more letters?

OFFICER (*hands him some*). Here.

WEISLINGEN. I had better look them through before I go to my bed. Good night to you, sir.

OFFICER. Good night, my lord.

> *Exit.*
> WEISLINGEN *sits reading the letters for a while.*
> MARIA *enters. He looks at her fixedly.*

WEISLINGEN. Where is he?

MARIA. Where is who?

WEISLINGEN. Berlichingen. You have come out of the forest with him, have you not? What do you want with me, both of you? You are trying to make me say I am guilty: and I am not – I am the instrument of the law.

> MARIA *looks at* FRANZ *in amazement.*

FRANZ. He thinks you are a ghost.

MARIA. No. I am alive, Adelbert. My brother is alive, but he will not be alive for very much longer. I have been asked to come and see you.

WEISLINGEN. Why? I am an instrument. Do you know what that means? I sign my name, I sign it again, and all of them die. And then after that, I shall die, too. I am dying already. Franz—

> FRANZ *passes him the cup as he feels another spasm.*
> *When he has drunk he takes up a parchment from the table and shows it to* MARIA.

Look, there is his name, with mine underneath it. As a nobleman, he has the privilege of a separate death-warrant; we do not have to look for *him* from among the common list – but it all means the same in the end. Why did you marry Sickingen? You could not have loved him.

MARIA. Of course I did not love him. But he was kind to me and honourable.

WEISLINGEN. You see what I mean, Franz? She wants me to say I am guilty. For your satisfaction, I am very guilty indeed, but I have not been able to think about you for quite a long time. I have had too much business – like this – and this – and – one hundred and seven this evening . . .

MARIA (*to* FRANZ). What is the matter with him? Why is he so ill?

FRANZ. He – he seems to be ill, madam . . .

MARIA. Yes, but what is wrong? Has he been looked at by a doctor?

WEISLINGEN. Do you hate me, Maria?

MARIA. For a time, I did, yes. And I hated your wife, too. When I see you as you are now, Adelbert, I hate her worse than ever.

WEISLINGEN (*with a grin*). My condition is not her fault, if that is what you are thinking. I would ascribe it to Justice. 'Naught but the Justice of God.'

FRANZ. Sir, you are wrong.

WEISLINGEN. What?

FRANZ. Wrong, wrong. She gave it to me and I put it in.

WEISLINGEN. Put it in what? What are you talking about?

FRANZ. She gave me the poison. She said it worked slowly. I put it in your wine every time you asked for it. I was her lover. I do not believe the Emperor ever got to bed with her at all.

WEISLINGEN. How long have you been doing this, Franz?

FRANZ. For over ten days. It's a powder in a little bag, and I put it in, you see. She told me it would take something like a week. Holy God, my lady, Holy God and Jesus Christ and Mary His Mother, can you forgive me . . .

He goes helplessly away.

MARIA (*embracing* WEISLINGEN *and weeping*). Adelbert—

WEISLINGEN (*putting her away*). No, don't do that; it's too late for that. I should have gone to Brabant many years ago with Goetz. I should have been like him, violent and stupid and a cheerful barbarian. But you know that was not possible. Because I knew that he was wrong and I knew that I was right. And I still *am* right. Oh yes, he deserves to lose his head; justice is absolute, chop off his head . . .

He looks at her and then slowly tears up GOETZ'S *death-warrant.*

This is for *your* sake and for no other consideration – I am denying my duty at the point of my death. What do you think of that? Now listen, I cannot release him – he will have to live in prison: but if I *am* at the point of death – and if I know Adelheid, that poison will be accurate – the Commissioners without me will be far more sympathetic. With the exception of Seckendorf, and *he* can be outvoted. Go to them and talk to them and they will see that his confinement is as easy as possible . . .

Another spasm.

Oh . . . oh . . . quick – drink, the drink – ha, I forgot; it's
Franz who poured it out; Franz poured it out and Franz put
it in, clever little fellow – Maria, please don't leave me. I
should like to think we *were* married, for just a few hours, and
let Sickingen go to the devil—

> One hundred bones and a hundred bones
> You shall see them grow together
> For the price you will have paid, my love,
> They will hold you tight for ever.

SCENE TWELVE

A dark vaulted cellar.
The Secret Justice in session – all wearing black cloaks and masks.

CHIEF JUDGE. Judges of the Tribunal of the Secret Justice,
sworn by knife and by rope to seek out justice where it is left
unperformed by those who ought to perform it, in secret to
judge and in secret to avenge, without pity and without
favour in this our pitiful country – let your hearts be pure and
your hands clean, raise up your hands and cry down punishment upon all unknown transgressors.

ALL. Punishment. Punishment.

CHIEF JUDGE. Crier, commence the Secret Justice.

CRIER. I am the Crier and I cry down punishment upon all
unknown transgressors. Whosoever has the hand is cleanest
and the heart is purest, let him bring the accusation and by
knife and by rope call forth our uncorrupted judgement.

> *The* ACCUSER *steps forward, and speaks as though for the*
> *first time, prompted in a whisper by the* CRIER.

ACCUSER. My heart is clean from misdoing and my hand from
guiltless blood. God pardon my unthought-of sin, and may
He bring my steps to virtue. I lift my hand and I make my
accusation.

CHIEF JUDGE. Whom do you accuse?

ACCUSER. By knife and by rope I make my accusation against Adelheid von Weislingen. She is adulteress and murderess; she poisoned her husband by the hand of his squire. The squire has confessed it; the husband is dead.

CHIEF JUDGE. Do you swear by the one true God of Truth that you make honest accusation?

ACCUSER. I do swear it, sirs.

CHIEF JUDGE. Should we find that you in this have borne false witness, do you take upon your own neck the punishment for adultery and murder?

ACCUSER. I do so take it, sirs.

CHIEF JUDGE. Let me have your voices.

The JUDGES *confer in whispers for a moment.*

CRIER. Judges of the Tribunal of the Secret Justice, have you taken counsel together?

CHIEF JUDGE. We have.

CRIER. What is your doom?

CHIEF JUDGE. Our doom is this: Adelheid von Weislingen, known to be guilty of adultery and murder, double transgressions, shall die the double death. By rope and by knife shall she die. Executioner of the Secret Justice, are you here?

EXECUTIONER (*steps forward with knife and cord*). Sirs, I am here.

CHIEF JUDGE. You shall strangle her with the rope till she be all but dead, and then with the knife you shall cut out her heart. Take your time, consult your safety – it matters not when she should meet her doom. We know it is inevitable.

EXECUTIONER. Sirs, it is inevitable.

CHIEF JUDGE. So be it. Judges of the Tribunal of the Secret Justice, in secret to judge and in secret to avenge, our business is now over for this time. God have mercy upon us.

ALL. God have mercy upon us.

They disperse. The last to go is the ACCUSER, *who, as she leaves the stage, takes off her hood to reveal the face of* MARIA.

SCENE THIRTEEN

Heilbronn.
A garden within the walls of the Prison.

ELISABETH *helps* GOETZ *to a seat. The* GAOLER *stands in the background.* GOETZ *wears leg-irons, but his hands are free.*

ELISABETH. You are allowed the use of this garden, we can send in your food from the town, you no longer have to wear the full weight of your chains. They are merciful, Goetz; you ought to be grateful.

GOETZ. Grateful? For what? You would have me die, after all, Elisabeth, in a kind of warm sunset of tranquility and reconciliation. With whom can I be reconciled? With Weislingen? He is dead. With the Bishop of Bamberg? He has forgotten about me. I am no more a nuisance to the commerce of his state. I am out of his life. The Emperor? I don't know this Emperor and he does not know me . . . What about my son? I have heard no word of my son. Where is he all this time?

ELISABETH. Karl is dead: you know that. We gave him away and he died. He was not like you: and he died.

GOETZ. No, no, no, not him. The other one. We rode into Miltenberg and told them to stop the burning, and I have never seen him since.

ELISABETH. Goetz, do you mean Georg? He was not your son.

GOETZ. He *was* to have been. I would have captured him a castle and set in it a garrison and there he would have lived, a Free Knight like myself. Where is he all this time?

ELISABETH. I do not know, Goetz.

Enter LERSE.

LERSE (*to* ELISABETH). The lady Maria has come to visit him. Is he well enough to see her ?

To the GAOLER.

His sister.

GAOLER *nods.*

ELISABETH. Bring her in, Lerse.

LERSE *goes out again.*

GOETZ. Is that my little Maria ? Weislingen's wife ?
ELISABETH. Sickingen's wife.
GOETZ. Weislingen should have married her. Sickingen had all his politics, his grand designs, his buzzings-up of power. Prince Elector he said he would be . . . Where is he now ?

Enter MARIA.

MARIA. He is at home, Goetz, in his castle. He has sent you a letter.
GOETZ. I don't want to read it. It is a tale of misfortune; we have all such tales to tell . . . Where is my son ? Have you brought me news of *him* ?
ELISABETH (*aside to* LERSE). Georg ? Have you heard any word ?
LERSE (*aside to her*). He was captured at Miltenberg by Weislingen's men. They hanged him on the spot.
GOETZ. What ? What was that ?
LERSE. I didn't say anything. We haven't got any news.
GOETZ. Oh yes, I heard you – you said that they hanged him. From a tree or from a gallows ?
LERSE. What difference does it make ?
GOETZ. I hope it was a tree. He was a free robber's man and he

should die in the green forest. Here is where *I* die, between these great stones. Eh, not entirely, you will tell me. They let me sit in this garden; it has one little bush . . . So am I, do you see, one little bush, and I was born a tall tree in the middle of a free forest. Weislingen told me I did not know what freedom was. He said it was not possible for me to be free when I inhibited the freedom of other good men. I told him they were treacherous. The peasants were treacherous because they burnt down Miltenberg when they swore they would not. Yet I believed in their cause. All they did was fight for it in the only way they knew. If we all fought for our causes we should all fight each other . . . Where's that dog-faced Lerse, where's that mercenary man? *You* would fight for anybody if they gave you the pay or a promise of good bloodshed – open your eyes, man, you should have asked them all why, you should know *why* you are fighting! Or else we are just wild animals, we must be shut up in boxes, and that's where I am. Because I stood by myself and I took no heed of nobody. All I said was freedom: all Weislingen said was some sort of order. To put the two together: all the world is broken up, and yet we must break it and break it and break it . . . Oh God, I am not strong enough – I don't think there's anyone can call himself strong enough – and yet it has to be done . . . After I am dead, should I expect my freedom then? But I inhibited the freedom of other good men and gave them no order. So what do I deserve? . . . By God's feet I will tell you. I deserve my true freedom and so do they all! And we deserve to be told what are the true questions and what are the answers, and we deserve to be able to tell them to our sons! And all that is impossible . . . You will break yourselves up, you will turn upside-down, you will destroy yourselves with it – there is always one possibility, that one day you will find it. You are made not to rest until you have found it. Freedom. And no warfare. Freedom. And good order. Freedom.

He falls back in his chair.
The two women bend over him. LERSE *looks keenly at him,*
then goes to the GAOLER, *who is leaning negligently against*
the wall.

LERSE. That's for your account-book one gaol-fee the less. But
I dare say you'll make up for it by overcharging on the others?

The GAOLER *grunts and shrugs his shoulders.* LERSE *whistles*
a little tune.

ELISABETH. He did not know what he was talking about. He
made a good living once and he did not need any grief then.
All this misfortune was brought upon him by others. If you
had held the love of Weislingen and not let him shame you,
my man would not be dead here in the garden of a gaol.

MARIA. That is true. I was not sufficient. Neither was Weislingen. Neither are you. Nobody can be. But we *can* remember and we can hold ourselves responsible—

She shouts across at LERSE.

—and hold our swords responsible for all the blood they
shed! And knowing that and knowing how the dead men of
Franconia and Swabia are lying among their fields like blue
lobsters on the deck of a fishing-boat, how can we talk about
freedom and justice without accusing ourselves? . . . On my
own neck by that rule should be murder and adultery, though
I have committed neither. But I do not see how I am going to
shake them off, except by remembering that God made mankind in the image of God, and that therefore it is possible. All
that my brother said, and that he failed to do, is nevertheless
possible . . . Learn, Elisabeth, every day learn. You cannot
afford not to.

Methuen's Theatre Classics

THE TROJAN WOMEN	Euripides *an English version by Neil Curry*
THE BACCHAE OF EURIPIDES	*an English version by Wole Soyinka*
THE REDEMPTION	Molière *translated by Richard Wilbur*
LADY PRECIOUS STREAM	*adapted by S. I. Hsiung from a* *sequence of traditional Chinese plays*
IRONHAND	Goethe *adapted by John Arden*
THE GOVERNMENT INSPECTOR	Gogol *an English version by Edward O.* *Marsh and Jeremy Brooks*
DANTON'S DEATH	Buechner *an English version by James Maxwell*
LONDON ASSURANCE	Boucicault *adapted and edited by Ronald Eyre*
BRAND	Ibsen
HEDDA GABLER	*translated by Michael Meyer*
THE WILD DUCK	
THE MASTER BUILDER	
GHOSTS	
PEER GYNT	
MISS JULIE	Strindberg
THE IMPORTANCE OF BEING EARNEST	Wilde
LADY WINDERMERE'S FAN	
THE UBU PLAYS	Jarry *translated by Cyril Connolly and* *Simon Watson Taylor*
ENEMIES	Gorky
THE LOWER DEPTHS	*an English version by Kitty* *Hunter-Blair and Jeremy Brooks*
THE PLAYBOY OF THE WESTERN WORLD	Synge

Methuen's Modern Plays

EDITED BY JOHN CULLEN AND GEOFFREY STRACHAN